## *What Readers Are Saying...*

Early in 2000, I had heard about Feng Shui and sought out a Master to do a radio show with me on "Feng Shui and Quitting Smoking." I wanted to dangle a carrot to the listening audience to get them to listen to my show. Sharyn Hatchcock stepped up to the task. It was a great show, but then I forgot about it. A year later, Feng Shui made its way into my life and I sought Sharyn out again... not for another show, but to continue her Feng Shui seminars for our community. She did, and I did everything she recommended! With intent set, I went from being a Tobacco Cessation Facilitator, to President/CEO of a Chamber of Commerce and on to my ***dream job*** – Promotions Manager and Radio Talk Show Host for SIX radio stations. My life is a FENG SHUI DREAM COME TRUE.

~ Barbara Bruce, White Mountain Radio personality,
former Director of the Show Low, Arizona Chamber of Commerce

The Home Whisperer is as elegant as it is full of rich content. It is a stunning accomplishment that honors the best traditions of Feng Shui and is a welcome, essential and fun tool for every house and home."

~ David Rippe, award-winning coauthor of The Flip: Turn Your World Around

To all who know her, Sharyn is an amazing individual, mentor, and blessing. Her positive energy and wisdom are relevant and vital no matter where you are in your life's journey.

~ Amie Rodgers, Owner/Publisher, Maverick Magazine

A must read for beginners and long time practitioners! Having studied Feng Shui, in various and often-conflicting forms, this book simplifies Feng Shui. As an energy worker, this book addresses numerous questions in a way I could internalize. FS became alive for me.

I now walk into a room and I can feel the energies, where they flow and where they are blocked or stagnant. As I make corrections in my own home and office, I am getting almost immediate results in the way of flowing creative energies, more stamina and increased sales in my business.

My living room now supports an inviting place to greet guests and doubles as a quiet retreat to read and relax. People comment that my home "feels" wonderful. Thank you Sharyn for taking the mystery out of Feng Shui. I will use this book as a handbook for years to come.

~ Diana Wesley Bay, Energy Psychology Therapist

Sharyn, you're awesome. I LOVETHIS BOOK!! I'm so happy that this is all coming full circle for you in your life right now. You have such a talent for writing that goes back to when you first began writing articles for the local newspaper. I always knew you were capable of doing something this amazing. It's going to be a best seller, and I know this because daily, you live the best of your life in order to share the knowledge you've gained to the rest of us. Everyone will be a better person for having read your book and sharing in your wisdom... I know I am. Thanks for all you do and for being one of my greatest mentors, motivators, and inspirations.

~ Amy Hathcock, Precious Daughter-In Law

Mom, I don't tell you often enough, but I am so lucky to have you for a mother. You have always been there for me. Thank you for all that you continue to do in James and my life. And now, your book will be there for so many other people to receive your help. This book is AWE-INSPIRING.

~ Olivia Smith, Beloved Daughter

The Home Whisperer is a magnificent gift; this book has empowered me to create a welcoming space that truly nurtures my family as well as my intentions. I have followed the teachings of the home whisperer and witnessed the transformation in my own life in ways that were only imaginable before. I am thankful for the opportunity to have these read this book.

~ Ian Hathcock loving son and Feng Shui enthusiast, Gilbert, AZ

Because I have witnessed its benefits, I am now learning about Feng Shui and energy work for that matter. After reading this book, I am capable of working with the energy of my inner home as well my outer home. I now take responsibility for my life and have agreed to listen to what my home is saying to me. Thank you for your wonderful contribution to our universe.

~ Tracy Parkinson Hathcock, Beautiful Daughter-In-Law

# The Home Whisperer

## Feng Shui Simplified

Sharyn Jordan Hathcock

Cedar Hill Publishing

The Home Whisperer™ – Feng Shui Simplified



The Meaning of Master Numbers contributed by Rebecca Hayes

Editing by Rebecca Hayes
Cover and book design by Rebecca Hayes

Published in the United States by
Cedar Hill Publishing
Show Low, AZ 85901
www.cedarhillpublishing.com

ISBN-13: 978-1-933324-89-0

Library of Congress Control Number 2007935783

Quotes from *I Ching - The Oracle of the Cosmic Way*, by Hanna Moog and Carol Anthony, used by permission

## *A Special Dedication to My Husband Jay*

In 1969, we met and married and our world as we knew it was focused pro-peace, adventure, enlightenment, and love for one another and humanity. The present world we continue to create beautifully carries on with these same passionate interests. Throughout these amazing years, we have served in a myriad of ways. However, our heart has always been and will always be on making a positive difference.

This is a special dedication to my loving husband, Jay. We share an exceptional love for home, enjoy our remarkable travels, adore our four children and their loving spouses, and we are wild about our grandchildren. Life is fulfilling, creative, inspired, and overflows with so much love. We are content to live in the joyous NOW.

Jay has been the person to keep everything going, while I have spent all of these years teaching, studying, dreaming, attending advanced classes all over the place, and documenting this work. In truth, he has given me the gift of living my passion. In turn, I have done the same for him, for his interests. All of these years, it still works magic in my heart.

Thank you, Jay. Your philosophical view of life is far reaching. Daily, your profound love and honesty inspires the best in me. To live our inner and outer lives in a place where the waters of joy sweetly flow and the graceful winds of blessings gently blow our way is a gift. Together we honor one another. Thank you for being my husband, friend, partner, and best friend. In our enchanted cottage in the woods, we live well in synchronicity and walk in complete gratitude.

## *Blessings*

*Blessings on my thoughts today*
*May they arrive in a beautiful bouquet*
*Being forever caring, creative and kind.*
*Please carry these noble thoughts on the wings*
*Of a clear heart and a de-cluttered mind.*

*Blessings on the words I write*
*I thank you, Sage, that they embody truth and light.*
*May this loving book go forth in cosmic delight*
*And resonate with joy, wisdom, and divine insight.*

*Namasté ~*

*Sharyn Jordan Hathcock*

# Dedication

This book is dedicated to you, the reader, the seeker, the adventurer, the detective, the wizened old soul, the sage, and especially the enlightened part of you that innately knows how Feng Shui works. You have responded to once more create a home replete with happiness, joy and contentment, where laughter abounds and music swirls within its walls; where its very essence feeds your sprit and supports your highest wishes and most splendid dreams.

Thank you for coming. Within these pages, you will discover the hidden treasures of your inner and outer home. This process enables you to remember who you are and why you are here.

# Acknowledgments

A warm and generous thank-you to Rebecca Hayes, my publisher/editor extraordinaire: Your humor and professionalism has made all of the difference. Thank you for the elegant cover design. The way of Wind and Water will be beautifully ushered into the hearts and minds of the readers.

To Barbara Bruce and Jacqueline Harte, my dear friends and fellow energy workers: Loving appreciation to each of you for not only blessing this book with your gracious forwards, but for your profound friendships and your loving support.

To my fantastic Focus Group: Dr. Richard Boatright, Amie Rodgers, Cheryl Ford, Jacqueline Harte, Barbara Bruce, and Jane Roberts. You are Chi-tastic!

To each and every attendee of my energy workshops and to each of my dear clients-residential and professional: Thank you for sharing your energy with me and enriching the world with your love.

Thank you to the Butterfly Garden Luncheonettes: May each of your intentions be manifested as you dance the joys of transformation into your lives.

Joyous blessings to Sheree Cannon and Tommie Covington for sharing such abundant love of home and hearth with me. Their remarkable creativity, gifted originality, and Texas charm is reflected throughout every room and in every heart. Through their generosity, I found my name, The Home Whisperer™.

Special Thanks to Jay and his remarkable Red Rock dream.

To our children-you are each a beautiful jewel:

Jason and his incredible wife Kirsten
Jeremy and his precious wife Amy
Ian and his wife beautiful Tracy
Olivia and her amazing husband James

From Gawni to our Grandchildren:
How blessed I am to have each of you… the prized treasures in my life
Shawn, Ryan, Alec, Abigail, Kali, Gabrielle, Koby, and Gavin Cruz

# *Preface*

In times past, the art, science and symbolism of quantum energy were honed by many cultures. This timeless information system is respectfully titled Feng Shui, pronounced Fung Schway! Easy enough, right? Right! From Chinese to English, it means wind and water. Inspired from this imagery is the universal symbolism of wind, the invisible - your inner consciousness - and water, the visible - your outer, physical home.

This book is dedicated to the positive alchemy (transformation) of your inner and outer home. These energies are always together and are forever influencing one another. When your home is aligned with your highest idea of life, your consciousness experiences what harmony and balance actually feels like. In turn, your discernment is heightened.

*"The soul of man is equal to water and the fate of man is equal to the wind."* ~ Goethe

Learning to flow with the unseen/wind and the seen/water is the mastering of life itself. The quest is to work with, rather than against wind and water. Water collects energy and wind scatters it. Water shows up in your life to unblock your path from old and stagnant past energies. It harmonizes the times of stillness and the times of flow in your life. It brings in the fresh and renewing waters of greater fluidity. Water works on a cellular level and cleanses the inner self to uncover courage.

Wind enables you to gracefully move through life's cycles and embrace change. The inner self grows, matures and learns to actually hear the voice of its genuine being. Wind is also your breath, and deep breathing connects us to the cosmic helpers. Being in alignment with Wind and Water allows your inner self to express itself and thus, guide you along our life-journey.

From this place of guidance, you gift yourself with the opportunity to be in the infinite flow of deep insight, intuition, illumination, and clarity. From this perception, an understanding that life itself is the vehicle for abundance, creativity, peace, serenity, contentment, fulfillment and overflowing joy are experienced. This path connects you to beauty, safety, and wholeness.

*The Home Whisperer - Feng Shui Simplified* expands the connection between your inner and outer home, allowing them to support and nurture your every intention. Hear what your home is actually saying and discover how to refine its language by energetic placement, color, and balance. Clarify and amplify its hushed tones, drawing upon the Feng Shui information system to bring forth comfort, stability, and increased awareness.

Hmmm, what else can there be? Well, okay, let's add in perfect harmony, resourcefulness, and wisdom, to inspire generosity. These values easily spring forth from the depth of your being. You awaken each and every day, fully cognizant of the abundance flowing around you.

The process of learning anything new can be quite daunting. *"The beginning is the most important part of any work." ~ Plato.*

The benefits of *The Home Whisperer* are novel, entertaining, highly effective, and user-friendly. Due to the book's simple teaching methods - thus the subtitle "Feng Shui Simplified" - your interest will remain keen. It was written for fun, practical application, and with the intent for you to easily decode the matrix of your inner/outer in other words… infinite potentialities.

In recent years, Feng Shui has become a multi-billion dollar industry; the mainstream business community has long since become aware of its power. A few of the successful people and companies that rely on this timeless information system are Oprah, Donald Trump, Merrill Lynch, Citibank, and Rupert Murdock.

You may include yourself, as you are now on a path to creating a supportive home to nurture your dreams and desires. Within these principles, the mystery of graceful embrace of life's challenges and changes is solved. Lend an ear and truly hear what your home is expressing. You will be surprised to learn how and why you've been experiencing life in the way you have.

Quantum physics validates the truth that you are comprised of tiny wave particles of energy. Otto Werner won the Noble Peace prize for proving that each of the body's organs has a frequency. It stands to reason, when raising your home's vibration, that clarity, wellness, flow, vigor, and creativity are thus inspired. Living in a balanced environment, such as a "feng-shui-correct" home, optimizes the body's healing potential. Re-discovering the hidden treasures of your inner and outer home is an adventure.

- *Sharyn Jordan Hathcock*

# About The Author

## Sharyn Jordan Hathcock

An accomplished entrepreneur and visionary, Sharyn easily shifts from consulting in the mainstream corporate world to her mystical and metaphysical clients. Her extensive background in both of these cultures has prepared her to work with people from all walks of life. In her early years as a devoted mom, she developed a business enterprise called Kids, Inc. Daycare. This evolved into Rosebud Preschool. Both endeavors enabled her to be with her four children during their tender years.

In 1989, she and her husband, Jay, founded Lakeside Entertainment Group, Inc. to own and operate Pinetop-Lakeside, Arizona's first movie theatre. Within a short time, they added three other towns to their developing venture and grew this endeavor in to a multi-million dollar corporation. In 2001, with the assistance of Sharyn's Feng Shui knowledge, the Hathcocks sold their company to a brilliant couple who continue to not only foster this business growth, but also have taken it to new heights. Together, they continue to enjoy great success, allowing Jay and Sharyn to pursue their travel passions and vast entrepreneurial interests.

However, prior to leaving the corporate world, during the construction of one of their movie theatres, conflict began to arise in their progressive business. In 1995, they sought mainstream counseling from their banks' brain trust, the Small Business Administration, and they even hired a new CPA, who remains their accountant to this day. Although they found ways to get their business back on track, there was still an undercurrent affecting their stability.

Sharyn discovered Feng Shui and soon, her old/new knowledge was put to the test, passing with flying colors. Immediately upon using Feng Shui's codes and precepts, positive shifts began to take place. The corporation was returned to a solid track of earnings. In the body of this book, these synchronistic details are further described.

Spurred by her success, Sharyn began working on friends and family's homes and businesses. She was a natural, because even as a child, she was able to understand connectivity and its underlying network. By working with Feng Shui, Sharyn discovered she is clair-tactictal (knowledge gained by touch). Along with the Feng Shui principles, she was able to intuitively create supportive environments. These nurturing spaces served her clientele so well that it enabled them to create the lives they desired.

In 1998, while browsing through a bookstore, Terah Kathryn Collins' best selling book titled *The Western Guide to Feng Shui* literally fell off the shelf in front of her. Upon reading this excellent teaching, Sharyn developed a professional and personal friendship with the author and founder of the Western School of Feng Shui. She is a 1999 graduate and continues to return for advanced training. Since she is able to decipher the hidden wisdom behind ancient codes, her practice developed into Feng Shui Simplified.

To better express what she has been doing all of her life, she adopted The Home Whisperer as her trademark. Sharyn deciphers the home's wisdom into a simple language that is easily understood. This book is dedicated to furthering her teaching that everything is energy. Our homes, our bodies, our gardens, our belongings, the food we choose to eat, the animals, and even the seemingly inanimate gemstones – all have a blueprint.

Sharyn wrote *The Home Whisperer – Feng Shui Simplified* to empower you toward the life of your dreams.

# Contents


Foreword 1 ........ i
Foreword 2 ........ ii
Introduction ........ 1
How Best to Use This Book ........ 3
A Brief History ........ 4
Glossary ........ 7

Part One: The Art of Placement - The Symbolism & Science of Feng Shui ........ 13
Everything is Energy ........ 14
1 - The Home Whisperer ........ 15
2 - We Are One ........ 18
3 - The Art of Placement, Symbolism & Quantum Science ........ 21
*Wind and Water* ........ *21*
4 - Chi – the Life Force ........ 27
5 - The Field of Intention ........ 31
6 - Space-Clearing – De-Cluttering for Your Highest Destiny ........ 34
7 - Yin & Yang - Balance & Harmony ........ 40
8 - The Timeless Five Elements ........ 45
9 - The Bagua - The Template of Alchemy ........ 54
*The Bagua* ........ *54*

Part Two - Alchemy of the Inner & Outer home ........ 65
10 - Missing Corners ........ 66
11 - Colorful Perceptions ........ 70
12 - Numerical Influences ........ 73
13 - Elemental Persuasion ........ 80
*Cultivating a Sustainable Life* ........ *80*
14 - Geometric Shape ........ 86
15 - Seasonal Cycles & I Ching Trigrams ........ 88
16 - Energy Patterns for Individual Rooms ........ 92
17 - Jewels to Re*Member ........ 95

Part Three - The Grid Of Empowerment ........ 97
18 - Family Tree Wisdom ........ 98
*Roots, Strength, Growth* ........ *99*
19 - Pure Abundance ........ 114

*Flowering Wisdom* ........ *123*
20 - Integrity & Illumination ........ 130
*Transcendent Radiance & Clarity* ........ *131*
21 - A Vitally Rich Intimate Relationship ........ 140
*Being Present: Developing Trust~ Receptivity ~ Well-Being ~ Balance, Harmony* ........ *141*
22 - Children & Creativity ........ 154
*Meet Your Personal Muse* ........ *155*
23 - Helpful People & Travel ........ 170
*Living in Synchronicity ~ Travel/Moving Forward ~ The Father Energy, Refinement* ........ *171*
24 - Career & Life Journey ........ 183
*Courageously Navigating the Waters of Life – the Flow* ........ *184*
25 - Self-Cultivation & Knowledge ........ 194
*Discern the Wisdom Within the Quiet* ........ *195*
26 - Unity/Chi ........ 205
*Dancing the Dance* ........ *206*
27 - Matrix of Your Miracles ........ 209
*The Matrix of the Bagua* ........ *213*

Part Four - Feng Shui Gardening ........ 215
28 - The Art of Energy Gardening ........ 216
*The Healing Garden* ........ *220*
*The Spiritual Garden* ........ *222*
*The Helpful People Garden* ........ *224*

End Word ........ 227
In Summation - Discovering the Hidden Treasures of Your Heart & Home ........ 229
The Western School of Feng Shui ........ 231

# *Foreword 1*

Jacqueline S. Harte, M.Ac.L.Ac.PT.

Sharyn Jordan Hathcock has provided us with a gift. Her mission is to help us bring energetic balance into our lives, and with this timely book she fulfills her goal.

We are living in an age of advanced technology and automation. People are working extremely long hours with little free time, constantly rushing and reaching out with computers, cell phones, text messaging, often literally running around meeting endless family commitments. It is easy to feel as though one's life is spiraling out of control. Relationships can be difficult, work may not be satisfying, the emotion of joy may be rare and fleeting.

It is time to slow down, take a breath, and look inward. We need help to organize our living and working environments in ways that will re-introduce balance into our lives. We have forgotten a truth known to the Chinese ancients for thousands of years: we are energetic beings, we are affected by every other being on the planet, and we are directly affected by the energies within our living space – this direct influence can and should be positive, but in many instances we are unaware of negative influences in our environment that may directly affect us.

The human body is quite capable of healing itself. The time has come to fully embrace the idea that we are pure energy. Every one of the 50 trillion cells within the human body is alive and pulsating at different frequencies. As energetic beings, when we re-introduce pure and balanced energy into our lives, we feel fully supported, healthy and peaceful.

Quantum physics tells us that every inanimate object, yes, even the chair upon which you sit, is pulsating with energy at the sub-atomic level, so let us not forget that our living environments are also pure energy. This energy is omnipresent – it only makes sense to work with it to enhance our lives.

Feng Shui is a remarkably effective method to gently manipulate the energies within our home and work environments so they fully support us in every aspect of our lives.

You have in your hands a tool, carefully crafted by Sharyn Jordan Hathcock, which will help you harmonize the energies within your environment. Allow Sharyn to guide you, and a happy, productive and successful life is within reach.

# Foreword 2

Barbara Bruce, Radio host of "BELIEVE"

In "***Simple Abundance,***" Sarah Ban Breathnach says that when in doubt, take a bath; in ***Until Today,*** Iyanla Vanzant says to ***S***top, ***D***rop (to your knees) and ***R***oll (it over to God); and, in the Ancient Oriental Tradition of Feng Shui, they say to move 27 things and your life will change. Sharyn Hathcock, in ***Home Whisperer,*** really gives you a combination of all three.

With her genuine Southern charm and sincerity, coupled with pure inspiration and intuition from within, Sharyn enters the home or business ***whispering*** the age-old secrets of Chi to its owner and or inhabitants. This woman's slogan is ***BE INSPIRED,*** and working with Sharyn, you can't help but truly be inspired… inspired for the moment and the intention she helps guide you to set for your future… the future you want, the future you deserve.

As a radio talk show host, I search for guests who can bring something to my listening audience that opens and uplifts people's consciousness – when I searched for someone who could explain "the way of wind and water" to my listeners, the Universe provided me with none other than Sharyn Jordan Hathcock. Knowing little about Feng Shui at that time, I wanted to dangle a carrot to my audience to capture them as a regular listener. Sharyn helped do that for me. But it actually wasn't until a year later that I realized what she had done… she had ***whispered*** so softly and succinctly that I had not realized how she stirred up the Chi for *me*!

I ran across an article in some magazine that told how General Motors, IBM, "The Donald," and others had embraced this ancient Oriental art of placement and had adopted it for the United States. That stirred up a desire and a greater curiosity within me, and I called Sharyn to find out if she could do local workshops.

To date, I now have been to about 18 or more of The ***Home Whisperer's*** workshops, and my life has changed significantly! I had one radio show when I met Sharyn and worked for County Government; then I moved on to 4 shows and President of the local Chamber of Commerce; today I have five shows and work for the largest radio group in The White Mountains of Arizona.

Sharyn is a devout follower of our Creator and possesses the skills of an Angel as she whispers the secrets of the ages to your home or business. Her goal is to ensure that you are living with what you love. Sharyn is a giver, a nurturer, and an encourager to all who cross her path. It is only fitting that she ***whisper*** her passion within the pages of a book to share with all who seek a better way of life.

The ***Home Whisperer*** will truly help you to follow Sharyn Hathcock's byline: ***BE INSPIRED.*** After you have read this "labor of love," you too will echo that sentiment. And, for those of you who think this is some kind of dark magic, let me challenge you to see it as I have: "If you open it, close it; if you take it out, put it back, if you throw it down, pick it up and if you take it off, hang it up. " Now, that is Feng Shui in a NUTSHELL – and today we actually call it LIVING SIMPLY, the same advice your Mama gave you, growing up.

Let Sharyn's love of the best life for everyone ***whisper*** to you through the pages of this manual and you, too, will BE INSPIRED!

*"May peace be inside your walls*
*and wealth inside your noble houses."*

*Psalms 122:7*

# *Introduction*

The Gift of Living in Beauty
**Sharyn Jordan Hathcock - The Home Whisperer**

*"If there is Righteousness in the heart, there will be
Beauty in the character. If there is beauty in the Character, there will be
Harmony in the home. If there is harmony in the home, there will be
Order in the nation. If there is order in the nation, there will be
Peace in the world."
-Celebrated Confucian Proverb*

Literally translated, Feng Shui (pronounced FUNG SHWAY) represents Wind and Water or the Unseen and the Seen. Wind and water are the weavers of intentions made manifest via movement. Wind and water's movement are powerful forces of nature. The winds and waters of transformation swirl around you daily creating awakened clarity, within and without. Feng Shui is the art, symbolism, and science of placement. It is an information system to enhance beauty, wellness, abundance, joy, self-actualization and harmony. Feng Shui, or geomancy as it is also known, has it roots in quantum physics and occurs naturally in the universe's magnetic field of energy. This beautiful energy upgrades a home's algorithm, revealing the matrix of its relationship to the universe and to humanity. This revelation brings peace into the world.

Feng Shui teaches how to harness the natural alchemy of wood, fire, earth, metal, and water. Living in beauty and being in alignment with these energies creates positive and powerful life transitions. Just ask to draw from the wisdom of flow, alignment, and connectivity. This trinity enhances the quality of your life's experiences and creates deep fulfillment. "Ask, and it shall be given to you; seek, and ye shall find; knock, and it shall be opened unto you." - *Matthew 7:7.* This awareness enriches your life. Know that you are connected to the greater Divine Web of Life that bestows inner peace and contentment.

In the Feng Shui tradition, there is a timeless and beautiful map called the Bagua. Each section of your environment demarcates specific energies in your home and workplace. These sections are called Guas and within this map are various aspects of life that enjoy a pattern projected by the innate flow of nature itself. Depending on your home or office's blue print, precious relationships, inspired creativity, harmony, and even your fame is influenced. Peace and harmony reside within you.

Since each of us is connected to one another, we are the channels of these blissful joys and blessings. This higher understanding creates a nurturing environment, furthering us, one and all, to be well, and to stand in the light of universal integrity and divine wisdom.

Feng Shui is a universal language comprehended by both the cosmic consciousness and humanity. Concurrently, it speaks through each Gua and supports what you desire most, generating a physical and mental response to manifest your deepest longings. Set an intention for beauty and experience the highest idea of life. Call forth all that is beautiful, sacred, and precious. Simply *be* with your blessings and create positive thoughts. Pay attention to your feelings and intuitions.

Rest in the knowledge that in perfect and divine order, the reciprocity of this beautiful energetic field brings everything you have ever desired into your path. For your longings clearly exist within time and space.

Once you are willing to do what it takes to hone your gifts and talents, bless others, as you would have them bless you, make wise decisions, and live in gratitude, YOU can resonate with beauty's higher frequency. Be one with abundance, be in the flow, be in alignment, and know that you are connected one to another. Accept and receive the gift of living in deep and abiding Beauty.

# How Best to Use This Book

The purpose of this book is to coach, inspire, illuminate and teach you how to create a "noble home," and to discover its hidden treasures. Feng Shui serves as a bridge that hones nurturing support for manifesting intentions. Relaxing into one's space and hearing the quiet affords a person serenity and deep contentment. Please read this book with a pen and notebook in hand. This will be your Feng Shui journal. You will be delighted to see the many changes/transformations occurring in your life as you apply these principles. Simply begin your Book of Alchemy by writing your name and the message, "I am a Beloved Child of the Universe. All is well in my inner & outer home."

Prior to reading the following chapters, you may skim them via the synopses. Everyone is always eager to move right into the art of placement. However, there are some highly important creeds to understand.

Before you can make any adjustments, you MUST de-clutter. I know – *"YUCK"* is what you are thinking. The reason for this first step is to avoid accentuating the very problems you are looking to release. When using Feng Shui "cures" in a disorderly environment, you will actually *enhance the problem*!

# A Brief History

By considering the quality of our home and workplace's energy, we become aware of how to invite harmony and true wealth. Fend Shui is a catalyst to enhance the life we are presently living and create the one we desire to experience tomorrow. The art and science of Feng Shui is about creating a nurturing and empowering environment. Feng Shui Simplified embodies these time-tested principles and teaches this process as a simple path. It is comprehensible and its mission is to bring clarity to the Feng Shui journey. Since Earth's energy is constantly changing, Feng Shui works with this transforming energy and adjusts accordingly. When we are flexible and open to living from achievement to greater awareness, this expedition is an adventure of abundance, fulfillment, and understanding.

Since energy moves in a spiral, both ascending and descending, star and inverted star patterns of energy also exist. Feng Shui honors these natural laws and explains them in useable terms. Studying Feng Shui's graceful approach to family bliss, true abundance, joyful recognition for our achievements, relationship synergy, inspired creativity, synchronicity, attracting a career in a profession that can be likened to a motivational calling, and of course, having the time for self-cultivation and knowledge that will complete you. The aforementioned areas of your life are actual age-old Feng Shui tenets. They correspond to your home and they exist in the NOW… their sweet waters and graceful winds are waiting to be invited into your life.

The words "Feng Shui" are of Chinese origin. I am often asked why these words were christened as the name of an energy practice. There are several reasons and upon reading about them, you will most likely agree with its wisdom. Since the Chinese understand that their structures are living entities and pay homage to Nature and her laws, it was accepted that wind and water were brought into the perception of blessings. Initially, the Chinese farmers watched after the wind. It was necessary for this early agricultural society to protect their crops against its mighty force. As a ten year old, I recall reading Pearl Buck's *The Good Earth.* This moving novel impressed upon me the attention paid to the elements. In order to shield the crops, they made it a custom to plant them on the south-facing slope of mountain.

The second component for a healthy harvest was water. It was indispensable and its liquidity nourished the plants and contributed to their growth. These two elements were always taken into consideration and contributed to a bountiful yield. In turn, an abundant crop return insured that the farmer would be richly rewarded. His family prospered and in this practice of honoring Wind and Water, Feng Shui has its roots.

As the farmer became more urbanized and absorbed into city living, water became the symbol for roads. Of course, all things that pertained to water continued to hold the energy of water. Buildings are synonymous with mountains and the wind still represents change or transformation. Geometric shapes were emblematic and had great meaning. A square epitomizes Earth, a circle characterizes Metal, and curvilinear lines signify Water, an upright rectangle or pillar such as a tree or column symbolizes Wood, and a triangle embodies Fire.

Every Chinese dynasty has revered Feng Shui principles. Since Feng Shui is the reading of Earth energy and Astrology is the understanding of heavenly energies, every Emperor had their personal Feng Shui Master and Astrologer. When our grandson Shawn (then age 11) and I went to the Forbidden City Exhibit at the Phoenix Art Museum in Arizona, he was amazed at the remarkable history laid out before our eyes. The children's curator approached him to answer any questions he may have had and of course, he was full of them. He was especially curious of the many devices that viewed the heavens and the hundreds of maps that detailed the known earth. What exactly did they have in common with the Emperor's lengthy meditations? The curator leaned closer to him, lowered her half-lensed glasses, and as though imparting secret knowledge that was tightly held among the select few, she whispered, "With their Astrologer and Feng Shui Master, they literally, and I do mean literally, controlled the heavens and the earth… they took care of their people and lands." We both felt a chill run down our backs. We could intuit this knowledge to be ever so true.

As we move through the study of Feng Shui, we will touch on many of the historical traditions of numerous cultures and their influence on the changing nature of Feng Shui. Throughout history, tribes and civilizations have honored Nature and her laws. To survive, indigenous people have always observed Nature's cycles. Instinctively, they integrated nature into their homes. Another way of life is that of the Native American tribes. They always faced their homes to the east. Upon rising, they greeted the sunrise with the full knowledge that this was a new day… yesterday was not their concern anymore. They lived fully in the present. Nature not only balanced their lives, but also fed and clothed them. As they listened and lived with Nature, they created and enjoyed harmony and great Spiritual understandings.

From the Roman Empire, Egyptian rule, pre- and post-Byzantine era; ad infinitum, there are countless stories of societies and their relationships to their cultural zymology. These rich tales are retold through famous archeological finds and we can oncc again understand how these articles enriched, encouraged and enlightened their walk of life. Archeological discoveries tell us how previous cultures lived and what the quality of their existence was. Our artifacts also reveal who we are. Whatever our timeline, environmental influences will dictate what kind of life we live. And eventually, it will create our culture and leave evidence of our historical relevance.

# Glossary

**Affirmations -** The process of affirming a positive statement through a spoken or written word. Some affirmations are even expressed through singing. To recite one's belief in what they want to see in their future. Affirmations are a catalyst for transformation and are always avowed in present tense and in first person.

**Altar** - A personal connection between Heaven (spirit) and Earth (physical). An expression of one's relationship with the Universe, Source, God, All-Knowing Spirit, and Cosmic Consciousness. It is a place for prayer, quiet reflection, and meditation.

**Archway** - Symbolic of the gates of heaven and as a portal into a magical garden

**Aromatherapy** – The use of essential oils, individually and in blends, for healing. May be applied directly to the body, or diluted in massage oil for therapeutic treatment. Pure therapeutic-grade essential oils contain their living essence and are capable of "turning on" the reflex trigger points on the body, and adjusting the energy flow for a person or in a room/environment.

**Bagua** - The grid of empowerment. It is a map that resembles a tic-tac-toe board. Bagua means eight-sided as there are eight sections surrounding the center of the Bagua. Each one of these sections has a corresponding life aspect. They are family/roots, pure abundance, integrity/illumination, intimate relationships, inner child/creativity, helpful people/travel, and career/life journey, self-cultivation/knowledge.

**Chakras** - Although there are seven energy centers that are connected to the body's brain, senses, organs and glands, in Feng Shui there are eight. Please see the Self Cultivation and Knowledge chapter for this teaching. The word Chakra means spinning wheels of light. The Egyptians first recognized chakras over 50,000 years ago. Each of these seven energy centers has a specific color, sound or tone, and a purpose. The first Chakra begins at the base of the spine and is called the Kundalini or root chakra. The second one is called the spleen chakra, the third is known as the solar plexus chakra, and the fourth is the heart chakra. The fifth chakra is located at the base of the neck and is called the throat chakra. The Brow or third-eye chakra is number six and the seventh one is the crown chakra and is located at the crown of the head. For further meanings, please see Self-Cultivation and Knowledge.

**Chatzkie** - This is a term I read about and it described the whimsical things we surround ourselves with. For workshops, I adopted the term to better identify an actual object as opposed to a section of the bagua or other Feng Shui teaching. A Chatzkie is always whispering something to your subconscious and when you are aware of what it is that is being said, you will do either of two things. If the message is not supportive, you will be happy to pass it back into the world. Or if it is the souvenir from your beautiful Tahitian vacation with your honey, that is a keeper! A chatzkie that allows you to tap into positive and nurturing energy is what you want to live with.

**Chi** - Prana, Ki, or also known as Qi = the life force; an invisible and powerful energy. Everything in the Universe consists of Chi and in its best idea of itself; it flows with vivacity-gently and continuously. Per Ms. Moog and Ms. Anthony-"There are different kinds of Chi energy, which the Sage has taught us to distinguish as follows:

- The life force that animates all of existence
- The will, which is the sum total of a person's or animals' psychic energy
- The electric energy that enables things outside the body to move.

Together, these different kinds of Chi energy form the Cosmic Consciousness. In the terminology of the *I Ching*, they are made up of the myriad of Helpers of the invisible world. All kinds of Chi energy have a light aspect and a dark aspect, which complement each other. Everything that exists in the Cosmos comes from the attraction between these complements. Chi energy, as in this electric energy, is the product of the interaction between the Cosmic Helpers and the Helpers of Nature. It can be pictured as an energy circuit that is constantly self-renewing."

**Columnar** - The upright symbol of growth and it is associated with the Family/Roots gua.

**Cosmic Consciousness** - The all knowing, all seeing, universal realm of wisdom and truth

**Cosmic Helpers** - per Ms. Moog and Ms. Anthony, "The helpers mentioned in the *I Ching* are not human beings, angels, or supernatural figures; they are individualized aspects of the Cosmic Consciousness and of Nature, and as such, are invisible. Every Helper fulfills a specific function within the harmonious flow of the Cosmos. Every aspect of Nature is a Helper with a unique function in the overall scheme of things. Thus, we learn that the correct way to name a particular Helper is to name it by its unique function… there is a Cosmic Banker that directs money to flow in accordance with the Cosmic Harmonics, there are Business Helpers, and Helpers that help us find lost things or something we need. All the Helpers in their totality maintain and restore the Cosmic Harmony through nourishing, healing, protection, and furthering everything that exists."

**Cosmos** - per Ms. Moog and Ms. Anthony, "Cosmos is the appropriate word to describe the Cosmic Whole. The Cosmic Whole consists of the invisible Cosmic Consciousness and the visible world of Nature. The Cosmic Whole is a system of harmonics."

- **Cure** - A remedy that is symbolic and oriented for transformation

**Curvilinear** - The meandering path water should be flowing in toward your home. Along this stream of good fortune, comes career opportunities and life path confidence.

**Dowsing** - Either a pendulum, a pendant, or a dowsing rod will suffice for clearing energy or asking a question. This method has been used for centuries and if down properly will accomplish all that you intend for it to.

**Dream Catcher** - This circle of webbed net is a Native American tradition to catch the dreams of the night and bring them into the day. It is considered to bring good luck and of course, beautiful dreams. A knot, or "mistake," is intentionally woven into each dream catcher to prevent and trap any possible bad dreams.

**EMF or Electromagnetic Fields** - These fields affect the home or workspace by way of energy. You can purchase a Gauss meter to help your understand how strong the fields of your television, computers, and other electrical sources are.

**Endless Knot** - In China, this important braid or knot represents the unceasing good luck and the promise of a long life. Since the knot turns back unto itself, it is never ending.
**Five Elements** - The ancients knew the connectivity of the universe and how all things as created from nature's five elements of Wood, Fire, Earth, Metal, and Water. In their productive cycle and in their controlling cycle, they create balance and harmony.

**Grounding** – Anchoring your spiritual presence in your physical body.

**Gua** – One of nine sections of the Bagua Map

**Guide** - a Cosmic Helper

**Harmony Balls** – Balls containing bells that make a light jingling sound as they are rolled between the palms of the hands. Useful for relaxation, or clearing the energy in a room.

**Intuition** – An inner feeling that something is either very right or very wrong. Living with intuition means listening to these feelings, honoring them, and acting on them.

**Journaling** – Keeping a written record of your daily thoughts and feelings. Can be very therapeutic. Helps mental and emotional clarity and understanding. Can be a catalyst for positive change.

**Karma** – The principle of balance in physical life, cause and effect, action and reaction. Has been interpreted as "fate", "destiny" or the ordering of life around actions and thoughts of the past.

**Quan Yin** – The Asian goddess of mercy, compassion, peace and healing.

**Labyrinth** - Along with the circle, the labyrinth is an important geometric shape. This is not a maze as there are sacred rules that apply to its design. There is a one way path to the center of the structure and through a labyrinth collects the energy in this center and sets it free. It represents life's journey with all of the challenges that are encountered along the way. Strength and vitality are enhanced when one walks the labyrinth.

**Lucid Dreaming** – Awareness of dreaming even as the dream is in progress. May even include the ability to consciously affect the events of the dream.

**Mandala** - The Sanskrit word means "holy or magic circle." A mandala is a cosmogram. The circle is heaven and the squares are the compass's four corners. It is the symbol of the universe. The Mandala's sacred geometry represents wholeness and symbolizes focus and transformation of the mind. It is a powerful tool

**Medicine Wheel** - The Native American's form of the Mandala. It represents their connection to the cycles of life. The Medicine Wheel is a mirror of our strengths and weaknesses. It provides a vision of what we are to become. This is the journey of authentic living and spiritual growth.

**Mentors** - People or saints who have inspired us to create a legacy that will serve seven generations after us, to live a life of integrity, generosity, and love. A mentor is an example of living well and living from the heart with compassion and dedication.

**Prayer Wheel** - This Tibetan implement sends blessings out into the world. They contain hand written prayers and spin prayers throughout the space.

**Residual Energy -** The energy of the person who originally built or owned a home, business, or crafted an object. This kind of energy can actually be very supportive, because of the care and love that went into the project or object. Every thing has residential energy, so if you want to be sure that you are free from any other person's karmic journey, it is best to cleanse and bless it.

**Sacred Items -** These are objects that have a special place in your heart and along your journey they have mile markers of your growth. With use, these sacred items enable you to expand your consciousness and focus. I have feathers, special gemstones, my Tibetan bell, my Chrysanthemum stone, my amber Kuan Yin, dolphins figurines, and too many items to name here. Honor your sacred objects and they will assist you on your journey.

**Symbolism** – One item represents or gives meaning to another or to a situation or place.

**Synchronicity** - a series of everyday coincidences that are actually linked by extraordinary circumstances. Carl Jung coined the phrase that means to be in the right place at the right time.

**Thunderbolt/Dorje** - The loud crashing of thunder represents the disruption of the cosmos and its mission per the Buddhist is "to split ignorance down the middle to liberate understanding." It releases stagnant energies.

**Tri gram -** The broken yin lines and the solid yang lines make up a trigram.

**Visualization** – The process of using inner imagery to "see" a desired outcome, or to assist with meditative focus.

**Yin & Yang -** We are surrounded by opposites. This symbolizes the feminine becoming the masculine as the masculine becomes the feminine. Without yin there would not be a yang and without yang, there would not be a yin. Without reset there is not movement and without the darkness there could not be light. Within this balance harmony and unity are created.

# Part One:

# The Art of Placement

# -

# The Symbolism & Science of Feng Shui

## *Everything is Energy*

A timeless map called the Template of Alchemy/Bagua demarcates specific areas in your home and work environments. Each section or Gua is in relation to various facets of life and enjoys a pattern projected by the innate flow of nature itself. Depending on your blueprint, cherished relationships, inspired creativity, harmony, and even your fame is influenced. Peace and harmony reside within you. In fact, each of us is connected to one another. This understanding creates a nurturing environment furthering us one and all to be well & positively transformed!

Feng Shui speaks a universal language comprehended by both cosmic consciousness & humanity. Concurrently, it speaks through each Gua and on all levels of consciousness, revealing what you desire most. These golden harmonious healing banners vibrate with the symbolism to transmit and manifest your deepest longings.

Set intention with these elegant scrolls and bring into one's life all that is beautiful, sacred, and precious. Simply BE with these golden symbolic banners of Integrity, Comfort, Peace, Wisdom, & Love. Reciprocity of each will joyfully ensue.

# 1

# The Home Whisperer

In the vastness of the Universe, humanity is an essential being able to contribute to cosmic evolvement. The inner home is how you advance, spiritually and intuitively. Your outer home is how you pave the path to these realizations and secure its progress. Since we now can appreciate that when translated, Feng Shui represents Wind and Water or the Unseen and the Seen, wind and water are the weavers of intentions manifested by movement. Wind and water's movements are powerful forces of nature. The wind and water of transformation swirl around you daily, creating awakened clarity-within and without. Feng Shui is the art, symbolism, and science of placement. It is an information system whose mission is to enhance beauty, wellness, abundance, joy, self-actualization and harmony. Feng Shui, or "geomancy" as it is also known, has it roots in quantum physics and occurs naturally in the universe's magnetic field of energy.

Subconsciously and consciously, the field of energy at play already influences you within your home. Whether you "believe" in Feng Shui or not, it works. When you learn to hear what your home is actually saying, you will have developed you Feng Shui ears. Along the way, you will learn how to "read" energy, too. Presently, your home's own alpha pattern of waves are determined by the following in your environment: Symbolism, the circulation (or lack of) Chi (life force), being clutter free, the choice of color, numerical influences, placement and their relationship to space.

The practice of Feng Shui upgrades a home's algorithm to a supportive energetic field of accelerating creativity, manifestation, and greater awareness. Decoding this matrix and establishing flow enhances your intuition, intentions and inspiration.

Discover how to mine the treasures of your inner and outer home and harness the Universe's energies. Through the study of Feng Shui, one can draw from its vast landscape to improve the quality of life's experiences. Embodying the flow of nature's elements, one is empowered to create positive life transitions. To be aware of being one with the web of life generates deep inner peace. Inner peace creates well-being and contentment.

Feng Shui speaks a universal language comprehended by both the cosmic consciousness & humanity. As a Home Whisperer, you will learn this language. Concurrently, it speaks through each Gua and on all levels of consciousness revealing what you desire most.

The Home Whisperer's journey is one of discovery and revelation knowledge. You are an energetic being and everything that surrounds you has a blueprint. At the heart of this book is the awareness of how to live in harmony and balance. Harmony holds the energy of infinite love and abundance. Balance transmits joy and healing back to us in the form of vibrations.

Look around your outer home and listen to what it is saying to you. Quiet your mind and still your heart… now, once again… listen closely. Your inner and outer treasures await you.

The Inner Home Nine-Year Life Cycle is based on Feng Shui's five-element pattern and Bagua system. Each person embodies a unique set of inner strengths and innate talents. This is considered your algorithm. Your innate traits and characteristics will be revealed within this teaching. Your Cosmic Algorithm will show you the highest idea of your path. This aligns and connects you with Universal flow.

Through one's life path, unique skill sets waft around you continually, desiring to be called forth. They are part of a universal pattern that, once discovered, brings joy. At last, you can recognize the brilliance of your life's path. This understanding helps you to finally *know* what strengths gently push you and, at the same time, creatively pulls you along. As it has been written in many texts and quoted by numerous masters, "You don't have to push the river; you can simply enjoy being in the flow." Within this place lie the treasures of your inner home.

Your exclusivity is influenced by the universal wisdom held within the elements of water, wood, fire, earth, and metal and how they relate to one another within your energetic pattern. This awareness enhances your strengths and cultivates your quantum potentiality. The Inner Home Nine-Year Cycle's support system is derived from the feminine-yin and masculine-yang properties of these elements. In order to create balance in one's life, it is essential to discover your personal expression. The map to these ancient insights shows you exactly how to mine the treasures of your inner and manifest them in your outer home. It paves a path to the clarity of your destiny, mission, and purpose.

Since life phases are cyclic, when you are made aware of where you are in your personal and yet universal pattern, you will be in the flow and enjoy clarity. Embracing the transformations along your life path gifts you with flexibility. Just like nature dictates the changing of the season, the weather patterns, and the evolution of time itself, the Inner Home forecasts your personal weather system. For instance, being grounded, calm and inspired helps you to focus in the moment.

# 2

# –

# We Are One

This imagery encapsulates all that is and all that has ever been. It is this interrelatedness that connects one to another. Feng Shui is the art, science, and symbolism of Life. It also includes the brilliant dimensions along one's inner life path. **We are connected in the web of life - we are all one.** All life or life matter is energy, frequency, vibration, or merely sound waves and light in a condensed form. When the treasures of our inner and outer homes are unearthed, the awareness of quantum wholeness emerges allowing us to live in fullness and purpose.

The archetypal images, animal totems, and symbolism found within numbers, colors, geometrical shapes, gemstones, plants, flowers and trees also have a living vibration. Even inanimate objects are alive as they are imbued with your memory and possess a consciousness. Their frequency pattern enables us to experience them as an energetic model. Together with this awareness, we create cohesive living.

The thought patterns we generate, the objects we surround ourselves with and the kind of personal energy we generate, all work together to not only enhance our outer homes, but also to transform our inner home. As we find ourselves more in sync with nature, our choices begin to resonate with cosmic harmony, our skill-sets are boosted and our natural talents are revealed, and thus, we are prospered. Through our success, we help others succeed.

In the Hindu tradition, there was A Web Of Indra. The legend told of energetic grids that criss-crossed and surrounded the earth. At each place where the grids met, there was a pearl and this beautiful pearl represented a person. It was said that when a candle was shown upon one pear, the entire web was aglow. This vital teaching portrays the truth of our connectivity. When one of us gains awakened enlightenment, we are all expanded and our lives are broadened.

Hexagram 42 from the I Ching by Hanna Moog and Carol Anthony, "Increasing the welfare of the whole is a Cosmic Principle that reveals the loving and caring nature of the Cosmos… the Whole." As we are able to feel the interconnection we have with one another, the fusion of wholeness takes place in the core of our beings. This shift creates a balance honoring the Universal laws. Please take to heart the ancient teachings of the Hoop of Life and the Web of Indra. Whether you recognize these traditions or not, they are at soul-play in your life.

## Change

Change is constant because all creation is in an eternal state of flux, or better yet, in a constant state of evolution. All of nature, including we humans, has the ability to grow and transform. If you are not living the life you love, it is within your grasp to change it. Through your self-talk and making the time to space clear your home, adjust it according to nature, and live in gratitude, you can live the life you so desire. You can enjoy a life of creativity, joy, wellness, happiness, and pure abundance.

## Deep Beauty

Beauty comes from within and is a gift of the heart. To see life as beautiful enables us to notice each and every situation possessing a hidden opportunity or treasure. Adversity is the seed of greatness. When seen through the eyes of beauty, this state of circumstance opens the heart to a magnificent journey. With beauty in your soul, you can quickly walk through to the end of old karmic challenges. Beauty allows you to step into the higher patterns of transformation.

## The Journey of Transformation

The journey of transformation begins with self. Using the map provided within this book as a mirror, you will discover the treasures of courage, strength, insight, compassion, trust, commitment, creativity, guidance, wisdom, and love that are hidden within your inner and outer home. It may very well be that you are already using some of these gifts to enrich your life. However, it is possible that you are stuck in using the same treasures repeatedly and do not develop the well roundedness that all of these treasures offer. This treasure map is a means of evaluating our steps forward. The transformational journey from the within to the without, reveals our interconnectivity with the universe and radiantly paves the life path with joy, wisdom, synchronicity, and love.

## A Jewel to Re*Member

*All things in the universe enjoy interrelatedness as everything is connected to one another. Truly, WE ARE ONE. – SJH*

# 3

# The Art of Placement, Symbolism & Quantum Science

## Wind and Water

Imagery: Goethe's quote "The Soul of Man is equal to water & The Fate of Man is equal to the Wind." Learning to flow with the unseen/wind and water/seen is the mastering of life itself. The quest is to work with rather than against wind and water. Water collects energy and wind scatters it.

Feng Shui (Feng Shui) literally translated means Wind and Water or the Unseen and the Seen. Wind and water are powerful forces within Nature and each has the ability to create change. They are a metaphor of how to stay centered, in harmony and at peace…regardless of the whirling energies surrounding us. Drawing upon these energy's power improves and enhances your life's experiences. Embodying their symbolic flow into your environment teaches you how to embrace and generate positive transitions in your life. When you are out of Nature's flow, you are open to experience conflict. Specific places in your environment, in relation to various facets of your life, enjoy a pattern projected by Nature. Depending on your home's blue print, your pure abundance, family comfort, health, cherished relationships, creativity, and even your fame and recognition are influenced.

## Wind ~ The Unseen

The unseen winds twirl about the world; these zephyrs gently and/or forcefully swirl through the lands inviting in active change in the climate. Wind powers up the wind turbines for energetic value; its cool breezes offer welcome relief from the "dog days" of summer. Airstreams transform and cleanse Mother Earth. In extreme currents of air, tornadoes or hurricanes (wind and water) are generated and mayhem can soon follow. When a microburst suddenly begins to white cap the water across a lake's otherwise calm surface, any boaters must seek refuge against the storm. It is our responsibility to be mindful of the moods of wind and water.

In the Disney film *Pocahontas*, the sound track lyrics to *"The Colors Of The Wind"* ask, "Can you paint with all the colors of the wind?" Below, draw a circle around the following words in the following place around this circle. On the left hand middle part of the circle, begin with * Green, proceed to the upper left of the same circle - Purple, the top center - Red, follow along to the top right hand part - Pink, down below it and in the center - Gold, underneath and in the bottom right area - Silver, the bottom center - Black, and bottom left - Blue, and the Center-Yellow.

RED

PURPLE PINK

* GREEN YELLOW GOLD

BLUE SILVER

BLACK

This exercise is a prelude to your work with the energy of color, patterns, universal form and function. Symbolically imagine of all of the colors of the wind's energy. Beginning at the circle's middle left, look at the cool, nurturing **Green** that spins healing through the air; in clockwise fashion move on to **Purple**'s true abundance calling forth the winds of fortune; envision the ruby **Red** winds churning up your enthusiasm and passions; the glow of **Pink** sparking romantic eddies; **Golden** spirals of wind ushering in creativity; **Silver** winds blowing through your angelic thoughts, stirring up the spiritual **Black**ness of energy that powers up your life's flow; **Blue** is then allowed open up wisdom and it is from this place that the **Yellow** winds produce vibrations or frequencies vital to your being centered.

*He makes WINDS his messenger...Psalms 104:4*

## Water ~ The Seen

The visible power of water is, in itself, life-giving. The vastness of the ocean, the stillness of a pond, the flow of a stream, lake, the meandering of a river or the waterfall's cascading energy. Water symbolizes the physical world. It's timeless as this energy speaks to your spirit, the inner yearning to simply be.

The down side of water is when excessive rainfall creates flash-flooding and torrential downpours flood the streets in a massive deluge. Or hurricanes pound the shoreline wreaking havoc for miles. When rushing waters race through the canyons or a tsunami swallows up entire villages, this is the darker side of water's fury.

Peaceful waters speak of floating, flowing, and being carefree. The stillness of a pond articulates the long-term benefits of being quiet. A lake's mirror-like reflection is reminiscent of serenity. The stream's rambling waters carry one forward into places of deep tranquility. The waterfall magically cascades into the deepest part of our being, transporting us into the heart of beauty. We are connected to this flow.

The dance of Wind and Water commenced at the beginning of creation. It is circuitous. As the wind spins the water and in turn, the water creates flow, energy moves, preventing our global environment from experiencing complete stagnation. Any time there are extreme changes in the environment, there is also an opportunity to create renewal in your awareness or your perception. Water renews and Wind rejuvenates. The integrity of Wind and Water are energetically vital. Find harmony within and between these two energies as they are made whole, we experience balance. Although we are reminded to respect these energies, the opportunity is to avoid being caught up in their fleeting dramas… staying centered.

## Your Noble Home

In the process of staying centered, we find how creating a noble home supports this place of agreement. Inherently, we understand that the spaces containing our most complimentary well-being are those in alignment with Nature and cosmic harmony. Our home is our place to grow, to evolve, to learn, to relax into the purest expression of our body/mind/spirit.

Our noble home is where we can untangle life's little knots and perceive what the next step on our life path should be. In the comfort and security of our noble home, we can know when it is time to pull back from a situation. To be open to spirit, hear it whisper in our heart, nurturing it through our self-talk and prayer/meditation. Think about the definite correlation to our present thoughts and your life's condition. On the space provided, write down everything you can think of to be thankful for. "Wake at dawn with a winged heart and give thanks for an other day of loving." ~ Kahlil Gibran

*My Gratitude List:*

My gifted Partner & her ever loving Love
That I can write these wonderful plays
My Cat friends and their furry ways
My friends that really are TRUE Blue
My car - My computer
My Printer, People who helped me get to [illegible] safe understanding of the Same
That I'm not in the hospital
My HOUSE especially Astara, Heating
[illegible] - My life is too full of good things too many to put in this format/list

Symbolism

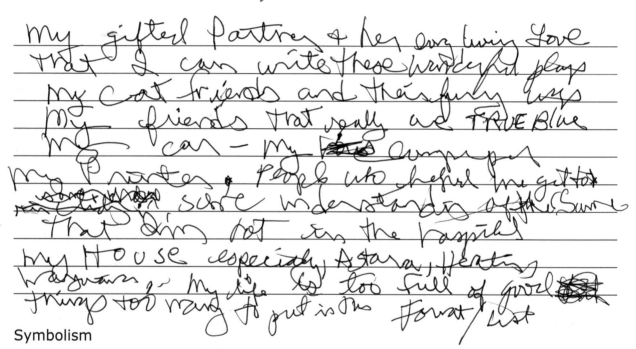

Symbols express meaning by way of universal and personal messages. As Psalms 104:4 shared, "Messages are carried on the winds." Our environments are richly textured with a symbolic messaging system. These messages are transformed to symbols - the hidden treasures of your inner and outer life. Their discernible meanings are indicative of exactly what the object is 'saying to you.' As you train yourself to be a home whisperer, you will understand the language of the seen and the unseen. Within, nurturing and highly supportive objects awaken you; you will discern their symbolic messages. The seen and the unseen evolve into a symbiotic process and live together harmoniously. In turn, you are able to enjoy a calmer, peaceful and integrated atmosphere. This is deeply healing.

As we create our heavenly haven, the unseen world and the seen world align with our harmony. This enables us to broaden our awareness of the intricacies of life. Where our spirit soars and our soul is fed, contentment flourishes with the ongoing flow of intelligence, peace and love. Throughout your entire life, you have been given clues to these messages that sparkle toward your refined quality of life. Look around the room you are reading this book in. Write down the first seven objects that you see. For discussion, I will describe the first seven items I see. I am at my desk and to the left of my computer monitor, I have the following: a lamp, 2 photos, a bell with a metal butterfly clipped to its handle, a Quan Yin figurine, and a silver box.

Within one look or pan of this area, my mind/body/spirit processes the meaning and the energy held within each of these items. This is what they are saying to me. 1. The Lamp - This hand painted lamp and its shade are reminders of fellowship, fun, and friends.

One of my photos is of Louis Hay, Terah Kathryn Collins and myself. The other is a wonderful picture of Denise Linn. These women are highly successful authors and widely published. For me, they represent inspiration and following through to the fulfillment of your intention.

The Tibetan bell is a gift from Denise Linn. According to Denise, this is a sign of personal attunement and celebration. The butterfly has amber gemstones on its wings and is a gift from my husband. Per Ted Andrews in *Animal Totems*, a butterfly symbolizes transformation and the dance of joy. Each item is especially dear to me and gives me cause to celebrate life with joy and embrace my transformation readily.

Quan Yin. She is the soul of compassion. This figurine is especially symbolic as she is carved from pure amber. According to the Crystal Bible, Amber is not a crystal at all. It is tree resin that solidified and became fossilized. It has strong connections with the earth and is a grounding stone for higher energies. Amber is a powerful healer and cleanser that draws dis-ease from the body and promotes tissue revitalization. It also cleans the environment and the chakras. It absorbs negative energies and transmutes them into positive forces that stimulate the body to heal itself. A powerful protector, it links the everyday self to the higher spiritual reality.

Psychologically, Amber brings stability to life but also motivates by linking what is wished for to the drive to achieve it. Its warm, bright energies translate into a sunny, spontaneous disposition that respects tradition. Mentally, Amber stimulates the intellect, clears depression and promotes a positive mental state and creative self-expression. It brings balance and patience, and encourages decision-making, being a useful memory aid. Its flexibility dissolves opposition. Emotionally, Amber encourages peacefulness and develops trust. Spiritually, Amber promotes altruism and brings wisdom.

Since the silver box is in my Helpful People/Travel area, it represents the assistance of the cosmic helpers in all that I do. I am a bridge of the matter-of-fact mind/soul to an intuitive, artistic, loving expression.

These symbolic objects serve and nurture the very core of my being. They align my life to the highest cosmic idea. Since they work on multiple layers, I joyously respond in the depth and height of my conscious and unconscious self. By living with what you love, your chatzkies speak to you in the language of love and integrity. The more aware you are of your surrounding items, the more focused you will become on wholeness and unity with the universe and with the wellness of your mind, body, and spirit.

## Quantum Science

We live in a new world. The old paradigm has faded away and it is indeed a new time. It is a fact that your thoughts, words, and deeds or consciousness affects the performance of subatomic particles. In quantum physics, particles move backwards as well as forwards in time and are seen in all possible places at once. As everything is made of energy, and energy affects energy, everything in your environment affects your inner state, and your thoughts affect your experience and environment. If you toss a pebble into the ocean, it isn't just the immediate trail of the pebble's fall that is affected by its passage – the whole ocean must shift to accommodate the pebble. The effects may be subtle, but they are there.

Be a part of this rewarding, creative, fulfilling, & uplifting experience and know that quantum physics supports this understanding.

# 4

# -

# Chi – the Life Force

**Visualization**: A circuitous flow of energy

Translating the Oriental word "Chi" into English means more than the word "energy." Chi is a complex concept that is fundamental to Chinese philosophy, medicine, and martial arts. Understanding that everything in the Universe possesses the Chi's invisible power helps to accept Chi as kinetic and potential energy and at the same time it is static matter capable of transforming into either kinetic or potential energy.

Chi is a circuitous flow of energy connecting humankind with wind and water's natural forces flowing from the Cosmic Consciousness of Heaven and the Earth. Chi is commonly used in Feng Shui as an explanation of life force. As in most Oriental words, our English language falls very short of their flowery expression.

Chi is the cosmic breath of the universe where all blessings flow, it is the interconnection of heaven and earth and when it isn't moving, stagnation sets in. This can be in our bodies, our inner and outer homes; even our thought processes must have brilliant or less than excellent Chi will settle in. Chi is the movement we invite into our life to bless us and advance our wisdom, our intuition and to open our perceptions with unconditional love.

This powerful field enhances the quality of life by working with the principles of movement and flow, and it gives life to all organic matter. Chi is considered life's breath, as it is the electromagnetic energy inherent in and circulating around all living things. Recognized by many cultures, this cosmic Chi is also called Ki by the Japanese and by the Indians, Prana.

Pronounced as chee and also spelled as Qi, Chi is constantly changing form. Just as our bodies must have healthy circulation, so must our living spaces. The flow of Chi in a space determines the quality of life experienced within the space. The flow of Chi decides its health, growth and abundance. There are many paths to improve the Chi of your inner and outer home.

Since Chi is fundamental to humankind, the cosmos and Earth, you can understand why its unrestricted flow is essential. This system has its roots in acupuncture's early beginnings and continues through to today. Just as Feng Shui works with the environment, acupuncture's mission is to stimulate and enhance Chi throughout the body. The body has meridians or channels where the energy moves or doesn't move, acupuncture works to clear those channels and removes the blockage. Therefore, Chi can once again move and health is restored to a deprived area. The same is true for our spaces. When the flow of Chi is stimulated, vitality and needed oxygen are restored.

Chi vibrates at a higher vibration when your home is cleared of negative energies and is re-energized with positive energies. Your home and you body are each a receptacle or vessel of loving vibrational energies. This book teaches you how to enhance these energies unlocking the mysteries of Feng Shui. Over the following chapters, you will learn how to wipe out inert energy and how to best accomplish instilling positive energies.

## Mouth of Chi

Your architectural front door is considered the mouth of Chi and plays a powerful part in the lives of the residents. Even if you use a side door or a garage door, the chi energy initially comes through the formal front door. This is where your expectations are generated. Since the front door connects you to the world, it graciously invites or shuns your blessings. The entrance also signifies who you are.

In order for the home to operate on higher levels of opportunities, it is important to keep the door free of debris and in good working order. Your main door should be most inviting and not a tree or tall bush impeding the entrance. It is best when your front door doesn't open onto a stairway, as your good fortune will flow right out of the door. If it is safe, place a potted plant at the foot of the stairs to slow the energy down. Plus, you can hang a large, dynamic picture at the top of the stairs as this will pull the energy up instead of down. Placing a crystal on the top rung of the stairs on a nine-inch red ribbon is a traditional cure.

Upon opening your front door, check to see if you have a door or large window lining up with this portal. This is indicative of great sums of money and/or Chi coming in and then pouring right back out the back door. I was introduced to Feng Shui by this very pattern.

Our front door lined up with the French door in the foyer and directly behind that through the living room was our large (9' wide!) arcadia window/door. Whoops!! Once I knew about this pattern, I hung a curtain sheer on the French door and placed a beautiful red velvet drape over the arcadia door panels. Two days later one of our employees resigned and unbeknownst to us, this person had been a source of great discontent. Their departure cleared the air for all of the other employees to be their very best selves. What a difference that made in our bottom line!

Make sure that your front entrance is well lit. This not only bodes well for potential visitors but especially for you. Also, placing a water fountain to the left of the door, as you look out of your front door, is an auspicious addition to your front entrance. During the cold winter mouths, place black rocks in the fountain to symbolize water. Select a fountain whose flow is directed towards the front door or circulates around the fountain itself. A fountain that pours out to the street is inauspicious. Which reminds me, please face all of your lawn statuaries toward your door. These blessings pour forth to your home and then you are a blessing back unto the world.

Attractive, decorative items placed around the door not only enliven the Chi, they create kismet. In late spring, summer and early fall, placing a healthy Jade plant by the doorway is symbolic of good fortune. During the late fall or winter, merely bring the plant indoors and place in a sunny location. Jade is associated with wealth and reliability.

To celebrate the joys of life, display a wreath (thematically appropriate) on your front door. For example, using ivy will promote trusted friendships and boxwood symbolizes a long life. For a detailed list of specific meanings, please refer to Chapter 22 on flowers. For example, wreaths are symbolic of unity, joy, togetherness (they are commonly used in marriage ceremonies), fame, honor and peace. Make sure your wreath is generous and embodies good will. Do not allow your wreath to whither; this will produce stagnate energy.

Wind socks, chimes and flags are excellent energy boosters and placed beside the front door can generate increased Chi. Be certain that these are not in front of your door because the opposite will occur, your energy will be blocked. Now you know how to enhance an abundant flow of energy to your home so enjoy following your instincts.

## A Jewel To Re*Member

*Our front doors are passageways transitioning all who enter into our sacred space from the world into our paradise. A door is a mystical portal into our universe of serenity. It is a gateway to peaceful tranquility. It is a threshold of majesty and lends entry to our sanctuary. Our magical entrance is truly meant to en-trance or to captivate us.*

*When we leave our abodes, we are refreshed, calm and collected. We are ready to return to the world in a state of knowing and a state of being fully present. Since we are walking in gratitude, we easily bless everyone who crosses our path. We delight in our enchanted life. The doors of opportunity are infinitely open to us. We joyfully and confidently step through them.*

*- SJH*

# 5

# –

# The Field of Intention

## Setting Intention

The fine art of manifestation begins with setting intentions. It is the process of aligning yourself with your dreams, heart desires or wishes. It is unraveling the elegant secret of drawing your treasured dreams to you. When you are very clear about what it is that you care to create, a commitment is formed. In turn, this commitment or promise, along with the universe, empowers you to attract exactly what you desire. From creating a peaceful home to an impeccable career where you express your calling, powerful intention is fulfilled. Intention is to live in the present of knowing your dreams are being manifested. Aligning with your intention allows greater focus to narrow the gap between now and then. As you make changes in your noble home, make them with your intentional steps towards creating the life you desire.

We must ask ourselves, "What is my deepest and highest purpose?" Through vertical and inner growth, we can enjoy fulfilling relationships, business excellence, pleasing travel experiences, health and wellness and of course pure abundance. A noble home attracts the realization of your intentions. You go from being a pretender to being an intender. After giving our intentions reflective thought, it is important to write our intentions down. After committing them to paper, it is as if we are beckoning them forth as they are already being created. When describing our intentions, we must be as explicit as possible. We can number them or we can even create a story around what we would like to experience in your life.

We are creating an agreement with our self. There is an exquisite quality of refined communications when we make a contract with our self…from the mystical ethers into tangible reality. Adding the phrase THIS OR BETTER to our lists opens up the universe's greater plans for us; preventing us from limiting ourselves. On too many occasions to mention, my Feng Shui clients have called me within hours of becoming intenders to exclaim, "You won't believe what just happened." They are amazed with their results and yet, they are the ones who created the manifestation. I was only the catalyst. They took the time to write down their wishes and the doors of fulfillment opened wide.

Be very present with the affirmation process. Awareness is only able to penetrate and bless you according to the focus and attention you give it. Going through the words of an affirmation without a connection or a feeling is simply a waste of your time. Make you time valuable and give it the attention it deserves. Intentions are the blueprint of your future…so what are you waiting for???? The following are intentions I have shared with my clients

Begin with "I easily live a productive and joyous life." Know that something is only as hard as you perceive it to be. The word easily flows out before you and smoothes your way. Life is lived through your perceptions so connect with a higher idea of life and ENJOY!

1. I radiate health and joyous vitality.
2. Enrichment flows freely to me for my personal use.
3. I am One with Unlimited Blessings.
4. I am whole in body/mind/spirit.
5. I travel in safe passage enjoying complete synchronicity.
6. My career is in alignment with my life's purpose.
7. Prosperity swirls around and I live a life of abundance.
8. I am content, at peace and I live in LOVE.
9. Balance and harmony reside in my home and in my world.
10. I am whole, holy, and perfect.
11. Harmonious family relationships abound.
12. My home gathers gratitude and permeates our walls.
13. I embrace the changes in my life and rejoice in my transformations.
14. I am a creative person who lives in spontaneity.
15. I have a balanced social life with like-minded yet diverse friends.
16. My home is my personal sanctuary.
17. Kindness weaves itself through my life tapestry.
18. I rest in the conscious awareness of richness.

19. Serenity and I are ONE.

My intentions are~

Write intentions in your notebook. Do not limit your goals and dreams. Think of yourself as an intentional person, living an intentional life, with intentional purpose. Through the support of your inner and outer home, you will find how things that you need and want all begin to flow to you. You are de-cluttering your mind and de-cluttering your home. When you do this, you have a clear heart. These newly opened spaces are now ready to receive all of the new and wonderful experiences just waiting to be infused into your life. Pull out the old and toss out that which no longer serves you. This helps you to connect with your intentions through generosity.

A Jewel To Re*Member

*Be Gentle To Yourself ~ Nurture Yourself with positive thoughts and your body knowingly responds. Rejoice with all your present blessings and your heart is filled with gratitude. Steep yourself into the deep contentment and the core of your being is satisfied. Develop a loving language and speak only tender words to yourself and others. Abide by these truths and grace will abide within you with the glow of inner peace and wisdom. – SJH*

# 6

# -

# Space-Clearing - De-Cluttering for Your Highest Destiny

Imagery: A beam of light shown forth, emitting radiance from the Cosmic Order

In order for energy to move through your space unencumbered, like a beam of light, it is important that order be present. Over the years, I have shown up for a scheduled Feng Shui consultation only to find the client's environment in chaos. The word "clutter" is likened to the word "coagulate" - and that's about as stuck as you can get. So let's get our home's arteries flowing, as this helps to create a noble home.

It is a fundamental Universal law when a home's energy is blocked, Chi will not freely flow in, around or through it. This principle influences your family bonds and creates dissention. Your finances will be challenged and you can become backed-up on your well-earned pay raise. Instead of a dazzling reputation, you will not shine. Clutter can strain intimate relationships, and instead of heart-to-heart interludes where mutual support thrives, disappointment can ensue. Creativity can find your muse MIA and projects will run long over their timeline. Helpful people will not be available and travel plans can be thwarted. Clutter will show up in your career and life journey by being uninspired or vague about exactly what your purpose is. Your time to meditate will be foiled and as a result, you will not hear wisdom's voice.

Once we establish that clutter is blocking the flow of positive energy through their environment, we reschedule their home or business's energy work for a later date. Privately, the client begins at their front door in a clock-wise fashion; and they take a conscious walk through their home. The client has a notebook and, with their head, heart and hand, writes down the items that immediately come to mind that no longer serve them. The notes help them realize if they are still emotionally connected to this item or not. The questions they ask of any item are as follows:

1. Do I love it? It is essential to live with what you absolutely and positively love. Doing so reminds you how joyous life is and supports the entirety of you.
2. Have I used in this year? Chances are that this item now longer serves you.
3. Is there a sentimental pull and if so, what is it attached to? If there is an object or objects in your home that call to you from a sad or tragic time, you will continue to relive this kind of low energy.
4. Would someone else benefit from having this item and who is that person? Very often we are not using some of our past interest in the way they could serve someone else. For example, I used to paint artistically and over the years, I moved on to other interests. I still had many useful items that I knew our granddaughters would thoroughly enjoy. Passing these along to them was a delight.

Each resident is responsible for his or her private space and as a family; they can decide what to discard in the communal areas. After they have worked through their home from one drawer at a time to large areas, they find they are motivated to move forward and even tackle their least favorite areas. The more they are willing to do, the easier it is to do. This plan does not overwhelm the client as it actually stimulates them!

Once we correlate the parts of the body to the sections of our home via the Feng Shui map (Chapter 9), we are sure to notice a connection to how well our body is being de-cluttered. I have personally had a significant improvement in my health when I began to stay organized. I am presently more casual in my task-orientation and put more emphasis on relationships. In my life, I have proven increased quality time with my beloved husband, treasured children, precious grandchildren and valued friends. When positive energy flows easily through our homes and heart, joy is present.

To begin your personal de-cluttering journey, take your note pad and walk through of your home, focused on de-cluttering. Notice everything in the room, open the drawers, look under the sofa and the beds… as Terah Kathryn Collins is famous for teaching, "There is no place to hide in Feng Shui!" This note pad will be your point of reference. At the top of each page, write an affirmation such as "I easily move outdated items out of my home." "Throughout my entire home, energy flows freely and abundantly." "I am at peace in my home."

In the late 1970s, Time Management seminars were plentiful. To fulfill one's goals, it was simple… select your priorities and then accordingly, you could bend time and space. Out of this era, the Day Planner, Day Runner, FiloFax and many other companies were birthed. Those workshops taught me some brilliant organizational skills and over the years, I have morphed them into my energetic de-cluttering knowledge.

It is a fact that, in this day and age, we are each a manager of great abundance. I have seen all too many garages that are filled to overflowing with stuff. In fact, one of the next trends to take off, as of this 2006 writing, is professional garage-organizers. I am fortunate in that my husband keeps our garages and his workshop in impeccable order.

However, for those of us who have to stay on task, I have some suggestions. In our offices and personal financial responsibilities, we will handle reams of paper work during the course of a lifetime. Years ago, my favorite Time Manager facilitator, Rita Davenport of Phoenix, Arizona, taught me the importance of handling a sheet of paper or mail only once. WOW, now that was a breakthrough. I can still hear her speaking this truth and it is essential that you apply this nugget to your organizational system. Plus, there are excellent containers to keep you life orderly once you are de-cluttered.

If you feel overwhelmed, please be mindful of staying in the energy of peace and clarity. There are only so many hours in a day, so dedicate a fifteen-minute timeline to just one drawer, one shelf or even one room. When my daughter was taking piano lessons, she did not like the idea of practicing for 30 minutes. When we reduced it to two separate fifteen-minute increments, she was able to move through the material and enjoyed the process of learning. Break up your time and soon, you too will be flowing freely within your space.

See how much you can accomplish by staying in a place of balance and harmony. My approach is non-clinical and its results, when followed, are highly effective. Once you decide to de-clutter, do not hesitate to follow through. You will find that by doing so, opportunities begin to show up for you. You are in the right place at the right time… Hmmm, go figure!!

## How To Be Decisive

To help you decide what items should go, pretend you are moving your entire house and ask yourself if this item is important enough to make the leap forward. After you have determined what items need to go, start small with your cupboards or drawers. As you take these baby steps, you will gain self-assurance. Then you can move into the midsize and onto the larger areas. When you are ready, gather together five containers made of either plastic, cardboard, wicker, and even paper sacks that will stand on their own will work. Label them as follows: THROW-AWAY, GIVE-AWAY, PUT-AWAY, SELL-AWAY, and last, but not least, a large container for REPAIR items. These are self-explanatory and as you move through the items after you have separated them, you will experience a great sense of peace. Allow relief to wash over you, because you have just stepped into a harmonious flow that relaxes and supports you.

To prevent future clutter from raising its ugly head and procreating over night, before purchasing any possible new items, ask yourself how this will benefit or increase your well being. Very often, you will determine that buying just for the sake of buying reduces your energy level. Once you recognize this truth, and there is ever a question, you will easily decide to pass. A great exercise to have your shopping and save too is Virtual Buying. Look through one of your favorite catalogs and mark all of the articles you want from what is offered on its dazzling pages. For a week, put the catalog away and then go back to it. Look over the items and see how many would have been impulse purchases. This is always a reality check. Also, when a real need does become known, use the mind-set that you already have what you need. You will be surprised what will turn up.

To free up mind clutter, at the end of every day make a list of the things you wanted to accomplish, but were unable to do so. Call this your Cosmic Helper List or title it anything that allows harmonious energy to flow in, around and through it. Think of this Cosmic Helper as a friend who has shown up to help you. The practice of releasing these items to the list frees up your mind chatter. You are now aware of what will be done tomorrow. Do not be discouraged by dwelling on the little things undone. Rejoice in what you did complete. You can now relax into the evening feeling serenity's peace and joy.

De-cluttering frees your home and body/mind/spirit in so many ways that you will be absolutely delighted with the process. It empowers your sense of fresh new energy that nourishes every part of your being and your home.

## Space-Clearing

Space-clearing is an art unto itself and the nuances are multifold. An actual energetic cleansing of a space lifts any pressure that might be communicated. It refreshes places that were void of nurturing energies infusing sparkle and vitality within the walls. I have always been a person who loved to burn pure incense and lovely candles. Fresh flowers both from our garden or from the local nursery always grace our home and when weather permits, we fling open our windows and doors.

The symbology of totems and geometric shapes has always fascinated me and I have utilized them in our décor. The enhanced energy of bells, angels, plants, gemstones of a great variety (I am a rock hound), wind chimes (they call to me) and prayer (I am a child of worship) blesses our home. Since I am naturally drawn to aromatherapy, healing herbs and salt baths speak of blissful completeness. Incorporating these elements into a space-clearing is ever so organic and you will love the feeling of wholeness they give you.

If these aspects are new for you, trust them and enjoy their being in your environment. One of the ways to dispel worry, frustration, and/or regrets is to journal. Writing about these areas in your life opens up a way to letting them go. These emotions will block energy just as much as clutter. In fact, this kind of clutter is most unhealthy and will eventually cause lymphatic, colon, kidney, bladder, skin and lung challenges. It is important for all of these to have a positive flow of energy. I have found that acupuncture and the V.I.B.E. machine help this to happen. The V.I.B.E. is an acronym for vibrational integrative bio-photonic energy. Gene Koontz of Greeley, Colorado invented it. To learn more about this remarkable machine, please check out www.sevenstreams.net.

Each phase of the space-clearing path has a beautiful ceremony associated with it. There is a long list of reasons you should consider space-clearing. The most significant are as follows: If you have moved into a different home that was occupied by previous residents, it is wise to clear the predecessor's energy. If you or someone close to you has been ill, it is sensible to space clear. There was a major disagreement and feelings were hurt. A graduation, marriage, new baby or any significant milestone of life can be celebrated with space-clearing.

## Simple Steps To Clear And Cleanse

Prior to my Feng Shui consultations, I take a cleansing sea salt or orange peel bath. You can also use an essential oil or sea salt. Even though you will be the one conducting the space-clearing ceremony, it is recommended that each household member also take a sea salt or essential oil bath. The cleansing of your home will initiate beautiful transformations and it is important to have everyone prepared to usher these changes in. Select an outfit that feels special to you. Take the time to reflect on what it is you are seeking to discover or accomplish through this ceremony. Be a conscious creator.

As mentioned, there were several items to consider while clearing your space. For reference, the following list provides the tools you will need: Flowers, a bowl of Blessing Water and a Bell will be on your altar. A Blessing Cloth will drape your altar, so think about the kind of experience you are creating. It is recommended that you refer to Chapter 11 as the significance of each color is referenced.

Your altar may be a tray or a portable table. Adorn this alter in beauty and dress it in your favorite symbols. For example, use a small angel pin that inspires you or the gemstone Kyanite that aligns all of the charkas, promotes communication and dream recall. Items that symbolize joy and renewal are a welcome addition. Sweet Alyssum represents worth beyond beauty and Queen Anne's Lace signifies haven… Chinese coins for abundance and rice for happiness can also be added to your altar.

Purifying a room creates the space for grace. Grace is the refinement of the cleansing process, where blessings are bestowed and positive energy can begin to flow. Awaken and heal your space. Gently call it forth to step into its highest energies and invite grace in. Pray for guidance and see your home in the heart of a healing circle. Know your intention and impress onto your heart space.

Take up your blessing/altar tray and begin in the left section of your home. Stand with your tray at the door of this part of your home. There will very likely be two rooms that occupy this space. If so, begin in one and, in a clockwise motion, move on to the next room. Take your bowl of blessing water and gently dip your fingers into its essence. Walk around the space lightly flicking this water evenly around the edges of the room. Remain in the consciousness of healing and renewal. Use your hands to clap away the corner energies. Corners are notorious for storing up stagnant energy. Once you feel the room has released and cleared all of its former sluggish energy, stand in the middle of the room and ground yourself. Allow Mother Earth to support you and Father Sky to illuminate you.

Ring your bell and listen for a pure sound to resonate within the room's walls. Repeating the clockwise pattern, walk around the room ringing the bell until you reach your place of origin. At this time, with your bell in hand, trace a fluid horizontal figure eight in the air. With this symbol of infinity, you are sealing the room. If you choose to further purify the room, repeat the process. Remember to finish each pass with the horizontal figure eight. Carry on into each of your home's individual rooms until you have completed the process.

Once all of the rooms in your home have been cleansed, return to the starting point and offer a blessing for your home and for each household member. Give thanks that peace (fill in the actual intention here) now dwells within your walls and blessings pour abundantly and freely forth.

To maintain this fresh and dazzling energy that you have christened into the home, bestow a specific name to your home. Listen, for it will whisper itself into your heart of hearts. You will be introduced to the soul of your home. The first time I honored this tradition, I was given such a sweet name that tears welled up inside me. I wrote this name on a beautiful flat stone and placed it underneath my permanent altar. To you, dear reader, I send Blessings to you, your sacred home and your fellow dwellers of the dawn in light and love.

A Jewel To Re*Member

*"Then your light shall break free like the dawn and your healing shall spring up quickly."*
*- Isaiah 58:8*

# 7

## Yin & Yang - Balance & Harmony

Imagery: The exquisite art of balance is danced in tune with Cosmic Order

It is said that when the winds are mild the sun is bright, the water is clear and the trees are lush, Heaven and Earth are in perfect harmony. Yin is birthed in Yang and in turn, Yang evolves into Yin where it develops into Yang. They are in an infinite dance of cosmic transformation. The Book of Transformation, more commonly called the I Ching, is the first book to ever invent an organized pattern based around the interaction of balancing the Yin and Yang energies. Through this union of opposites, Yin and Yang interplay with one another and depict universal transformations. Symbolically, a solid line represents Yang and a broken line signifies Yin.

Yin is the feminine aspect of the two. She is the way of the earth, receptive. She condenses and contracts, she is passive, static, wet, cold, inward and quiet. The white space within the black yin symbolizes potential for transformation. An excellent example is the understanding that night without a doubt moves into day and after day is done, gone is the sun and it is night again, readying itself for the dawn of the morning sun. Yin also represents sadness, meditation, yoga, tai Chi, intuitive, sleep, creativity, night, moon, winter, imaginative, soft, reading, depression, mother, daughter, angular, religious philosophy, fragility and green/blue.

Yang is masculine, and the way of Heaven. Yang expands and represents the dry area, the light and heat. The sun is Yang; it is dynamic. Yang is alive. Yang deals with science, mathematics, finance and aggression. It is the father and the son where football, karate, speed, running and wrestling are emphasized. Yang is firm, out going, analytical, heavenly, logical and rounded.

In concert, Yin and Yang embody Nature's Laws of everlasting and unending transformation. The Curve of the S dividing/joining the Yin and Yang is indicative of harmony and that nothing is simply black. Within Yang's whiteness, observe a small black Yin eye. Within Yin's blackness, therein lies Yang's white-eye. The dance of the Yin and Yang births beauty and wholeness.

As all occurrences transform into their opposites, this infinite cycle of exchange has one principle generating the other. All states of energy have within them the potential of their opposite where they are merely one and the same. Again, this union moves back and forth. At some point, we find our center and experience complete balance without being pulled off by the mood swings of outer circumstances. Finding this balance is the key to harmony.

## Establishing Balance & Harmony

Our home's blueprint, the symbolism in it, the culture we subscribe to, how, when and where we spend our time creates the pattern of our life. This pattern overlays itself into every one of our life experiences and defines its quality or lack of. For example, if we try to squeeze 36 hours of activity into 24 hours, we will live an unbalanced life. Our time is possibly divided up and spread thinly between our significant other, aging parents, and our children. To excel in the professional world, career excellence is essential and of course the commute to and from takes time; so use these found moments to learn a foreign language, listen to book on CD, if you have a speaker phone on your cell or blue tooth in your car call your mother-in-law or anyone you like. You can even slide a show tune CD in and sing away. The necessity to exercise or at least benefit from recreational walking is a must.

Spiritual and personal development along with fellowship are necessary; a movie or stolen moments to read a favorite book are essential, spending creative time on projects or scrap-booking enables us to become lost in time, and the precious occasions to write in our Journey Book is critical. And lest we forget, the eight hours of sleep our bodies truly must have are neatly folded somewhere in our schedule.

Oh, dear reader, the above certainly looks closer to a juggling act than living in balance and harmony. Yes, life is demanding. However, we are the captains of our own ships and it is you and I who make up our own personal rules. You may say you are simply the one going along with everyone else's schedule, and that might be the case. But now that you have commenced your Feng Shui journey, transformations will reframe and reshape your pattern. It is a process and in time, all of the above will find its own rhythm within your new life patterning.

A pattern is a customary way of operating or a standard of behavior. It is only fulfilled according to a model, set of rules, design plan, formula, practiced routine, set of habitual actions or a blueprint. As we learn how to abide by the cosmic order, we deepen our sense of belonging while a smooth flow of energy seems to gently guide us.

Finding balance and harmony is the goal of the following chapters. Implementing them into your present life pattern empowers the discovery of hidden time to simply BE. One by one, each of your present demands will evolve into a more even pace. This new framework will generously support everything you love. The additional bonus is that everyone around you will benefit, too.

The following exercise asks that you take your "Journey" notebook. In this log, write down your day-to-day schedule. This differs from a day planner. Dedicate two pages (side by side) to a day of the week and across the top, create a header with that day's name. To the left margin, write down the hours of the day, into the time of evening you usually retire. Please begin with Sunday and, even though you think your Monday through Friday schedule might look the same, describe each day individually. A well-rounded day incorporates a sense of balance in your activities. An example is as follows:

Sunday:

6:00 a.m. - Awaken ~ Take the time to revisit my dreams and jot them down on the note pad next to my bed. Stretch my entire body so that I am ready to arise.
6:30 a.m. - Spend 30 minutes in meditation in my personal space and reflect on anything my dreams were saying. Be in a place of Gratitude.
7:00 a.m. - Write down my thoughts about the day and what I would like to experience.
7:30 a.m. - Prepare and enjoy a healthy breakfast
9:00 a.m. - Fellowship of spiritual pursuit of your choice
10:00 a.m. - Healthy snack per your dietary choice
11:00 a.m. – Walk, listen/talk with the sage and the cosmic helpers... re*member to call upon them for your assistance
12:00 p.m. - Yard work, laundry, closet clearing, de-clutter at least three drawers, anything productive may be listed here for a Saturday….
1:00 p.m. - Healthy Sunday feast with family/friends
2:00 p.m. - Time for a visit with family/friends, read book aloud with family/friends, watch a DVD together, play a board game, charades or card game together, scrapbook with family members, plan the next family vacation by creating a story board of the destination; investigate genealogy.

5:00 p.m. - If weather permits, plan an early evening picnic in your back yard or nearby park. Enjoy Nature.

7:00 p.m. - Place a DO NOT DISTURB sign on the bathroom door and enjoy a long, soothing bath. Soak your cares away by adding rose petals or organic sea salts to your bath. Play soothing music and light jasmine or your favorite incense. If you want, you can leisurely read one of thousands of uplifting books (make sure your light is right) or simply relax into the warmth of the bath. Spend this time dreaming about new frontiers, giving thanks for all of your blessings. Focus on what you have, instead of what you think you may lack… for in truth, you already have everything you truly require to live a quality life. It is *buried* deep within your being and the Feng Shui process will empower you to *unearth* it.

8:00 p.m. - Time to read or relax into the moment, enjoying music… this nurtures you.

9:00 p.m. - Sip your favorite nighttime tea. Our favorite is Celestial Seasonings Sleepy Time mixed with any of their caffeine free flavored teas. Retire whenever you wish.

Per Jacqueline Harte, acupuncturist, "The earlier you turn in before midnight, you happier your liver, gall bladder, heart and lungs will be."

After you have written out your weekly schedule, look for the following:

1. Where you can create the time to organize your home or your daily, weekly, monthly and even yearly scheduling.
2. Plan for flexibility so that if the traffic light changes to red, your entire day doesn't tip into the domino factor.
3. Time to record your dreams and not dash out of bed. Greet the day, meditate/pray and think good thoughts.
4. Quality family time can be the breakfast or dinner table time, the commute to school or while traveling to your children's clubs or sporting obligations. Prioritize these events and learn to delegate many of the tasks you are now doing for your children to them - work as a team. Preparing the meals and cleaning up together adds value into your day.
5. Socializing can be combined with business/community interest projects by meeting for lunch, an afternoon tea or planned dinner.
6. Exercise! Can you walk during your lunch hour with a friend? If so, you can enjoy nature at the same time. Or do as our daughter did and install a personal gym. She purchased pre-owned equipment and is disciplined enough to wake up an hour earlier to exercise each morning. She readily shaved off 2 hours from the commute she once endured to go to the gym after work. To enjoy nature, she hikes, takes her dog for a walk, swims and whenever possible, she enjoys fishing.

7. Enjoy spending valuable time *on a daily basis,* with your spouse or the Sage within. The two of you can share each other's day. Keep in mind that only positive experiences are allowed. It is a Universal Law that in the light of upbeat energy, negativity cannot abide and will dissolve.
8. Spend some time in touch with Nature. If you live in an apartment or condominium, plant indoor flowers and tend to them.
9. Take time to read, relax, and enjoy a long bath.

When you deliberately slow your life down, you are resonating with earth's heartbeat. For hundreds of years, the majority of humankind has been living in a manmade sequential time phase. This synthetic rhythm robs a person of the opportunity to be in tune with the planet's energy. Being in tune actually affords one the opportunity to increase their personal energy. Enhancing this capacity creates a receptivity of remarkable awareness. Overbooking your life holds the possibility to move your timeline too fast. Slow down - see what happens. Connect to the order and the flow of heaven and earth.

As you are creating a safe haven/noble home, to reveal the hidden truth of your inner self, experience the ability to re*ceive, re*trieve, a*chieve, light*en, re*new and re*store your personal energy to accom*plish all that your heart desires.

A Jewel To Re*Member

*"Happiness is when what you think, what you say and what you do are in harmony,"*
*- Mahatma Gandhi*

# 8

-

# The Timeless Five Elements

Imagery: A new door of perception opened and inside, the mystery of the column, triangle, circle, square and curvilinear lines stretched to infinity where all truth was revealed.

It has been established that Chi is a circuitous flow of energy connecting human kind with the Cosmic Consciousness and the Earth. The energy of life itself can only stay alive through dynamic movement. If there were only static energy, transformation would not occur. Stagnant and inert energy cannot move forward. The five elements describe how the diverse expressions of Chi flow and, although separate in their energy field, they each complement and oppose one of the others, providing a coalescing force. These powerful forces act to unify you and I to one Source.

The Home Whisperer works with environmental laws operating parallel to the Laws of Gravity. Gravity is the simplest of all known forces behaving on essentially every level. Gravity pulls things together in a steady and foreseeable way. Just like Chi, gravity is a universal force. Chi's movement translates the wonder of life into yin and yang and then transforms this energy into five specific phases. These five-element models explain the cyclical nature of natural forces wherein the five elements exist. They consist of the elemental forces of wood, fire, earth, metal and water. These patterns determine how energy moves in an environment. By enhancing or playing down these elements, we can effect positive change.

They possess a productive and a controlling pattern. The productive cycle exists when wood feeds fire, fire creates earth (volcanic ash), earth creates metal (gemstones), metal holds water and water feeds wood (plants). The controlling cycle is the opposite as water extinguishes fire, fire melts metal, metal cuts wood (as in the ax chopping trees), wood covers the earth and earth dams water. Creating a proper and healthy balance between all five elements generates harmony. These cycles each have a purpose.

Think about being in a beautifully forested mountainside where you are in total alignment with nature's complete peace and harmony. The tall and graceful trees symbolize reaching to Father Sky (higher consciousness), lifting your spirit upward, allowing you to be one with heaven's infinite abundance. Below, the trees' roots go deep into Mother Earth, where you are grounded with support and sustainability. The animals of the forest playfully symbolize living within nature's balance and being provided for. The creek water rushes freely throughout the mountainside, tumbling over the rocks, all the while renewing your spirit and gifting you with emotional release. From this experience, clarity and fresh creative potential are forever yours. In that scenario, you have been enjoined with wood, fire, earth, metal and water.

Through her elements, Nature speaks to us daily. For an overview, it is helpful to envision all five of the elements. Following this synopsis is an in depth study of each element. The wood element embodies the power of upward growth, creativity, the renewal of springtime, and the colors of green & blue.

**Fire** holds the energy of both destruction and creation, which burns away the negative and inspires the positive. It is summer time, the color red, passion, enthusiasm, and stepping into who we are known as with integrity and truth.

**Earth** is the power of stability, where we can build solid foundations, and it has the ability to break down our highest visions into a step-by-step process. Yin Earth is associated with Indian Summer, when we see the colors of brick red, golden harvest, sable brown, terracotta, and sienna orange. Its attributes are reliability and centeredness.

**Metal** feels like a fresh breeze blowing creative and clear ideas into our thought processes. Its energy contracts and condenses and its energies are at their best during the early autumn. White, pastels and gold are associated with the metal energy.

**Water** washes away old patterns and calms the deepest parts of our being. The water energy is all about being in the flow. Associated with intuition, water's season is winter when we can quiet our hearts and minds to renew our spirits. Black, navy blue and dark burgundy are the colors for the curvilinear fluidity of water as it conforms and powers up our ability to summon courage for any situation that takes place.

The first of the five elements is **Wood**. It is deemed the beginning of the five elemental cycles. When it is in a state of balance, wood is both dynamic and level. Wood qualities are associated with being aware and focused, trusting, progressive, creative, intuitive, decisive, organized and nurturing. Upward movement and personal growth are wood's hallmark. When you plant a seed, it takes dynamic energy bringing it forth to blossom. Wood transforms the shapeless into the definitive process of being.

Trees epitomize wood and once you experience their force field or aura, their guardianship is assured. The tall and graceful tree limbs (Wood) are reaching for Father Sky (Metal). Being in Nature's bounty lifts your spirit upward, allowing you to be one with heaven and earth's abundance. The tree's roots are deep within Mother Earth (Earth). The earth gifts you with the experience of being grounded, supported and grants you sustainability. The animals (Fire) of the forest playfully symbolize living within nature's balance being provided for. The creek water (Water) flows freely. Being steeped into this oneness affords you the refreshing and renewing energies of Nature. Clarity and innovatively creative ideas are flowing through your Being enjoined with the bounty of nature has blessed you.

Their strong root systems symbolize family lineages where unwavering support prevents a person from being blown away by life crises. Yet the flowing tree branches permit flexibility and the ability to bend with the forceful winds of life. For it is in times of challenge that seeds of purpose are planted. It is then up to you to encourage these seeds to their fullest potential. In our favor, we can think of the roots and the branches and how we are the union that receives these tree-wisdom blessings.

Along with the imagery of a tree, an excellent example of wood energy is the bamboo plant. Just like the tree's ability to withstand the storms of life, the resilient bamboo is known for its ability to right itself after the storms of life have passed. It then continues to move forward along its chosen path of growth. Again, when life offers you a challenge, look for the hidden value within the situation. The Asian community correlates the bamboo plant with the harmonious ordering of one's life to attract positive Chi and live in balance.

Wood energy is also associated with flowers, plant life and all types of vegetation. Plus, all objects made of wood anchor and enhance this encouraging energy. The geometric symbolism for wood is the columnar or pillar shape. Too much wood in an environment creates a feeling of being overwhelmed… too much growth too quickly will not possess enough of a root system or focus. Too little wood generates a closed, distrustful attitude. The right balance engenders harmony. The colors of wood are bright green, royal blue and vivid purple. It is associated with the season of spring and with the early morning. Wood is an energizer and a catalyst. It possesses the drive to be truly alive.

In acupuncture, the body holds certain patterns of the elements. However, if they have an excess of wood, stubborn traits and lack of flexibility will be present. A lack of wood is a lack of being rooted and grounded. Projects will not be completed, as there is also a lack of focus and commitment. When a person is considered a wood personality, they are active, outgoing, expressive, productive, empathetic and interested in creating a positive change for the better.

## Fire

Fire possesses the longest angstrom wavelength color of all the elements. It is related to expansion and change. Fire's energy motivates us to be more dynamic, enthusiastic, exuberant, passionate, joyous, inspired and original. Fire insures the ability to lead, and assures the energy for being emotionally balanced is available. Summer is fire's prime time, as it is the time of enhancement and great activity. The sound of fire is laughter, the emotion is pure joy and the climate is heat. The energy of Fire is exciting. It moves upward and outward. It is exuberant, vivacious, physically affectionate, and humorous. It desires intimacy and loves change.

The energy of fire references how at ease you are with accepting respect and/or admiration. This energy allows your inner light and your radiance to shine. Fire encourages you to love life, and enjoy being fully alive. The passion of living life thoroughly and abundantly comes into fuller meaning. Fire personalities' inner warmth will literally light up their friends and families' lives.

Fiery folks have a sparkle in their eyes, are easy to smile and laugh, have quick movements and fast speech patterns. A dead giveaway of a fire personality is that they may have freckles, pink flush to their complexion, have dimples and/or they have points at the tips of their mouth, nose, ears, and even their eyebrows. Fire people are considered forward thinking, rousing, unconventional and certainly playful.

Too much fire in an environment produces aggression and sets up the possibility to burning the candle at both ends… burn out! With fire's energy and fast pace, you might need to draw it off a bit. If so, simply sprinkle water or add a water feature. Too little fire and a cold, uninspiring lethargy will weigh a home or its residents down with apathy. To enhance Fire's intensity, feed it with wood (anything made of wood, green or blue). Fire's color is red. Red is associated with fire as it holds the energy of passion and love. However, in balance, fire is enthusiastic and radiant.

When fire consumes wood or whenever anything burns, it is changed and transcended. Fire's energy holds the desire to be partnered with the Cosmic Harmonics. Since the power of Fire is the heart center of your being, the fire energy raises the body's Chi. Fire energy also beckons you to open your heart and move beyond self-imposed limitations. To provide an outlet for fire, allow Earth's balance (ceramic pottery or a sand garden) to create safety and discernment. To avoid being vulnerable, it is necessary for fire to be reduced by metal. Metal is analytical and by adding stones to your environment, your decision making ability is furthered.

The scientific influence of fire relates to transformation. Fire's energy makes available the key to unlock your creative gifts, empowering you to share them with the world. Fire provides the illumination and enthusiasm to carry out your life's intentions. Your passions are fueled by fire's energy. Passions change over time and, as you mature, you will understand yourself more clearly. Pursuing your passion or following the fires of your heart will bring you closer to the wisdom of your Destiny. Enjoy and allow fire's exuberance and excitement to expand and enlarge your life.

Fire's geometric shape is the triangle, which can be found in the diamond, the pyramid, the sunburst, and the fire (as in a campfire) shape itself. These shapes certainly keep the energy moving upwards. You can enhance this energy by adding a fireplace to the room, candles, bright light, the sun, animals and any of their by-products. People are also considered fire elements. Since your stove is a source of great abundance, please use your stove and keep the surface and interior spotless. A stove that is used very little is indicative that you are not utilizing your resources very well. Stand in front of your stove and mindfully light each of the burners and give thanks for your many blessings. Since Fire's energy is about transformation, this brief little ritual will charge and ignite the atmosphere with positive energy.

Fire's body parts are the heart (passion), the eyes (to see life's illumination), and the small intestine (to digest all that life has to offer). The animal sign is the Horse. A horse is symbolic of mobility, power and the ability to cope in light of challenging circumstances, love, loyalty, intellect, wisdom, power, nobility, energy, freedom, wildness, divination, prophecy, fertility.

## Earth

Earth… ah, sweet earth… herein is our stability and our safety. Consider the people known as down to earth; they are reliable. In today's rapidly changing world, this element is a must in all environments as it moves more slowly. It bestows calmness and is devoid of struggle. Earth's colors are of yellow, terracotta, brown, ocher, red clay orange gold and beige. They are soothing and serene colors. The stability of earth is echoed in its geometric shape the square. Think of the cornerstone of a strong foundation, here you will find earth's permanence. Any items of sand, pottery, brick, clay or tile enhance earth's energy. Too much earth and we become fearful, even earthbound and overly protective. Too little and we become flighty and/or disorganized. Balanced earth produces sustainable living, reminding us that peace of mind and body creates inner peacefulness and security. In balance, earth is grounded, fertile and supportive, and our grounding cord is connected.

Mother Earth is a timeless support system that sustains all life. She is also remembered as the Great Mother, Devi, Ishtar, Isis, Brigid, Sacred Feminine, Goddess, and Gaia. She is the bountiful embodiment of Mother Earth. The Great Mother is the fertile womb from which all life comes.

Mother Earth represents the receptive, the nurturer, the maternal, acceptance, devotion and bliss. It is where you find and express unconditional love. Just as the energy of fire asks you to have an open heart and spread your love abroad, this energy asks you to *receive* love openly.

Since Earth energy loves to take care of others, it is essential to take care of yourself, too. In fact, you are always in relationship with self, so why not foster a healthy sense of self?

Cultivate relationships of openness, mutual support and trust. Earth energy is sacred and supportive. At its core, it is calling you to move beyond yourself and *trust the process*. It is about taking on something greater than yourself, such as creating a loving home, nurturing your own self, a mate or partner, developing a career that you *absolutely* love, not living miserably in "survival" mode... learn what the difference is by making a commitment to enhance your quality of life. Earth's entreaty is about connecting, being grounded and embracing reciprocity.

People who are considered to possess earth's energy are sympathetic and truly care about their friends. An earthy person will have a round face, roundness to their body... especially their stomach, large mouth with full lips, and full and or softly rounded lower cheeks, thick calves (men and women), and a yellow hue to their complexion. They love cozy rooms, beloved possessions and special family photos on display, large easy chairs or sofas; they prefer loose and comfortable clothes and have an easy-to-keep hairstyle. Well-known Earth people are: Oprah Winfrey, Hillary Clinton and Rosie O'Donnell.

Indian summer is the season of the Earth element; this is where abundance and fullness are at their peak. It is the Harvest... the gathering up or reaping of what you have sown. Nurture and invest in yourself... stay in earth's balance of joyous relationship. Jesus inspired us to, "Be Ye the salt of the earth." So go forth and flavor the earth and its people with nurturing kindness, devotion, commitment and integrity. Remember, peace resides in your walls and wealth lives in your noble house.

## Metal

Metal is the energy of being refined; the accomplished... it encompasses the mind and clarity. It moves inward, contracting and condensing, spinning, pulling and pushing. It is forever creating a pattern of various energies coming together in a unified composition. Metal inspires, is aware, idealistic, gracious, genuine, creative, powerful, the Father energy and it must create beauty.

As metal melts, little circular droplets form. In a circle, energy is considered yang, powerful and in constant movement. The circle spins energy outward and at the same time, it draws energies together. In the collective consciousness, this is viewed as the merging of individual awareness with the greater community of consciousness. Whenever possible, sit at a round table for group discussions, as it is inclusive and will draw everyone into the topic at hand.

The arch is also associated with the Metal Gua. Could the golden arches play a role in McDonald's success? This form of energy is considered the yin form of the yang circle. The colors for the right-brained aspect of this energy are reflected in the rainbow. It is bringing in seven of the pastels and primary colors of Red, Orange, Yellow, Green, Blue, Indigo, and Violet or ROYGBIV. Actually, the rainbow colors merge gradually into one another and it is only in our perception that we see them separately. The color order of the rainbow starts with red at the outer edge and moves through the colors to violet. The vividness of the colors and the width of the bands of colors will vary. While watching a rainbow, we can now be aware that it is related to the size of the drops that form the bow. The colors at the base of a rainbow are different from those at the top. Usually, red is near the ground. It is uncommon for red to be viewed at the top of the rainbow. The width of the arch measured from red to violet is about four times as wide as the full moon. The arch, the circle and the egg are the metal shapes.

The left-brain vibrates to the colors of white, silver, and black. These colors promote dynamic thought processes and although they can be sharp, a creamy white will take the edge off. White in social settings is not an optimal choice, because the guest will be far too serious to have fun. Too much metal causes rigid thought patterns to emerge, and over analyzing will show up. Too little metal and lack of clarity or purpose ensues. The perfect balance of metal produces the state of being accomplished, the state of knowing. Metal is associated with all things mental, clearing the space to bring in the new and pushing the horizons back. The most gracious hostess derives their warm hospitality from the metal influences. They truly love to plan parties and they love to serve.

The Spiritual Father is associated with the realm of brilliant light, the heavens, and being illuminated. The Father archetype is best explained in Thomas Moore's *Care Of The Soul*, where he describes a father as being a mentor who teaches by example, leads without pushing and allows the child to learn by being loved. The loving father protects and directs; reminds you to be true to yourself, all the while fostering the understanding of the law of cause and effect. The Father archetype influences your sense of order and your feelings of being in or out of control of life circumstances. Your Father subconscious shines in balanced service, reflecting effectual living.

In addition to the ethereal Father, metal governs heavenly aspects, the angelic realm and effects sacred guidance by walking in spirit and living in synchronistic bliss; having a charted path to be in the right place at the right time. Displaying drawings, sculptures, or photos of St. Francis, Quan Yin, favorite teachers, angels, mentors and/or your own dad in your environment, enhances metal energies. To welcome this Chi, introduce objects made from mctal, such as stainless steel, copper, brass, gold and silver. Place a silver box or silver envelope in this area and write your "wish notes" to the angels. Deposit these little notes into this box of alchemy and allow belief to manifest your wish. This area also governs patron luck excellence and is enhanced by installing metal wind chimes on the outside of your home where this area corresponds. The colors are light pastels, silver, whites and blacks.

In addition to metal objects such as a Tibetan bell, stones enhance this Chi. For example, Celestite encourages the flow of life… synchronicity. It is a stone for balance, assists in the clairaudient, wisdom and the search for bliss. When compressed, it bears a resemblance to angel wings and is called Angelite. This stone embodies peace and will aid in your spiritual journey. It promotes conscious awareness and provides protection. One finds their muse within the metal energy of creativity. Stones such as Kyanite, Jade, Amethyst, Rose Quartz, Jet, Jasper, Amber and too many to share here (see Chapter 26). Each stone possesses an energetic value of inspiration, motivation, visionary talents, and holds a healing vibration. Their dazzling beauty and therapeutic qualities enhances your level of consciousness.

## Water

Water is symbolic of remarkable internal resources capable of refreshing your spirit. The graceful flow of water represents the mystery of life. It releases emotions and embodies the natural order of the cosmos. In many cultures water is considered the Source of all life. It can be the stormy floodwaters or the calm of a reflective pool. Water is presented in streams, lakes, rivers, and oceans. Of course, the water that courses throughout our body is a major influence on our life path. To remain in healthy, it is essential to drink water daily to re-hydrate your body. When water effortlessly flows, it unconditionally provides clarity and pure life's real meaning. Water is the most yielding of all of the energies, reminding us to be flexible. However, murky water represents being indecisive and vague.

Water has two forms: moving (yang) and still (yin). Moving water creates the energy pattern of attracting abundance, career excellence and the flow of financial increase into your life. You have heard that still waters run deep. This watery pattern is about going within. It represents germination and gestation… birthing new paths. Water/womb is associated with birthing. It represents the transformation and rejuvenation of life itself.

Water represents wisdom, bravery to venture into uncharted oceans, willful, independent, dreamy, intuitive, unconventional, truth seeking, sensual, exotic, wintertime and nighttime. It is the return of the stillness where this last cycle in the circle of energies bathes and then renews itself. The body parts are the ear, where we must listen to our inner truth, the kidney and bladder where trust, fear, and courage all reside… which shall we summon? The aspiration is destiny, motivation, career and the journey of life itself.

Living our life purposefully allows water's stream of consciousness to lend lucidity to the other four elements of wood, fire, earth and metal. Water seeks new paths through the mountain, extinguishes fire, reduces metal, and nurtures wood. The presence of excessive water by way of colors and symbolism creates a mood of being wishy-washy and disorganized. Too little water promotes passivity.

One of my clients lived in an extremely 'watery' home. She had blue carpet and blue furnishings, glass table (also considered a water symbol), paintings of the ocean adorned every wall and even her little Chaska's were of watery creatures such as dolphins, whales. Although lovely, her indoor fountain only added to this room's watery excess. She was experiencing wishy-washy moods and she was never able stay with one path. To correct this situation, we moved many of her items into other parts of her home. In order to 'absorb the watery excess', we added greenery (wood energy) and earth items. Once we cleared this room of its watery tomb-like feeling, she was able to better concentrate. Plus, she was not as emotional and began enjoying stability in her finances and health.

In balance, the water element opens the door to cosmic attunement where we feel at one with Source, relaxed and refreshed. The bathroom is a prime water room. To keep your finances flowing, be sure to plug up the bath and sink drain, when not I in use, as water energy moves downward. Since water is associated with abundance, avoid water's financial leakage. Create a spa like atmosphere by adding greenery in the bathroom where you can directly benefit from this room's energy of renewal. Enjoy thick and thirsty towels placed on a towel warmer, waterproof pillows for the bath, lovely artwork, aromatic candles, basins of scented soaps, a dimmer on your light switch and a CD player to pipe in soothing music. My bath time is also my meditation time. My mind/body/spirit is thoroughly prospered here.

The unblocked flow of Water in your life is unswervingly associated with the stream of money in your life and your career success. Improve the water energy by adding a water fountain, mirrors, actual crystal and items made from crystal or glass art featuring water and/or an aquarium. Objects in the color of black, navy, maroon, or very deep brown certainly anchor water's energetic values. In Chapter 28, we discuss the appropriate places for these water enhancements.

Curvilinear lines move freely to create the geometric shape of water. Shapes of paisley designs, curves or rounded lines emulate water's flowing essence.

A Jewel To Re*Member

*Jade that has not been polished is of no use.*
*Chinese Proverb*

# 9

# -

# The Bagua - The Template of Alchemy

*"Your home shall not be an anchor but a mast." -Kahlil Gibran*

In Joseph Campbell's book The Power of Myth, he cites the historical passages of cultural myth. Within each civilization, the story behind the myth, therefore the myth itself was perpetuated only as long as its people had confidence in its principles. The confidence is the power of belief and actually powers up the codes themselves to have value. We are only as strong as the belief system that we focus on. Over centuries, there have been numerous belief systems and some, although evolved remain with us today. This epistemology holds a set of convictions or opinions inspired by a mentor, saint, teacher, intuitive, and even by one's own heart or inner truth.

Through our life decisions, belief system, career choices, place of residence, and the preference of friends, each of us has created our own myth. In the creation of our myth or sage, there is an energetic cycle in place that supports its growth and evolvement. At the heart of this maturation process is the Jewels to RE*MEMBER. For truly, you already have the information you need to make as Hanna Moog and Carol Anthony teach, a "spontaneously correct choice." It is the understanding that we already possess the capability, the capacity, and the ability to be the person we know we can be.

Observing the laws of natures and their order or energetic cycles created the Bagua. It is beyond myth and yet it is myth itself as it has been manifested throughout history. Pythagoras, Plato, Einstein, Frank Lloyd Wright worked within and were each inspired by nature. As a child, nature expressed her beauty to me in the forests, mountains and streams of Ruidoso, New Mexico. Our family would spend time there each summer and early on, I recognized I really liked who I was within the sanctuary of nature's beauty. There was serenity, a calm that spoke to my heart. Over the years, I began to collect information of how cosmic nature actually is present within us.

This knowing or wisdom was furthered in the 1960's when I studied Carl Jung, as a college freshman when a Native American shaman introduced me to The Tree of Life, as a newlywed upon "randomly" finding little booklet in the supermarket checkout lane regarding Oriental astrology, when we lived Mazatlan, Mexico, and upon being the student of a wizened woman who could read people's energy by the laws of nature and their birth. And certainly, the study of the Bible and the I Ching further enriched my life path. There have been far too many synchronistic experiences to list that led me to Feng Shui's information system. I recognized the parallels of each teaching or belief system and saw it reflected in all that been in my life's legend or myth.

Many years ago, we were guests in Sante Fe at the home that Witter Bynner built in the early 1900's. He translated the TAO of *The Way of Life* from Chinese into English, which is considered to be a brilliant translation. The integrity of the Tao, Golden Rule, the Golden Mean, and the Bagua, were each birthed from these intrinsic laws of order and have survived because they are the highest idea of the Cosmos. Our inner and outer homes are connected and work in concert to create our personal saga or myth. In these next pages, please note the teachings of the Bagua's energetic pattern. When in alignment with nature's laws of order, our focused intentions can be manifested revealing our highest idea of life. Then, the inner Bagua teaches how us how we can best utilize our hidden treasures. With these timeless energy teachings, you are evolving your personal myth or saga where you can "live happily ever after."

## The Bagua

**Imagery: A house is the canvas that makes known the state of our inner home. Our inner home is the brush that paints destiny's portrait.**

The Bagua (bah-gwah) is a map of energy or a grid that determines how Chi (life force) flows through an environment. This grid analyzes and corresponds to central aspects of the life journey. It is an information system based on the I Ching (Book of Changes). Each trigram contains the Universe's essential DNA from which all life flows.

The Bagua is made up of eight I Ching trigrams. From the observation of universal laws, the art, placement, and symbolism of Feng Shui has evolved. Feng Shui's mission is to create balance and harmony in each of the Bagua areas called a Gua. Ushering in deep peace brings well-being into the home. This serenity is reciprocated and infused into the fabric of life. This seamless cycle has threads of self-awareness, joy, insight, intuition, integrity, and stability. It also symbolizes nature's ageless system of beauty within and order without. The external environment mirrors the inner.

Concurrently, the outer space supports and furthers the inner truth of a person. The gifts of the Bagua are expressed through Family/Roots, Pure Abundance, Fame/Integrity, Intimate Relationship, Creativity/Children, Helpful People/Travel, Career/Life Journey, and are interconnected with the middle section - Health or the Cosmic Jewel of the Lotus.

As a Home Whisperer, listen now to hear what your home is saying to you. You can develop your Feng Shui ears by taking responsibility for your life. This is the first step in securing harmony and balance. Secondly, I have found that most of my clients are surprised when they become aware of their home's consciousness. In fact, when they begin to delve into the symbolic value of their space and the shape of their home, they begin to better understand why their life has been spiraling out of control and/or why they have been experiencing certain blockages. This clarity lends itself to renewal and restores their balance and harmony.

The Inner Home journey is one of discovery and revelation. We are each energetic beings and everything we surround ourselves with has an energetic value. At the heart of Feng Shui, is the awareness of how to live in harmony and balance. Harmony holds the energy of divine love and abundance. Balance transmits infinite joy and healing. Look around your home and listen to what it is saying to you. Quiet your mind and still you heart… now, once again… listen closely.

The Bagua is the map that is a visual imprint of how nature flows through a space. Each section of this tic-tac-toe-looking map is called a Gua. Every Gua is an aspect of your home that has a correlation to your life pattern. When any part of your home is blocked, this aspect of your life becomes stagnant. If any corners of your home are missing, its parallel or life characteristic in this blueprint becomes vacuous. For example, the right hand part of your home is designated as the Relationship section of your home. Two of my clients were going to buy a condo in Hawaii. Although I urged them to not to purchase it because the entire section of their Relationship Gua was missing, they bought it, anyway. Within six months, they were divorced and although they continue to deeply miss one another, they are not open to reconciling.

To create harmony and balance it is essential for you to completely understand your own home's blueprint. For purposes of this study, we will only focus on your home. Once you have mastered this blueprint, you may move on to your office, your desk and even your town. To continue to experience oneness, Feng Shui consciously connects us to our space. This connection is our lifeline to harmony and balance, which in turn creates and inspires love, abundance, healing and joy to be part of the quality of our life. In the vastness of the Universe, we are essential beings responsible for humankind's evolvement. Our inner home is where is we advance and our outer home is how we secure our progress. So please… enjoy the journey!

The Bagua grid has numbers assigned to each one of its sections or Guas. When tallied up in either direction, the sides equal 15. Interestingly enough, this is the same number of days in the moon's waxing or waning. To locate the Bagua map in reference to your home, simply think of yourself as looking down upon your home. Sketch the grid or Bagua over your home. To do so, line the bottom of the map up with your entrance quadrant-your original architectural door. Even if you enter through your garage or a back door, you must honor the designed entrance. You will see how the squares find their way into each room of your home. This is the process of analyzing the parts of your home where certain influences exist. Face inside to your home and draw off the sections of your home according to the Bagua map.

To properly map the Bagua, include any structure that is attached to your home and has a roof or a hand rail. For example, this could be a front porch, garage, a patio deck, or a workshop. Notice the general shape of your home. If it is a U, L, S, or Horseshoe shape, please consult Chapter 10 titled Missing Corners. You will become quite adept with this process once you begin to get a feel for how the energy is moving around your home. This map can be used in an office space, desk, and of course, each room has its own bagua. You always lay it out with the bottom of the map lined up with the front door facing into the home.

Now the adventure is heightened.

The Bagua has the following life patterns associated with its magical square or map. This map is not the territory. The grid creates an awareness of how energy is moving around and through your home. The Guas are as follows:

- Left Hand Mid-Section-Family/Roots
- Upper Left Hand Side-Pure Abundance
- Upper Middle-Integrity/Illumination
- Upper Right Hand Side-Intimate Relations
- Right Hand Mid-Section-Creativity/Children
- Bottom Right Hand Section-Helpful People/Travel
- Bottom Middle-Career/Life Journey
- Bottom Left Hand Section-Self Cultivation/Knowledge'
- Center-Unity/Tai Chi

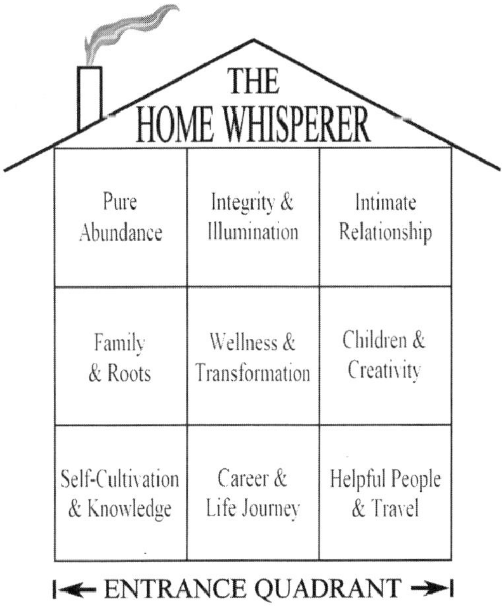

Please refer to the illustration in the previous chapter and notice the middle section. Around this center area, or as it is commonly referred to, a Gua, there are eight other sections. With the exception of this middle square, each Gua expresses an I Ching insight and enjoys a specific family posturing. In addition to these support systems, they each have a numerical influence, an element such as wood, fire, earth, metal, or water, and a feminine or masculine energy. They all collaborate to influence your personality traits. They are based on your birth date, month and year. This is the time and space continuum you agreed to be born into as it supports the reason you are here today.

| Number | Element | Family Position | Cosmos |
|---|---|---|---|
| | | | |
| 1 | Water | Middle Son | K'uan – the Void |
| 2 | Yin Earth | Mother | K'un – the Receptive |
| 3 | Thunder | Eldest Son | Chen – Dynamic |
| 4 | Wind | Eldest Daughter | Sun – Clarity |
| 5 | Earth | | Endurance |
| 6 | Yang Metal | Father | Ch'ien – Harvest |
| 7 | Yin Metal | Youngest daughter | Tui – Joyous Lake |
| 8 | Yang Earth | Youngest Son | Ken – the Mountain |
| 9 | Fire | Middle Daughter | Li - Passion |

The Principle number is who you showed up to be. To find this number, count backwards from the year 2000. For example, if you were born in the year 1966, please subtract 1966 from 2000 and you arrive at the number 34. Further reduce it by adding these numbers together 4 +3 and you will receive the number 7. This person's principle number is indeed a SEVEN. For those born after 2000, subtract your birth year from 2045.

The following profiles are in-depth personality traits of each number. In addition to the Principle position, there is also a character number and an energetic number. For fuller Inner Home Algorithm/Nine-Year Cycle insights, please go to my website, *www.homewhisperer.net*. The main number will teach you how and why you are at your very best when with certain people and not so much with others. Everyone has a frequency or algorithm pattern, and we can learn how to always live in the highest idea of Cosmic Consciousness by honoring others and ourselves, our passions and patterns. Plus, knowing how we are wired answers *so* many questions!

The Number Three: Chen-Yang Wood. This highly yang energy expresses the Can-Do attitude of the optimist, the executive, the achiever, and the drive to be alive. Even while resting, this person's toes will tend to move. No, they do not slow down. They possess incredible energy and do not waste time in getting things done. A youthful demeanor supports their enthusiastic approach to life. They are the first to try new things and are considered trendsetters.

Due to the pattern of this upward moving energy of wood, they will have outbursts or their tempers will flair up easily. They will spout off critical phrases to co-workers and even family, and then they are fine. The challenge is for those around them to know this is their trait and they should take the truth of the flare-up to heart, but not take it personally. This bluntness should be better understood, so check out your spouse, boss, or co-worker's principle number and save your self from unnecessary grief. Even though they are easily frustrated, remember they can quickly recover from these flare-ups. This anger must be vented because the liver can become compromised when they do not work through any grudges. Forgiveness is a key lesson for them to master. In Louise Hay's book, *You Can Heal Your Life*, the liver is considered the seat of one's anger. A three can become angry and it is important for them to learn to process their feelings.

The trigram Chen is symbolized by thunder, the big bolt. This drive is a major power force for transformation. Creativity, new beginnings, and strength are also associated with this pattern. A three is also assertive and highly capable of great feats. They are able to multitask… even *hyper-task* like no other person. They are delightful individuals whose single mindedness serves them. Since they are strong, resilient, punctual, and decisive, setbacks drive them up the wall. When a three incorporates a routine of Yoga or Tai Chi, they will cultivate the ability to work through their delays with wisdom and balance. Another interesting trait of a three is their love of debating. What others might consider as an argument, a three will simply think of it as having a lively discussion.

A three thrives on being outdoors. Plant a tree, plant a rose bush, plant veggies, and create a new pathway for the garden. Just being outside enables a three to live in perfect balance and harmony. They love to be in nature. They are enthusiastic and when cultivated, they have a deep sense of organizational skills. Yes, they are impulsive and action-oriented, but they do champion and answer the call to make the world a better place for generations to come. They are born humanitarians.

**The Number Four: Persistent Wind/Yin Wood.** This gentle natured soul is likened to the wind, hard to take hold of, for how do you catch the wind? Since their nature is forever changing directions, they are poised to step into the new and the extraordinary… so much so that they live in anticipation of transformation. A four is graceful, makes an excellent first impression, and they have a gift for gently guiding others without being pushy. The energy of the Wind/Wood is that of being inquisitive, stubborn, dynamic, upbeat, creative, and vulnerable in love. Because they are fascinated with every aspect of life, they can be indecisiveness and will miss many opportunities. They are charismatic and their excellent listening skills make them a sensitive and compassionate counselor. People trust them with their most intimate secrets and rightly so because a Four is trustworthy.

A four is passionate about their beliefs and articulates them beautifully. A four enjoys discussing idealistic topics. From the core of their being, they are always being pulled along a higher path. All of their life, they will cultivate a deeper connection to source. Since a four will have many choices to select from, they can become overwhelmed with all of the tasks they take on. It is important for a four to become clear about their ultimate vision and learn to trust in their generous heart.

At the same time, they are highly influenced by others and must choose their associates carefully. Since there are different states of awareness, it is essential for fours to evaluate their company. In balance, a four will glow in knowing who they truly are and why they are here. Their tomorrows are filled with promise and their ongoing experience is a journey of opportunities, harmony and balance. Swirling around this personality is Wind/Wood's beautiful energy of a pioneering and graceful spirit. They are usually highly esteemed.

**The Number Five: Tai Chi/Unity; Earth**. A strong leader who is resilient - these robust folks epitomize being a survivor. They are natural corporate directors as they flourish in the Center or the Soul of an organization. Whatever the mission, a five will exceed others' expectations and become the expert in their field. A five's Mother Earth traits cause them to knowingly support very dependent people. Even though they are highly practical, they toss common sense to the wind and exercise their unique ability to help the less fortunate. True to the law of reciprocity, a five will always be given assistance by strangers in their hour of need.

A five thrives in a world that is safe and responsible and works tirelessly to create this kind of stability. One of my clients is a triple five energetic pattern. She chose not to take a vacation with a multi-billion-dollar company for years. It was in the start up years of this famous corporation that she loyally served as the second person in command to the CEO. Her professionalism took her on and beyond the call of duty. However, she enjoyed beauty and balance by creating an enriching and private life.

Whether a five is a male or female, they are excellent parents. They set a moral code for their children to follow and they walk their talk. They are shining examples and their children usually become people who know how to give their very best to the world. Five's are overachievers and love to be at the center of attention - so they are located in the hub of the Gua. Since they will go the extra mile, they fully expect others to do the same. It is inherent in their nature to be the protector and sustain a high quality of life at all costs. They will not tolerate being left out of the circle, so don't make them mad!

Travel is important to a five because they are deeply invested in CHANGE… not for the sake of change itself, but for spiritual transformation and growth. They understand life's numerous ups and downs, because it is often through these very challenges that they are able to turn an obstacle into a stepping-stone for great good success. Their goals are lofty, but they know exactly how to pave the path to accomplishment. They are over-comers and innately know what to do in any given situation. A five is a remarkable mentor, parent, wellness coach, and best friend, all rolled into one.

**The Number Six: Ch'ien Creative Heaven/Father Energy, Yang Metal.** A six is considered highly efficient and can be depended upon to be on time. These folks are a paradox as they at once linear and yet very spiritual. These people can literally strike fear in the hearts of their cohorts. Their work ethic is strong. Since they are sharp tongued, they easily speak their truth. Due to the way they come across, they are challenged on every level of their relationship. However, they will always live in the energy of blessings, synchronicity, and heavenly influences.

A six is a visionary with a far-reaching plan. Residing in the heavenly planes is the father/protector energy. Inherent within a six are those same heavenly planes, as an angelic energy is present within a six's energetic pattern. They will forever want to rise above everyone and everything. Even though they are the models of how to view life from the highest possible places, they can also see it in black and white terms. They can be unyielding and, at the same time, spiritually aware. A six is always willing to help anyone in need; they are an inspiration, a mentor and must abide by the golden rule. They embody compassion and community.

A six follows the speed limit, does not bend policy, and will not appreciate anyone who may challenge his or her hard earned authority. They are focused and rise to the top of any endeavor. They are detail oriented and sticklers for the minutest of factors. They could easily write an operating procedures manual for a large corporation, home, or life itself. They inherently know how to get things done!

They are perfectionists, and along with this trait come the tendency to be considered superior, they truly cannot help this propensity, so it is important for them to become less critical of themselves and others. When they develop the truth of "walking a mile in another man's moccasins," they can be softer and less judgmental. They may appear to be peaceful, but they have the resolve and forceful drive to refine the world.

**The Number Seven: Tui The Joyous Lake, Yin Metal**. This charming and highly sociable pattern truly enjoys life. Sevens make the most of their life experiences to gain wisdom. A seven has excellent communication skills and is considered a refined speaker. However, they'll do whatever it takes to get what they want, even if it includes losing their dignity. Until they develop a sense of responsibility, they can be somewhat like a child. They must learn to keep an organized home/work space. They are elegant people and they love luxury.

The executive abilities of a seven are well defined. The sky is the limit with a seven. They have the ability to work at a global level and can take a company to international heights. Words/phrases that define this accomplishment are clarity, a broad philosophy, symphony, the ability to reach a target, and refinement.

Of all the energy patterns, a three and a seven possess the greatest capacity for creativity. A seven can create something out of nothing. They are highly cerebral and must refrain from living in their head. When they are out of balance, they will get so caught up in their own thoughts that they spiral into separateness and isolation, which sets up a sense of lack.

As everyone knows, lack is an illusion and exists on the mental and spiritual plane. When a seven separates his or her self from Cosmic Consciousness, anxiety and grief will attempt to set in. If this occurs, anxiety and grief will attempt to set in. The good news is that a seven will eventually learn how to break this destructive pattern. This realization activates their inner compass to direct them back to the infinite resources of spirit and divine wisdom.

Appearance is keen to a seven and they are always fashionably well dressed. They exude confidence and this inspires others to dial their life up to a higher code of living. A seven is a gracious host and makes everyone feel at ease. Sevens are multi-talented and ingenious. By showing how to set one's inner child free, play and spontaneity come forth. Thus, they empower others to live with great joy.

A seven is connected to breath. Letting go of stress is found by exhaling. Sevens must learn to move with the rhythm of receiving and releasing. From breathing, fresh insight, originality, and inspiration are brought forth.

**The Number Eight: Ken, Yang Earth**. An eight is loved because people discern their sincerity. Eights live from the deepest part of their heart. They have a tendency to be childlike and will sometimes reinvent the wheel, learning the same lessons several times over. When in doubt, they return to a cave like retreat and this safe place enables an eight to find divine wisdom to work through any and all challenges. It is within this place of quiet reserve where true transformation comes from within. An eight has tremendous amounts of energy coming in and deep reserves of strength from which to draw. An eight knows the value of being still.

Eights give, give, give, and give. In the aftermath, they might try to balance this extreme behavior by controlling others. They can be demanding, but when fully rested, they are steadfast, reliable, tenacious, and innovative. Gifted and well put together, they are always beautifully groomed.

They love to be in love and romance is high on their list of priorities. Regardless of the years of their long-term marriage or relationship, an eight will continue to woo the one they love and appreciate being remembered in this same fashion. Eights are sensuous, loving, and extremely thoughtful of others. An eight has pleasing, captivating mannerisms and they are witty. They tell good jokes and deliver an impressive punch line. They enjoy spectacular good fortune and are very nice people.

**The Number Nine: Li, Fire**. True to the fire element nines are luminaries. They prosper in show business, careers such as public speakers, ambassadors, fashion designers or runway models. Our grandson Shawn is a triple nine. Since he was a toddler, he has known or remembered who he is supposed to be in this life. At the time of this book's birth, he is sixteen. He is compassionate, multi-talented, uninhibited and shines as a song and dance man. He expresses the beauty and grace assigned to nine's energetic pattern.

A Nine has the energy of exuberance and is action-oriented. Nine folks take great pride in their accomplishments, naturally garner respect, attract loyal friends and are themselves a very faithful friend. A Nine is highly passionate about their life choices. Because they can accomplish things at the speed of light, they have to be careful to not scatter their energies too far. Since their active mind clips along at a rapid pace, it can create a little impatience with regard to the other people who are taking the slower route.

Nines have always had an inner pull into the extraordinary. They live their lives in spiritual awareness and see beauty in every aspect of life. They thrive on variety and must mix things up a bit. Just like our grandson, nines are natural performers and love the movies, theatres, and television.

They love to create excitement, because life for them will never roll along on at a ho-hum pace. In fact, a nine can be a bit of a drama king or queen. Nines are proud of their appearance and always compete for the spotlight. Similar to Leos in Western Astrology, Nines - a fire element - have an air of superiority around them. Impulsive behavior can make them inconsiderate to others. When out of balance, a nine will go to great lengths to compete for attention.

A nine is bright and effervescent, talented, and is at ease in all social situations. They love to learn and are highly intellectual. Couple their advanced verbal skills with their well-earned knowledge, they are a joy to listen to and in turn, they are excellent listeners. They are naturally creative and can gracefully express this talent via the written word. The number nine is advanced energy, a brightly shining star that warms the world. This inner glow radiates outer auspiciousness.

Divine Love is of the utmost importance to a nine as its fiery spirit has an open heart that transcends all fears. This energy sparks joyous transformations to the highest ideal of cosmic expression. They are compassionate, passionate, vivacious, love change, self-engrossed (they are full of life and lose sight of others' paths), can even have panic-attacks, are huggers, can be scattered (their other Chi energies can balance this tendency), and when in balance and rested, they are fun and witty folks. Rest is essential because they will want to burn the candle at both ends…'tis the nature of fire.

**Number One: K'an trigram, Water.** Water is the element supporting this energetic pattern. There is always so much going under the surface in this person. They are sensual, spiritual, mysterious, and gravitate towards solving life's mysteries. They are private, love their free flowing freedom, artistic, love to lie down - notice drivers who appear to be reclined in their cars — this is a water trait. They are lucid dreamers and intuitive. They are overly sensitive. It is essential for a one to have time alone, but they must not become a recluse. In their optimal state of being, the one should stay in the flow.

Since water Chi can be calm and at other times chaotic, they will experience mood swings. These temperamental yet very sweet and often misunderstood people, will go from high to low. Their challenge is to find the still waters that run deeply within them and develop courage to overcome the dark night of the soul.

If out of balance, a one can find fault with the most beneficial of circumstances and be overly fearful. Although they build life on a slower path, they do prefer to live in different places. Due to their deeply penetrating thought patterns, they can have emotional issues that will manifest into health challenges. They are independent and do not work well within a hierarchy.

**Number Two: Kun trigram, Yin Earth.** This represents the Great Mother, a person who is simply the best friend anyone can ever have. They are loyal and totally committed to all relationships. They are forever willing to help others and because of this, they must make sure to take care of themselves, as well. In fact, we have a family member who is a two and she is precious, but treats her husband like he is her baby. Of course, he loves it! A two is nurturing, gentle, motherly, frugal, and is detail oriented. They will seek out better ways to do things. They are known for getting things done and are reliable. Although they prefer to build their lives in the slow lane, they are highly committed to the long haul. They thrive when they are nourishing others.

Their biggest challenge is their tendency to become overly concerned. When they can truly build on a positive belief system that supports their caring and grounded nature, they will move beyond worry and indecisiveness. This shift enables them to fully express their generosity, thoughtfulness and to live in the balance of giving and receiving. They are loving and thoughtful individuals who truly care.

# Part Two

-

# Alchemy of the Inner & Outer home

# 10

# Missing Corners

Now, turn your attention to your home's blueprint and note any missing corners, protrusion or irregularly designed shape. If you have this situation, do not fret because you can energetically and symbolically correct these. Missing corners are prevalent in western building or architectural design.

As an example, my home was once missing the Helpful People and Travel Gua. When I filled this Gua in, the negativity and lack of support I had been experiencing simply shifted. This section was located in our steep driveway. Since this element was metal (re*member Chapter 7's teachings), I elected to bury a smoky quartz crystal, pointed side up. Smoky Quartz promotes joy in living, provides protection from negative energies and grounding for all endeavors.

Several people who were less than inspiring in my life, literally moved out of my circle. At the same time, I was introduced to some wonderful mentors who changed my life for the absolute best! These amazing people continue to be in my life today.

As you can imagine, these incomplete areas of your home would have you experience the opposite or lack of what this Gua intends to manifest for you. Just like my missing "helpful people" Gua, you might have a missing "career" Gua, which would look like a U-shaped home. It is possible that you are in a job with out a future for a promotion or you have topped out on your salary quotient.

There are many cures for this challenge. Prior to making any changes, reflect on this missing area. Consider the potential and status in reference to your life experiences in relationship to the Gua's attributes. A missing section warps the natural flow of this Gua's energetic value. The following teaches you how to create a supportive Gua. Standard cures for building-in missing Guas are placing mirrors on the inside of the space, planting a garden inside the missing corner, or burying a stone to symbolically fill in this room.

As you read through this, feel free to reference the Bagua Map on page 55.

## MISSING FAMILY GUA

**Family** - The lack of this area being filled in holds a pattern of family discord or a felling of not being well cared for. To correct this situation, plant a tree, shrub, or flowers. Arrange a group of three garden statuaries or three outdoor chairs here to anchor this energy. An excellent cure is to create an ancestor garden and dedicating this space in honor of family members.

## MISSING PURE ABUNDANCE CORNER

**Pure Abundance -** as mentioned above, can interrupt the flow of your finances and produce a sense of life being lack luster. Plant flowers (can be in containers) in the colors of red, blue or purple, hang a wind sock, install a water fountain pointing toward your home with a pump that is in excellent working order, and you can even place a beautiful statuary (please avoid any statues that symbolize those folks who took a vow of poverty!) in this wealth garden. Plant bamboo and set Jade plants out. Butterfly and Lilac bushes, rose bushes and garden furniture in a group of four, are wonderful cures.

## MISSING INTEGRITY GUA

**Integrity -** A missing area here is indicative of not receiving credit where credit is due or you have a challenge with accepting recognition. An outdoor fireplace with a triangle seating arrangement is ideal for filling in this missing space, plant climbing red trumpet vines or red roses here, outdoor lighting of any kind, but the torches especially fashioned for outdoor use are truly perfect here and a square table with nine candles or nine flames painted on top anchors this energy.

## MISSING RELATIONSHIP CORNER

**Relationship** - Whenever this Gua is absent, intimate relationships or business partnerships can become rocky. This is an opportunity to create a cozy space where a beautiful garden bench or swing for two can be placed. Erect a garden arbor where coupled rose bushes, two Rose of

Sharon, or any two of the same plants that blooms in red, pink, yellow or white can flourish. Locate a pair of garden statuaries here.

I have two garden angels side by side, anchoring my outdoor relationship Gua. You can also enhance this Gua by burying two stones of your choosing such as amber, which according to Melody, is the stone for marriage renewal vows and to assure promises.

Frankckette (also per Melody), "…sustains one in both the recognition of and the stability of one's identity. It furthers interaction between business and emotional partners, cooperative efforts…" It may also be employed to expedite ones finding a marriage partner; and lastly Melody says, "Sardonyx is a mineral that can assist in bringing happiness in marriage and 'live-in' relationships. It allows one to realize the delightfulness of living, is used to attract friends and good fortune (wow, bury two of these stones even if you have this corner filled in!). It is also known as a 'stone of virtue,' and is said to have been one of the stones used in the breastplate of the high priest." You can use any two gemstones you choose, but please look them up and create a ceremony when you place them within Mother Earth.

## MISSING CREATIVITY/ CHILD GUA

**Creativity/Children -** When this area is missing, you will find yourself without the muse that sparks your imagination. Your inventiveness will be flat and life will seem out of sorts. Without ingenuity, even when extraordinary opportunities show up, you might not recognize them. This area is an excellent spot for a beautiful Zen rock garden. Place a garden bench here to reflect and consider all that good and wonderful fosters in the spiritual aspect of this Gua. Garden shops and nurseries offer beautiful benches fashioned from concrete, but take it from me, please have it professionally delivered, as they can be heavy.

This Gua also represents the children or projects in your life. When this Gua is missing, you can experience a stalemate in your heartfelt endeavors and not have much fun. Pettiness or childish behavior can rear its immature head in your home or workplace. This can come from you or your playmates. There are playful sculptures of children. I have one with a little boy and girl (in metal) flying a kite. Let your inner child come out to play.

## MISSING HELPFUL PEOPLE / TRAVEL CORNER

**Helpful People /Travel -** When this Gua goes missing, it is certain that you will just miss your plane, have your flight cancelled or stand in an endless line for refunds. You will be under the influence of folks who are nagging and complaining about everything from the weather to the missed opportunity. Yikes… please fill this one in fast!

This is a fun corner to take care of. You can place statuary of an angel, St. Francis or Buddha in this missing space. Or if you are like, pour silver dust into a prepared hole in the ground. Bless this space and know that your dreams are coming true.

## MISSING CAREER GUA

**Career** - This missing space is indicative of job challenges or blockages. Because water rules this station, place a water fountain here - make sure it flows in the direction of your front door. In the winter, it is appropriate to use black river rock for water. Another excellent cure is to place a turtle in front of your front door and point it towards the door. Geraniums are considered a water plant and its round leaves are symbolic of coins, silk ones in the winter are also perfect here. Also, wind chimes or windsocks are wonderful ways to invite in the Chi.

## MISSING SELF-CULTIVATION / KNOWLEDGE CORNER

**Self-Cultivation/ Knowledge -** This area is the station of wisdom. I have a lovely little fairy statue and she reading a book. She balances my protruding self-cultivation and knowledge area. The other consideration is to activate this room by keeping lights on and battery operated chimes rotating. The tendency for a protruding room is that it will not fully realized its potential. We are fortunate in that this is our library and the room our grandchildren dubbed the Dream Room.

# 11

# -

# Colorful Perceptions

Color, color, color… it is everywhere we turn. This morning, I visited my hair-colorist, Minda. As color was swirling around me, I was ever so cognizant of her richly colored plum apron and her flowing turquoise skirt. She appeared to be draped in the essence of jewels. As an organic colorist, she was returning my once auburn hair full circle to its red radiance. Yes, it is time for me to stand in the fire of my passion and allow this book to color the world with its blessings, information, and knowledge.

The experience of writing this book has indeed been a colorful journey. Beginning with the gift from source to share my Feng Shui wisdom, the concept was birthed in amethyst (thus the book cover's color) where I was "given" this beloved project in my dreams. The workshops are forever steeped in the feel and look of royal blue, reminiscent of the sacred, the intellect, and spirit. My commercial consultations feel like black, the color for career/life journey, where flow and deep reflection are each important to be of the best service for my client. My residential meetings are forever green… the heart and growth of a family stepping into their new life. The Inner Home Nine-Year Cycles are the hue of happy yellow… compassion. The vibrancy and warmth of orange denotes my monthly magazine article. Red is the passion and enthusiasm that serves everything I do.

Color is an essential part of discovering the hidden treasures of the inner and outer home. Understanding color's timeless codes of truth is vital. In the Eckankar practice, the word Hu (pronounced as Hue which is synonymous with color) is sung as a love song to God and it is their practice to know this vibration can transform life and open hearts to God's love.

Throughout history, color has been used to express tribal or cultural identification, and specific colors wave freely in national flags. Color evokes strong emotional and physical responses, has social relevance, is considered to have strong metaphysical essences, and plays a major epistemological role in our lives. Color is found in the oceans, the skies, the mountains, the meadows, the forests, and of course, we are each influenced by the color of and in our homes. The study or truth of color denotes a significant part of how energy moves through a space.

Since everything that exists is alive and consists of atoms, these atoms or molecules contain movement or oscillation and the speed at which they travel is called frequency. Within this frequency is an inner energy that has a certain vibration. Quantum physics states the process of this vibration is measured as wavelengths or angstrom units. Depending on the angstrom unit, when light reaches the retina, the brain reads it as color.

An angstrom unit is a hundred-millionth of a centimeter on the electromagnetic energy spectrum. Each of the seven colors has a position on this spectrum.

Is it a color or not? Black actually is not a color, but it does absorb color. Think of how hot you can become if you are outside on a bright sunny day, wearing black. Uh-Huh! White is the blending of all colors and reflects color. Color flourishes around us. Think of how powerful colored signs are in our daily lives. The colors of the traffic light instruct drivers when to slow down, stop, or go. The red stop sign, yellow says to yield, and even the speed limit is denoted on the black and white roadway signage.

Color is a visibly sensuous experience. Within color's vibration are hidden treasures that calm the mind, ease the heart, and heal the body, each creating a specific awareness.

**Red - Passion** is a mighty color resonating with an obvious link to blood. For centuries, red has been used to promote fertility, invoke protection and invisibility, and inspire and call forth magic. A bride in China wears a beautiful red wedding dress with a red veil and walks to her groom on a red carpet. The red rose is associated with long lasting love and fidelity. The fiery Phoenix is symbolic of revival and rebuilding your life in a stronger vein. Red is considered a life giving color.

**Pink - Love.** It is youthful, calming, symbolizes awareness, encourages action and has the exact same energy as red, without being too aggressive. When we are tickled pink, we are happy. In the pink means good health is being enjoyed.

**Orange - Creativity.** It is warm, radiant, and shows brilliantly in the sunsets, autumn leaves, and pumpkins. Orange itself is a healing medium, connecting a person to the vibrancy, wholeness, and balance. The flamboyance of orange is fun. It is vitality with endurance and longevity.

**Yellow - Joy**. As a trend, the whimsical yellow smiley face sent a message to be happy. On a more spiritual note, the Buddhist Monks wear saffron robes representing the highest of symbolic value of daylight. Daylight is considered the penultimate transitional state of meditation in which matter begins to be transformed in to pure light… the awakening of the inner self. Sunshine yellow is perky and when wearing this color, you actually spread joy. Place a bouquet of yellow flowers on your dining room table – it reminds you to smile.

**Silver - Inspiration.** It enriches communication. Set a silver box in the Helpful People (Chapter 24) area of your home and call forth blessings.

**Green - Growth and Strength.** Green brings to mind green grass, green leaves, clover, and green meadows. In the Emerald Isle of Ireland, there are fifty-nine different shades of green, hence luck is associated with this color. Green is the color of abundance. The Jade and Bamboo plants are forever green, as are the forests. Green is associated with renewal, and next to blue, is the second most favorite color. Green denotes peace and ecology.

**Blue - Wisdom.** When we are true blue, we are considered a loyal friend. Blue waters and blue skies come to mind with the color of blue. Blue is trustworthy, spiritual, committed, and restful. This blue is conservative.

**Indigo - Focus.** This deeper shade of blue is contemplative and inspires calm focus. It is about cosmic knowledge, profound insights, the mystical self, where mastery is achieved.

**Purple - Abundance.** The color purple is associated with royalty, nobility, spiritual awareness, enrichment in one's life journey, and luxurious elegance.

Be mindful of the colors you are living with and the colors you choose to wear. See how they influence your creativity, focus, abundance, inspiration, growth, joy, passion and above all, love. Enjoy the energy of color and allow it to enhance your life. Discover the hidden treasures of color and awaken your highest potentialities.

*A Jewel To Re*Member*

*"The richness I achieve comes from Nature, the source of my inspiration."*
*-Claude Monet (1840-1926)*

# 12

# -



# nerical Influences

## The Energy of Your Address Revealed

***"Were it not for Numbers, and its nature, nothing that exists would be clear to anyone either in itself or in relation to other things. You can observe the power of Number in all the acts and thoughts of man."* - Pythagoras**

Isaac Newton believed that special numbers governed all natural phenomena. Pythargorus of Samos defined numbers as the language of God. His contributions advanced geometry, mathematics, philosophy and musical theory to greater awareness. Galileo believed that all of nature is written in the language of mathematics. Plato insisted that as a prerequisite to his academy, his students must understand Geometry. Numerology is the actual study of the numbers themselves. What does this mean for the energy of your address? By converting letters into numbers, you will find a pattern or a profile of the prevailing energy of your home. To determine your home's influences, apply the following template accordingly.

Numbers exceed their value by merely adding or subtracting items in the mathematical and world of commerce. In Feng Shui, all even numbers are yin and odd are yang. Numerical laws actually create the harmony necessary to scores of music. Numbers rule the progression of the planets and they underscore Greek philosopher Pythagoras' association of numbers and the laws of our universe. He established the mystical energy of a number to more than the quantity it symbolized.

In the Hebrew and Greek tradition, each letter of the alphabet was assigned a number value. Based on this tradition, Nomenology is the study of one's name… it is fair to research this and find out what your name says about you. It combines the art of numerology, runes, and the wisdom of the Kabala. Which comes first, the chicken or the egg… do we live up to our name's expectations or do we create our lives around the energy of our name. I submit that we can create more than our name suggests, however valuing the inherent positive energies within the name supports our greater selves. So it is with our home or office's address, this is merely a jumping off place to better understand the location's energy. By harnessing the vital forces of nature, practicing positive thinking, cultivating wisdom and living in gratitude, we have the ability to exceed the following descriptions.

| 1 | 2 | 3 | 4 | 5 | 6 | 7 | 8 | 9 |
|---|---|---|---|---|---|---|---|---|
| A | B | C | D | E | F | G | H | I |
| J | K | L | M | N | O | P | Q | R |
| S | T | U | V | W | X | Y | Z | |

<u>701 7955 12</u>

For example, if the address is 701 Pine St., the value is 7+1+7+9+5+5+1+2=37.

The value is 37…unless you have an 11, 22, 33, 44, 55, 66, 77, 88, 99, please continue to reduce it down…3+7=10=1. The Energy of the House is ONE.

**ONE:** Individuality, originality, fresh new beginnings, purpose, advancement, innovation, pioneer… blazes new trails, confidence, follows feelings.

**Living in a one home** is conducive to an entrepreneurial spirit. One who is confident enough to embark on the journey of heart and follow his/ her dreams. This energy supports the self-employed or the driven person to succeed by doing most of the work alone. A one home is nurturing of self and if by any chance, there are a several strong individuals at this address, they will learn to creatively work through this strong energy and be healed of any past isolation they may have experienced. The number of one encourages determination, leadership, and taking the initiative to see things through.

**TWO:** Empathetic, romantic, cooperative, consideration, kindness, diplomacy, co-dependent, friendship, the dance of yin and yang in perfect harmony, self-less, passion, the balance of polarities, the deepening of the mystical self.

**Living in a two home** creates a pattern of sensitivity to everyone within this domain. When two is the energy, the art of true love exist in splendor. Closeness prevails and thoughtfulness is an unwritten rule joyously abided by everyone in residence. Lovely grounds, metaphysical music, the ability to look within and find the deeper core of one's being is available in a two home… relationship of self in the circle of the cosmic consciousness. The desire to foster one's marriage or relationship is important in this home. Gentleness and harmony abide in this home.

**THREE:** Artistic expression, creativity, rooted, strength, joy, laughter, sociability, the trinity, optimism, growth, and divinity of the mind, body, & spirit.

**Living in a three home** opens the door to enthusiasm as joy abounds in this home. The lively and hospitable energy of this home supports expansiveness. The laughter reverberated around the home, but the opportunity for greater communication and pushing beyond limited boundaries prevailed. A three home opens up nurturing relationships and positive thinking assists its residence in living an empowered life. Although this home's entertainment calendar will be full, it will never exceed the host's ability to find their social balance. This home supports activity, comfort, nurturing, diversity, and spirituality.

**FOUR:** Practicality, stability, self-discipline, loyalty, security, dedication, beauty, courage, four corners of a foundation, career enjoyment, and safety.

**Living in a four home** feels like one has finally arrived. The security of having four walls around one, living close to the earth as the four home has a solid foundational energy attached to it. It is grounded and enables one to beautifully express the practical side of living. Career opportunities flourish in this home and it is quite likely that the careers or schooling experiences of the residents are fulfilling. The rewards of working beyond the call of duty or making that extra push to pass with honors can be realized in this home. The ordinary will have an extraordinary quality about it as the every day tasks are considered blessings. The joy of taking care of home and pride in ownership will keep this home in top condition. Again, the residents will enjoy taking care of this four home, as it is more than an investment it is a home. The stability of this home connects one to gardening and craft or woodworking. A four home supports a higher calling to volunteer one's services to the community with the willingness to take responsibility for something greater than one's self, creating a better world in which to live.

**FIVE:** Travel, transformation, adaptability, versatility, freedom, resourcefulness, energetic, enterprising, bold, valiant, dauntless, impromptu and adventurous.

**Living in a five home** is dynamic! Surely the life of the party, who remembers and better yet, can deliver all the jokes with such panache, lives in a five home. This home creates a whirlwind of activity and constant change. Spontaneity is standard rule of thumb. Innovative thinking lends itself to a great job as a travel guide, a journalist covering exotic lands, or simply a person who enjoys a garden variety of experiences. This home supports major transitions so if one has been in a boring existence, this house will liven things up. The diversification of this home must be thought through so that impulsive decisions are thoroughly considered… well, as much as a five home will allow anyway. However, set your sails toward universal balance where you enjoy the wisdom of thinking decisions through. Enjoy the diversification of this energy and allow the adventure to bless you.

**SIX:** Service, understanding, synchronicity, inner truth, harmony, inspiration, beauty, art community, generosity, philanthropist deeds and volunteerism.

**Living in a six home** is all about compassion and comfort. The harmony afforded in this energy creates an opportunity for balance. However, the deep sensitivities of the residents of this home might become sequestered. This can be avoided by keeping one's activity in the world flowing. The reclusive energies are usually spent in meditation or reading to enlighten the residents, within and without. A healthy balance is attained through generosity and receiving. A six home creates a synergistic pattern where one will find synchronicity is regular occurrence. The support of a six home engenders intimate marriages and close friendships. When a family resides in a six home, the loving nature of the home stimulates open communication and caring relationships. Inspiration and compassion set the stage for innovative ways to make the world a better place. A six home is an excellent place for budding artist, poets, and writers. The energy is conducive to getting in touch with the rhythm of the universe. The beauty and serenity of a six home nourishes one deep within. This kind of nurturing enables one to give and successfully teach those who have not discovered how they too can prosper… mentally, physically and spiritually. Mentors, counselors, philanthropist, anyone wishing to express and experience beauty and art will flourish in a six home.

**SEVEN:** Spirituality, perfection, mental analysis, clear thinking, wisdom, musings, triumph over limitations, meditation and mystical realms, solitude, reflection, and sagacity.

**Living in a seven home** conjures up the patterns of creativity; the seven days of the week, the seven chakras, seven seas, seven deadly sins, seven dwarfs, seven orders of the architectural code, and the seventh son of the seventh son. There are seven continents and located within the Milky Way the seven sisters of Pleiades' constellation. King Solomon took seven years to build the Temple. It was then dedicated to God's glory and in the seventh month, the festival celebrating it's completion continued for seven days. And of course, *The Seven Habits of Highly*

*Effective People* by Stephen Covey is a prime system of order. The wisdom of one's inner life is relevant in a seven vibration.

The number seven is associated with spirituality. Referencing the seven days of the week and how we can best enjoy each day, let us consider the following Sanskrit hymn:

"Look to this day, for it is life, the very best of life." - a Sanskrit Hymn. In its brief course lie all the realities and truth of existence, the joy of growth, the splendor of action, the glory of power. For yesterday is but a memory, and tomorrow is only a vision, but today well-lived makes every yesterday a memory of happiness, and every tomorrow a vision of hope. Look well therefore to this day.

Living in a seven home is similar to living in a monastic way of life. The spiritual aspect of this home engenders solitary pursuits such as researching one's genealogy or seeking a higher order in life's purpose through prayer and meditation. Dream analysis and visions will part of the resident's interest including all of the traditional faiths and metaphysical studies will be highlighted in a seven home. The reclusive seven template will serve the resident in their reflective times and material pursuits will not be a topic for consideration. A seven home is an excellent abode for a student, investigative journalist, pastor, philosopher, psychic, guru, scientist, teacher, savant, academician, architect, artist, and or savant. When there are contemplative souls sharing a seven home, there will be balance. Although the energy of a seven is social, the residential energy is more spiritual. A seven home serves everyone as we are all on our path.

**EIGHT:** The cultivation of knowledge, financial gain, self-empowerment, perspicacity, wealth, achievement, gifts, compensation, dividends, benefits, profit, global conscious awareness, abundance, and infinity.

**Living in an eight home** can be compared to hitting the lottery. As you cultivate self-mastery and financial acumen, your worldly possessions will be plentiful as you apply discipline. Even before financial comfort is evident, the flow of many friends and family in and around you will always be present. Omnitude is the operative word in an eight home. Balancing financial responsibilities and being sensitive to the cares of others is extremely important. The fullness of life pours forth for the residents of an eight home. As they develop greater skills and higher education, leadership and recognition of their many accomplishments is supported. Where integrity is present, honor and prestige will follow. Organization is essential in an eight home. By paying homage to the clutter-free life style, the residents avoid self-imposed blockages. The eight home residents will not sit on their laurels, as they know they the importance and responsibilities of opulence and abundance. Through managerial excellence and keeping their priorities clear, great good success can be acquired in this energy field.

**NINE:** Universality, wholeness, benevolence, good will, tender-heartedness, charity, consideration, altruism, humanity, honorable.

**Living in a nine home** affords the residents to reap the benefits of their past accomplishments. Sowing what one reaps or as Pearl Buck once said, "In order to reap the whirlwind, one must sow the wind." This home offers the occupant recognition for earlier interests and these are usually of the universal sort. This home attracts the compassionate and creates the prophetic. It's sympathetic ear listens to the needs of humanity and does something about them. This proactive wisdom serves mankind in the highest of fashion. Whether one is a visionary, a mentor, equal rights activist, or a full time caregiver, the common thread is empathy. This home is about planting the healing seeds and harvesting their bounty. In the truth that we are all connected, the universal family will be more apparent in this home. This vibration personifies the law of attraction. The residents will find themselves being a shoulder for humanity's cry for help. Their mercy comes through to comfort and support those in need. The compassion and discernment of the nine vibrations are strong enough to stand in the gap for humanity. Generosity of self gifts mankind with their wisdom and refined insights. This altruism creates foresight that will be enlarged and allow old limitations or boundaries to be dissolved. This home may encourage old friends or past co-workers to look the residents up. When this occurs, it is purely an opportunity for the nine residents to spread their goodwill abroad via one person at a time. They take their role of humanitarian seriously and care deeply for the people they meet throughout life's journey. They are able to separate the individual from the mass cause they are passionate about. After all, it is the individual who makes up the need to make this world a better place.

## The Meaning of the Master Numbers

**11** – Eleven is the Student, learning new things, having already mastered many levels of Self.

**22** – Twenty-two is the Teacher, passing along what they have learned through personal experience.

**33** – Thirty-three is the merging of Student and Teacher, knowing they are one and the same, aware that what they are teaching is what they most need to learn, and the more they teach it, the more real it becomes for them.

**44** – Forty-four is dedicated to Earth, the environment, coming out of the focus on Self to focus on the outer world.

**55** – Fifty-five is a catalyst for change, aware that their very presence in the lives of others is helpful for initiating course-corrections, inspiring new beginnings, prompting the arrival of Cosmic 2 x 4s to remove blockages and initiate new flow… not always comfortable, but always necessary.

**66** – Sixty-six is the Healer, the energy-worker, the Shaman, committed to healing in all forms, inner and outer, and helping others.

**77** – Seventy-seven is the Manifester, knowing that spiritual lessons manifest on the physical level, able to manifest whatever is needed or desired, understanding the dynamics of the Law of Attraction and able to use it for Self and others.

**88** – Eighty-eight is the Master, aware of their responsibilities and power, capable of making clear-headed decisions that affect their own life and the lives of others, the Leader, leading by example, taking charge without questioning what might be required and willing to take responsibility for their choices.

**99** – Ninety-nine is the Humanitarian, having the big picture, aware of the flow of consciousness and the power of mass-thought-forms, the Universalist helping with the greater cause for good, unconcerned with their own needs, focusing on the needs of others, desiring to make the world a better place. Ninety-nine is also completion and preparing the way for a new beginning, but always for many, not for the Self.

# 13

# Elemental Persuasion

## Cultivating a Sustainable Life

The elements we speak of are timeless. They were here before time began and they continue to support us. Within their free-flowing Chi, we find them everywhere. They are wood, fire, earth, metal, and water. Everything in the Universe has an element associated with it and people are even considered a "fire" element. Of themselves, the elements are a treasure map for cultivating a sustainable inner and outer expression of an enriched life. This endurance is found when we can decode their meanings and allow the balance and order of their energies to support us. Instead of swimming upstream, we can flow with the river.

Each element has a symbolic place in our life, it has a color, a numerical code, a geometric shape, a season, a feminine or a masculine energy, and it has a body of energetic patterns such as creativity, love, spirit, and how to embrace change.

The element's interrelatedness to one another has a specific effect on the earth and on us. Their relationship to one another creates either a productive or a diminishing cycle. When these five forms of Chi or elemental energies are in their enhancing cycle, they create harmony and balance. When they are in the controlling cycle, they control or reduce one another. In fact, it is the art of balancing of these energies where this harmony is produced. Each cycle teaches us wholeness and it is within these teachings where we find our place in the web of life.

This is an excellent model of how energy flows not only through the universe, but also through our spaces… both personal and professional.

*"Everything in the Universe is a pitcher brimming with wisdom and beauty."*
*- Rumi ~ 13th Century Poet and Mystic*

These five elements represent five unique movements of Chi and, as stated, they also have seasons as well as other characteristics. These elements determine how energy will move through your home and should be considered equally as important as your blueprints and building materials.

All objects in our environment, such as a Bamboo plant, are of themselves not the elements. An object merely symbolizes an element; for instance, Bamboo is considered a wood influence. To further expand this teaching, let us consider the movement or the Chi of the elements. In fact, we will begin with the **Wood** element.

For this understanding to be clear, think of the forest, the upward growth of trees, plants, and flowers. Think spring, when all of the buds begin to burst through the ground. This dynamic power of nature is replete within our souls as we feel the energy of new beginnings and of fresh opportunities to create. After the winter, we take in the buds, the bulbs, the greenery, and we experience the upward movement of spring within and without. Spring evolves into late spring and we delight with the flower and trees as they unfold their blossoms.

For you to re*member, Wood's sacred shape is the upright column or the tree form. It is supported by the colors green and blue. Creativity, optimism, and dynamic ideas are being put into action, vitality, and we are part of the nature's movement of pushing upwards. The ease of focus and planning is balanced by a deep and knowing flexibility… embrace the transformations at hand. Be like the Bamboo plant, it bends but it does not break.

Too much wood and you will become rigid. If there is too little, there is a lack of creativity and a lack of strength and trust in our relationships with family and friends. Water feeds wood and metal controls it. When in balance, WOOD teaches us to TRUST.

**Fire** symbolizes the flaming upward movement of Chi at its peak, when it is completely directed and fully burning. In balance, it's enthusiastic, passionate, comforting, warm, and uplifting. Fire burns off the excess and leaves the highest idea of who are we. From this place, we live with integrity and are illuminated from within. Our bright flame of universal love warms our life and allows us to go forth with clarity. When fire burns out of control, it can ravage the inner and outer landscape. Once it is contained, it seeks rest. Instead of burning out, be the sunshine, the bright light and shine radiantly from within to the without and back again.

Re*member, the triangle is its sacred shape and the color red is its energetic pattern. The Universal number nine is in its energy grid. The season of summer is associated with the fire element. Think of the blazing sun at noontime in the heat of a summer's day. The blazing energy of the element of fire creates growth and a desire for swift action. An excess of fire will have you seeing red where tempers will easily flare up. Burning the candle at both ends will create burnout. Too little fire creates a lack of enthusiasm and compassion, lifelessness, laziness and all of these create an apathetic attitude. Water controls fire and wood feeds it. Fire teaches us INTEGRITY.

**Earth** is where we cultivate our plants to harvest vegetables and our trees for fruit. As a gardener, I love to dig in the soil and be connected to Mother Earth. She is the nurturer, and the giver. This energy is reliable, receptive, caring, and loving. This energy is the center of all the other movements. She represents all seasons and at the same time, the transitions between seasons; it symbolizes a horizontal movement around an axis as she spins, she sustains full force of movement, while the other elements move and change. Her energy is constant, as she is loyal.

When there is an overabundance of earth there will be imbalance. This creates a tendency to be slow, stuck and forever fearful of change. For example, a living room that is brown, upon beige, upon gold—I knew some folks who had this color scheme and change was not in their vocabulary, because it terrified them. In fact, wearing earth colors is okay but do not make them a uniform. Mix them up with reds, pinks, blues, and black. When there is not enough earth, there is flightiness. Environments such as these will influence folks to be indecisive and have their flight or fight adrenal glands wide open. Worry will be a preoccupation, they will want to move around, and people in this environment are not content… they are hard to please.

When in balance, earth is majestically stable and grounded. In balance, earth is centered and contented. Think of the 'salt of the earth' this - implies dependability. A balanced earth environment encourages the ability to make good on a long-term commitment.

Re*member the earth is square, has the colors of terra cotta, sable brown, golden yellow, sienna, and all earth tones such as ocher and beige. It is all of the seasons. In the productive cycle, earth is created by fire. Envision the volcanic ash creating the islands. Wood controls earth. The trees of wood can dig its roots into the ground and break up the density of earth. Earth teaches to BE PRESENT.

**Metal** is the Chi of inward, condensing, and the hardening movement of energy. Metal is symbolized by the mind and is associated with Mercurial thought processes. Many cultures consider metal to be almost magical, because it was relentlessly unyielding. Swords and armor were made from metal as it held high stature in the days of old. Metal is associated with financial $ucce$$ and bu$ine$$ $ucce$$. Coinage was fashioned from silver and gold and forged for material barter. Metal is considered an element of success and yet it represents the spiritual matters in life. Metal is about refining and defining the best life has to offer. It is the breath where we breathe in the great the beauty and pleasures of life.

Metal is the season of fall. Think of autumn's pageantry when the wheat fields are yielding their golden stalks of grain and the harvest moon lights the sky with warmth and comfort. It looks as if Midas himself has touched all of the trees, as their golden hue is replete in the apples on the nearby branches and the leaves of the Ashes and Oaks. Row after row of golden pumpkins rise, ready and willing to be transformed into happy Jack O' Lanterns or a delicious fall pie. Amber ribbons around the sunrise and the sunset as harvest gold enriches the land of fall.

Metal coalesces, so it is essential for one to have purposeful intentions. Just like the magnet, metal is a strong attractor factor. When there is too much metal present, it will have the tendency to implode. An overabundance of metal creates an environment with the propensity to over-analyze everyone and every situation. Think of the office spaces where the sea of gray cubicles goes back as far as the eye can see. No wonder folks get road rage… they sit in these little metal spaces and drive home in a metal car on black and white roads, in congestion and with little mind energy available to process or respond.

It is essential for these cubicles to have a desk water fountain, red flowers and even a red rug. In an overdrive mode, metal will change its mind a thousand times and create chaos from within and without. Too little metal and you will miss out on golden or silver opportunities to invest and can create a poverty mentality. When it is in perfect balance, it symbolizes refinement.

Re*member the Earth enhances metal and fire controls it. The colors are white and gold and its shape is the circle. Metal teaches us how to have MENTAL CLARITY.

**Water** runs downwards and is always seeking the darkness and the restful quiet. Water is considered to be renewing and refreshing. It is a mysterious energy where its hidden power lies beneath the surface. Water is associated with the curvilinear or freely flowing movement. It is associated with spirit and courage. The essence of water can run from the peaceful stream gently flowing along to the violent surge of hurricanes. Its emotions can run from high to low and just like the ebb and flow of the ocean rolling onto the sand, it is infinite.

Water is present is a myriad of forms such as the ocean, lakes, rivers, streams, ponds, and even ice. In order to live fully, we must have water to hydrate our bodies. Water symbolizes intelligence, determination, willfulness, intuition, and independence. Water is reflective, philosophical, preoccupied, and possesses great strength. The experience of water teaches how to go through the dark night of the soul and find courage to face the challenges in life. The energy is to be in the flow and accept life's changes.

Winter is the season for water. This is a still time of year when all of the bulbs are beneath the surface, wintering-over. It is a time of rest and reflection. A time when we plan ahead and when we experience new beginnings. Hibernate and enjoy this winter wonderland time of life where it is opportune to curl up and dream or read, or bring out our dormant artistic abilities.

Re*member, if there is too much water in one's environment, we surely become wishy-washy and overly sensitive. Too little and we become brittle and aloof. When water flows freely, it can be artistically expressive. The expansive energy for water is metal. The controlling element is earth. Black and blue are the colors and the energy is meandering. Water at its very best it is INTUITIVE.

## The Enhancing and Controlling Cycles

Each object has a relationship to the specific characteristics of each element. It can either be enhancing or controlling, one to the other. This process is considered a "cure." The enhancing cycle is supportive of each of the five Elements.

### Enhancing Cycle

Wood enhances Fire. The expansion of Fire is carried out with wood, as it feeds fire and gives it fuel.

Fire enhances Earth. The upward energy of Fire spins and the smoke swirls; this builds up the Earth energy. Think of the pottery process when clay is fired.

Earth enhances Metal. The spinning energy of Earth and the inward, condensing, and contracting energy of Metal enables earth to be as mother to Metal; all gemstones come from, and are created from, earth.

Metal enhances Water. The descending energy of Water condenses out of the contracting movement of Metal. Think of the metal as a container for water, giving it focus, shape and purpose.

Water enhances Wood. The regenerative nature of water is like a womb and gives birth to the creative, expanding force of Wood. Water refreshes and replenishes plants and enables them to grow.

### Controlling Cycle

Just as Elements can support and enhance other elements, to create balance they can control one another.

Wood controls Earth: The roots of a tree break up earth, and a plant depletes the soil of nutrients.

Earth controls Water: Earth dams water and prevent it from flowing. Also water and earth make mud.

Water controls Fire: Water extinguishes the flames of fire.

Fire controls Metal: The rising heat of fire melts metal.

Metal controls Wood: As an ax, metal chops wood - the tree.

Harmony and Balance

The field of harmony is always seeking to have all of the Elements by way of their sacred geometry, colors, and strengths, and even their weakness… to be in balance, in size proportionate to the space. Allow the elements to balance and harmonize your sacred spaces.

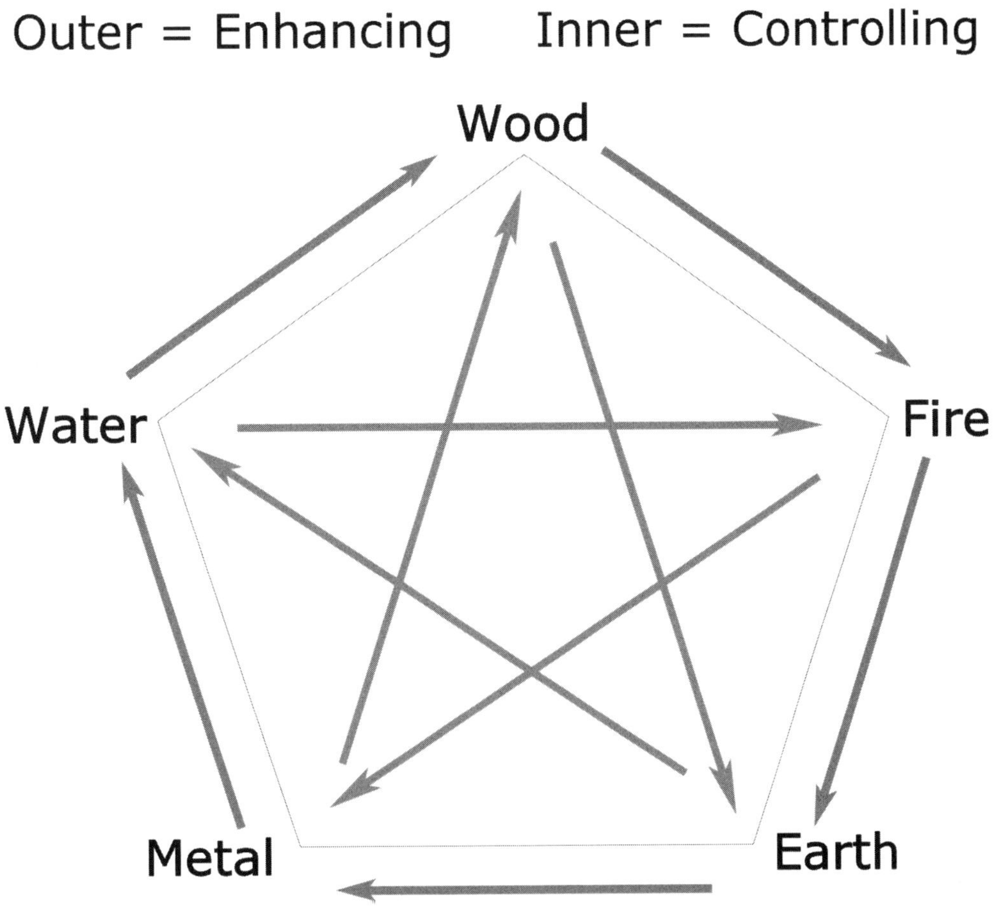


ELEMENTS - ENHANCING & CONTROLLING

# 14

# Geometric Shape

The shape of an object defines its form, and the form contains information coded within its matrix. This information reveals the energetic pattern of movement in time and space. The grid of information forms fractal images that balance the right and left-brain. In fact, the brain is always trying to recognize patterns and when it sees a pattern it recognizes, it can relax in safety and peace.

Our subconscious mind registers all of the energetic information coded within certain shapes and forms. We were there when time began and although it doesn't register at the surface of daily awareness, at a very deep level, we are responding to everything around us… the seen and the unseen.

We are actually "reading" between the lines of an environmental space with our feelings and our senses of smell, hearing, taste, sight, touch and intuition. This is how can either exclaim, "I love that home," or, "Yuck, that was not the home for me." We know that we know, and the certainty is almost tangible.

When we pull it down from the ethers, we are all energy-workers, because everything is made up of energy. We are energetic beings and the environments that surround us are rich in geometric shapes that should be nurturing and supporting our every wish or desire.

Geometric shapes have a blueprint with a basic pattern of physical reality attached to them. These models are meshed with the very fabric of the universe. They influence our decision-making, our emotions, thinking, intentions, health - overall; they play a major role in the quality of our lives.

From the spirals of the golden mean to the square of stability, we recognize who we are within these shapes. Energy is forever moving within, around and through us. The shapes are interconnected with the spiritual planes of heaven. They are more than mere shapes; they are sacred to us and are the hidden treasures of our inner and outer homes. As it is on the inner, so it is on the outer. The concentric circles of time and space spiraling through our lives move forward so that we may know who we are. For a fact, we are the beloved children of the Universe. In poised certainty, we are free to make spontaneously correct decisions and we can enjoy a life of enrichment, balance and harmony.

Geometric shapes are as follows:

| | |
|---|---|
| Wood: | Pillar or Columnar shape |
| Fire: | Triangle or Pyramidal |
| Earth: | Square or Flat |
| Metal: | Circle or Arch |
| Water: | Curvilinear or Meandering |

# 15

# -

# Seasonal Cycles & I Ching Trigrams

"For everything there is a season,
a time to be born, and a time to die;
a time to plant, and a time to pluck up what is planted;
a time to kill, and a time to heal;
a time to break down, and a time to build up;
a time to weep, and a time to laugh;
a time to mourn, and a time to dance;
a time to throw away stones, and a time to gather stones together;
a time to embrace, and a time to refrain from embracing;
a time to seek, and a time to lose;
a time to keep, and a time to throw away;
a time to tear, and a time to sew;
a time to keep silence, and a time to speak;
a time to love, and a time to hate;
a time for war, and a time for peace."
Ecclesiastes 3: 1-8

Seasonal cycles are associated with every element. It defines how energy will move through a space. Its inherent energetic blueprint determines whether it is in the meandering pattern of water or in the rapidly expanding energy of fire as it spreads throughout a flame-engulfed area.

Along with seasonal cycles are colors, sound, emotions, sense organs, tastes, spiritual resources, positive aspect, value, Resolution for Imbalances.

| | **WOOD** | **FIRE** | **EARTH** | **METAL** | **WATER** |
|---|---|---|---|---|---|
| | | | | | |
| **Season** | Spring | Summer | All Seasons | Fall | Winter |
| **Sound** | Shouting | Laughter | Singing | Weeping | Sighing |
| **Emotion** | Anger | Joy | Worry | Grief | Fear<br>Lack of Joy |
| **Sense Organ** | Eyes | Tongue | Mouth | Nose | Lower Orifices |
| **Tastes** | Sour | Bitter | Sweet | Pungent | Salty |
| **Spiritual Resources** | Spiritual | Heavenly | Thought | Animal Spirit | Will |
| **Positive Aspect** | Bursting Forth | Love | Thoughtfulness | Spirituality | Courage |
| **Value** | Creativity | Compassion | Caring | Meaning<br>Inspiration | Inner Courage |
| **Resolution For Imbalance** | Forgiveness | Stillness<br>Surrender | Service | Connection | Faith |

I was first introduced to the timeless *I Ching = The Book of Changes* in 1969. Being a student and seeking truth, I found its truths to be rich with enduring insights. I recall opening this book and as I drank in its words of wisdom, my awareness shifted. The wakefulness of being immersed in the web life flooded through me and I knew I was connected to the entire cosmos. Its universal perspective gave meaning to the sustainable joy and profound transformations.

In Chinese, the "I" in I Ching means *change* and Ching means *classic*. It does indeed provide a wealth of classic change. This may be the oldest book on earth. It possesses the treasures of wisdom and creativity. Confucius said, "*By following the counsels of the book, and studying it continuously, we can attain creative awareness in every situation.*"

The I Ching identifies order in what may seem like a chance occurrence. It is the dynamic balance of opposites. It reveals the unfoldment of events as a process and shows how we are all connected.

In 1913, Richard Wilhelm began the ambitious task of translating the I Ching into English. Wilhelm is considered the Marco Polo of his time and clearly is responsible for opening the east up to the west. He wrote, "*Lao first opened my mind to the wonders of the Book of Changes. Under his experienced guidance, I wandered entranced through this strange yet familiar world. The translation of the text was made after detailed discussion. Then the German version was retranslated into Chinese and it was only after the meaning of the text had been fully brought out that we considered our version to be truly a translation."*

His was the first text I referenced and although, for a span of twenty some odd years, I set it aside, the eternal wisdom of its truths continued to bloom in my heart. In 1995, when I discovered Feng Shui, I, like Wilhelm, knew this information system to be quite familiar and yet, all so very new. It revived my I Ching studies, which proved to enrich my life on every level.

The creativity and wisdom of wind and water is birthed from the I Ching. In 2004, I discovered Hanna Moog and Carol Anthony's I Ching translated version. In their foreword, they have written, "As the title indicates, this is a book about the Cosmic Way. To we humans, learning the Cosmic Way is about understanding. Transformation is the natural activity of the Cosmos, and of all that exists within it. As such it is among the enduring Cosmic Principles, discussed in the I Ching, that governs all existence. The authors are careful in distinguishing transformation and from "changes"... But isn't transformation simply change of a sort, or perhaps a vaunted kind of change?"

Ms. Moog and Ms. Anthony ask their readers - as I am asking of you - to "look beyond this rather circular definition. The further difference between transformation in the Cosmic Way and 'change' lies in the source and direction of the movement. Change is movement confined to the outer plane of experience, while transformation is movement on the inner plane, to which the outer plane responds spontaneously."

Within *The Home Whisperer*, you will discover the hidden treasures - the jewels of the inner that reveal the wealth of the outer. Be prepared to step into what Wilhelm described as 'this strange, but familiar world.' You will recognize it, as you have it encoded within your being. The adventure of person and place began long before you reached for this book. But now, we can wrap words around your inner knowing and find the balance and harmony of our outer that nurtures our inner treasures. In turn, our deep and wise inner world is a source of great nourishment and truth. Enjoy the process.

## The Binary Code & the Yin & Yang

In the I Ching, the broken lines represent yin and the solid lines are yang. For 6,000 years, this early form was a binary code and the combination of eight basic tri grams when expanded, forms the sixty-four patterns or hexagrams. It denotes the way the energy is moving. In the world of computers, the basic code used is the binary system. The sixty-four characters are symbolic and possess intrinsic qualities that the intellect can recognize. Just like my first experience with the I Ching, I was immediately transformed by its wisdom. Instantly, my brain recognized its use of Universal code.

In fact, a fractal image provides a similar experience. Given that the brain is always trying to recognize a familiar pattern. When it sees one, it becomes balanced and much more productive. Music can have a similar effect, as the tonal quality of the vibrations induces a higher frequency within our brain. Listening to Mozart has proven to improve test scores and for creative types, and inspire greater works in their chosen field of artistic expression.

Waves and frequencies are in the flow mixture of the matrix of space and time. This is how we know our connectivity is actually enmeshed in the fabric of cosmic consciousness. Regardless of the world's trends, know that you can be in alignment with the cosmos and live in the infinite place of potentiality. What you see is truly what you get in life.

The binary system hints at the nature of Duality, the extremes of the spectrum and everything it contains. Duality pertains to physical experience, where energies have been separated in order for us to have experiences with them. This system can bring us experiences that are harmonious and happy or chaotic and painful. Understanding this system allows us to consciously choose which we will experience.

When you see the beauty and order of the sixty-four cosmic characters that play themselves out against the yin and yang energies moving through time, you will get a deep sense of inner peace. You will recognize the timeless patterns and overlay them onto you life, and not be drawn off by linear time. Yes, you must be responsible and honor your timeline, but do so from the perspective that you are unlimited.

# 16

# Energy Patterns for Individual Rooms

Each room in our home has a unique purpose or meaning attached to it. In order to take full advantage of the room's potentiality there are certain auspicious principles to keep in mind. These codes do not fall under the numerical influences, however there will be an element attached to it. As you can surmise, color is always a consideration.

First of all, let us highlight the living or great room. Regardless of where this room is located within your home's blueprint, this room is considered a fire element. Just like the Integrity and Illumination gua, it reveals who you are and what you are known for.

The **living room** is the heart of your home. This is an excellent place to enjoy fellowship and to spend quality time with your family and friends. Arrange your furniture to honor one another. When all of the seating is gathered around the television set or the computer, these items will take precedence over your family and friends. If there is a media system in the room, be certain there are doors so you can readily close it off. If not, drape fabric over it. It is fine to enjoy a movie or sporting event, however, to have television or radio on all of the time delivers too many EMFs into your home.

Dress the living room in comfortable fabrics and colors you love. Consider the kinds of activities that your family enjoys. Do you host a monthly book club in this room, play family games, or listen to music in this room? If your space affords, create little rooms within the large room dedicated to reading or playing music. A large over sized chair in the corner by a window offers privacy and proper lighting so that the space can be doubled for anyone's reading pleasure.

The **dining room** is associated with the earth element and highlights the stomach. Earth is about nourishment and giving of one's self. What better way to express these attributes than in a calm and comfortable dining area? Plan your time around being able to relax into the meal and be present with everyone who is in attendance. Pay attention to your meals and make certain they are healthy and satisfying. Gathering at the table and enjoying a meal at home is a gift.

The preferred shape of a table is round or oval. This form is known to promote community and lively conversation. If this is not possible, place a large round bowl on the table. Fill it with fruit or flowers. It is said that whatever we have on our table is indicative of the experiences we have in our life. A bamboo plant is always a welcome addition to a dining table as it symbolizes auspiciousness. Prior to eating, cup your hands over your food and ask that it match the highest vibration possible. Then give thanks.

The **kitchen** is represented by the wood element and the liver is associated with it. The liver is where we might hold any anger so how perfect is it that we can be in a nurturing room such as the kitchen to process any misgiving we may have about life. When we cook with love, we add the most powerful energy available. Wood is the energy of growth and creativity so add cookbooks to your collection of books. Reading a cookbook like an adventure novel is a great way to come up with unique ways to feed your family.

If your kitchen is like ours, everyone gathers together in this room. Be sure that your stove, refrigerator, or sink do not face one another. If so, these power units will create power struggles. If this is the case, safely secure a round blue rug in between the appliances that are in contention with one another.

One of the first things I learned along my Feng Shui journey was to closet the knife block. Plus, I have my trash inside a pantry and I empty it often. Others tips are as follows:

- Keep your counters clear of clutter.
- Shine your stove daily. When you are not eating at home, please turn on each burner and then turn it off. As you do so, give thanks for your abundance. The stove is a powerful financial assistant.
- Room with a view… it is nice if your kitchen has window. If not, place a mirror over your stove and double your pro$perity. Be certain you do place your mirror so low that it crops off anyone's head.
- Even though it is always important, it is essential to have good lighting in this room. Working in a dim kitchen is a challenge.
- Surround yourself with the things that encourage you and for more information, each chapter will have specific insights for each section.

The **bedroom** is represented by the element of metal and the lungs. What better place to breathe the pleasures of life deeply into our being. Since metal is the energy of the mind, it is important to quiet the mind by sleeping peacefully and truly being rested. A bedroom is a sanctuary and beckons us to forget the outside world and be enfolded into the rapture of this space. The yin metal is the number seven and the yang metal is supported by heaven… that says seventh heaven to while away in this place of ecstasy. Directional sleeping comes into play by affecting your dreams and energy level. They are as follows: The top of your head pointing:

**South** - Expect to be more intuitive in your waking life and perhaps a lucid dreamer in your nighttime life.

**North -** The minute you open your eyes, you will want to get-up-and-go.

**East -** Regenerative and A New Lease of Life

**West** - A deeper and more tranquil sleep

If you have NW, NE, SW or SE as your direction, simply bring together the two and you will have your sleep decrees.

The **bathroom** is considered a water element and emphasizes the kidney. In Chinese medicine, the kidneys are more important than any other organ in the body. I have had clients who were terrified that their bathroom was in the wrong place. No, no, no, and no. There isn't a wrong place because there are always cures available. Look at the actual place where you bathroom is located within your home's footprint. In short, think of it as a spa and create a restful and sensual. Keep your toilet lid down. Otherwise, you will be leaking $$$ and enrichment opportunities. Consider this room to be most auspicious because water is always beneficial.

**Storage rooms** can be a curiosity. We can either pile them high with outdated stuff that we never use, wear, or need and think we can just forget about all of it. Wrong! It is much more preferred to only store things we love, care about and use often. For example, we frequently move our decorative things around and keep them on rotation. I have a linen closet that is perfect for this purpose. I also store out of season and thematic objects here.

**Hallways and Stairways -** The energy in a hallway or stairway are always fast and furious. It can whip through so fast that you cannot benefit from it at all. To slow it down, check out the sections within each of the aforementioned chapters. However for a heads up, if your stairway and your front door are lined up, please place a round rug with a mandala (see glossary) pattern on it. Or you can pull the energy up the stairs by hanging a large and very distinct painting or photo that draws the eye up. Please do not cascade your pictures in the hallway or stairway.

**Home office** - all of the principles you will learn in the following chapters can enhance this room profitability. Please set boundaries for this room. Depending on what your profession is, it is best to have designated work hours. Otherwise, you create the possibility to working harder not smarter. I have always had a home office and I love it. I have surrounded myself with nurturing chatzkies that help me to stay focused. In the Helpful People and Travel chapter, find out the importance of a Tibetan bell on your desk. You will love it!

The most important thing to re*member is to live with what inspires you and makes you smile from the inside out.

# 17

# -

# Jewels to Re*Member

Jewels to Re*Member are the truths that we already know, but have simply forgotten. When we come back to earth, we are given a contract that we agree to follow our destiny. If per chance we miss it, not to worry for Nature has a way of finding us and inspiring us to fulfill our true purpose.

When we begin to transform our inner and outer homes into something marvelous, mystical, magical, and magnificent, there is an alchemical process that we go through. Although this mind-set makes us think of King Arthur and his round table oh so many years ago, it is actually a present day process that enjoys the assistance of the sage, cosmic helpers, Chi, and willingness to be transformed, increased and renewed.

This is creating your home in the model of the most elegant spa, the most blessed of sanctuaries, as a heavenly haven, and recognizing the profound connection between person and place. Along the way, you will discover the hidden treasures of your inner and outer home. We are the Alchemists.

Outer Home - When we think upon a treasure, we are reminded of a beautiful jewel box. In fact, your noble and loving home is this box and holds jewels in the form of the enrichment of well-being, wealth of a loving family, the riches of happiness, the fortunes creativity brings forth, and of course, the treasure trove of creating balance and harmony. The analogy of your home and that of an elegant jewel box reveals your outer home's hidden treasure or rich potential.

Your outer or physical home nurtures, supports, inspires, and blesses you in very possible aspect of pure abundance and true wealth. The jewels of your home have intrinsic value in that energy always resonates with powerful vibrations. We are all energy and the homes we create have a frequency. It is up to us to bring forth this hidden treasure and live in the richest fashion that balance and harmony offer. Seeing our homes as the timeless jewel boxes they truly are enables us to live with what inspires us, supports us, nurtures us, and prospers us.

Our outer homes are vibrating with the electric Chi energy that enables the movement of Chi that is self-renewing, supportive, abundant and harmonious. Fortunate blessings and profound enrichment are available when we recognize our homes as a treasure chest.

Trust that we have all done this work before. We are energetic beings and everything in the universe is comprised of energy. As you discover your home's hidden treasures, you are permitting it to enjoy the highest frequency possible. Through the art of placement, science, dreams, optimism, signs, and symbolism, re*member we are the Alchemists.

**Inner Home** - This inner treasure chest is brimming over with millions of golden and silver coins, jewel-encrusted with brilliant sapphires, emeralds, and rubies, long strands of pearls and glistening diamonds. This treasure chest is something you already possess. This is where you discover the inner truth of intuition, wisdom, sustainable joy, insight, integrity, and love.

Per Ms. Moog and Ms. Anthony, "Everything in the Cosmos is imbued with life force, with the exception of crystallized forms (although they also have a specific kind of consciousness). The transformation of life force into the visible occurs in the sphere of the atom. With regard to humans, every person is born with a reservoir of life force in every body cell. This life force is part of his "inner truth," which is also his *feeling memory* (in the form of imprints, or DNA) of what Cosmic Harmony feels like. Under normal circumstances, the life force is constantly renewed, in the atomic realm, through the person's contact with his feelings and the totality of his senses. The life force brings the Cosmic nourishment to the person's whole being. It is felt as caring and loving energy that makes him feel at one with the Cosmos."

To fully access the jewels and discover the treasures of our inner and outer homes, it is essential that we learn how to be centered, willing to release blame, shame, guilt, de-clutter our inner and outer homes so that the electrical and Cosmic energies surrounding and imbued within us are not blocked. These principles allow loving Chi to move elegantly and beautifully around and through us. May we always re*member to see the highest idea of the Cosmos exist within everything and everyone.

Jewels to RE*MEMBER is the understanding that we possess the capability, the ability and now we have the map to help us discover the hidden treasures of inner and outer home.

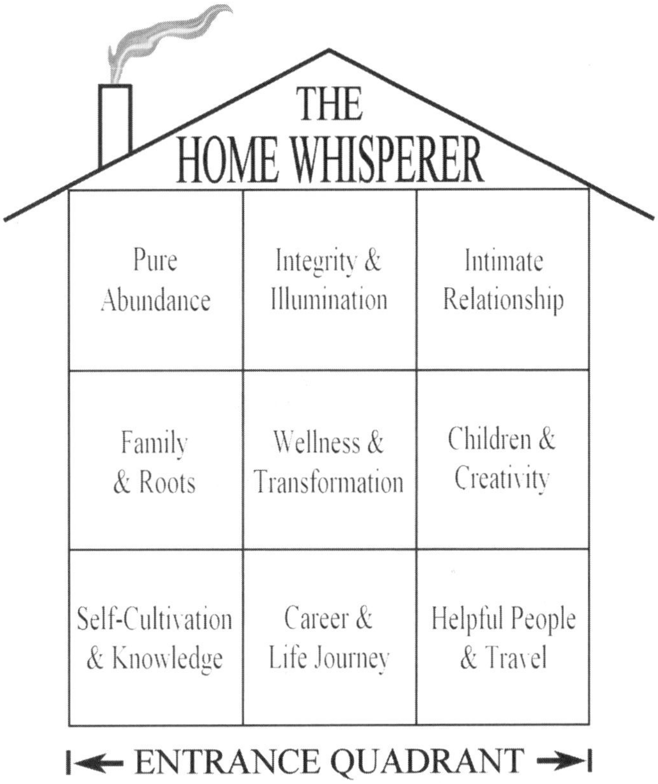


# Part Three

-

# The Grid Of Empowerment

## MAPPING THE BAGUA

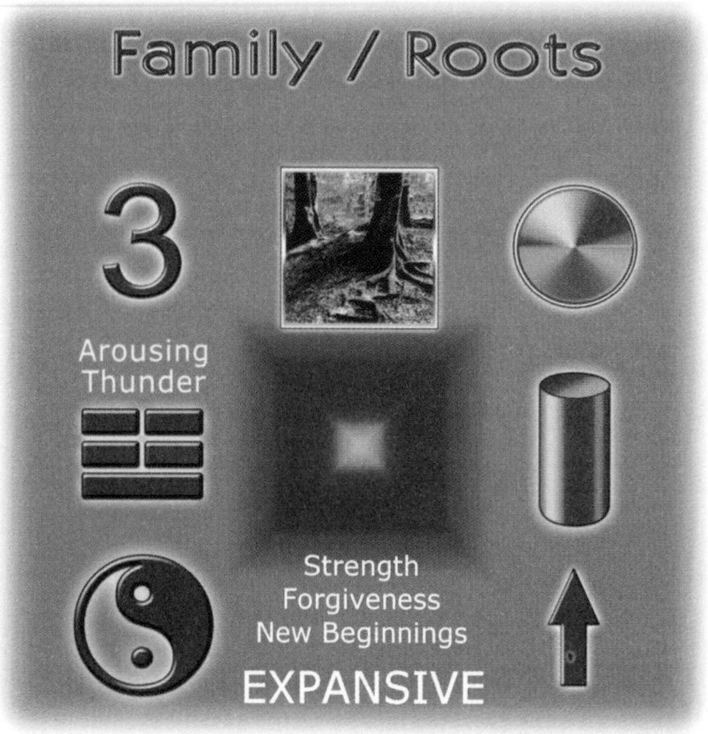


# *18*

*-*

# *Family Tree Wisdom*

## Be Strong

## Roots, Strength, Growth

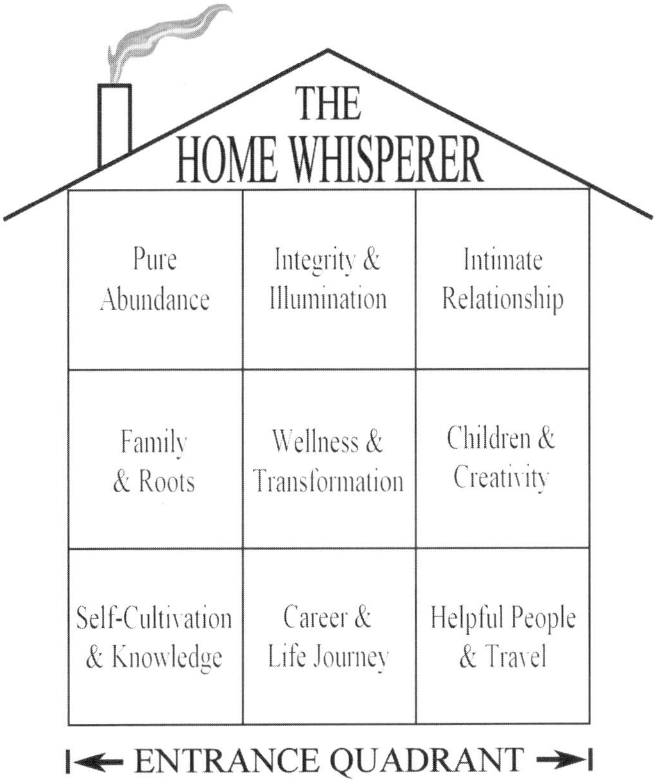


- **Location:** Left middle of the Bagua
- **Sacred Geometry:** The verticality of a column or tree-like shape
- **Numerical Influence:** Three
- **Color:** Green & Blue
- **Element:** Yang Wood, Eldest Son
- **I Ching Trigram:** Chen, Shocking Thunder
- **Operative Words:** Focus, strength, dynamic, growth, creativity, roots, forgiveness, expansion
- **Gemstones:** Emerald, Chrysanthemum Stone, & Phantom Quartz
- **Chi Imagery:** Photos/artwork of plants, trees, forest and/or flowers, objects of wood, columns/pillars, fresh plants/flowers, antiques
- **Season:** Spring
- **Directional Energy:** Upwards
- **Affirmations:** I cultivate and live a dynamic life of strength & purpose. I am joyous, fulfilled, and strong!

I trust the process.
My life is in perfect & harmonious balance… I forgive others and myself.
I fill my home and each room with the vibration of unconditional love so that all who enter, myself included, are nourished by this love!

## Visualization

*The tree's graceful branches soared into the skies and found guidance and its root system reached deep into the ground and found strength.*

Traditionally, I begin my Feng Shui Simplified consultations with the Family Gua. As you develop your Home Whispering skills, it is vital that you align with fresh beginnings and the expansive energy this Gua holds. The Family Gua's potentiality for fulfilling its purposes lies hidden within the family dynamic. Our cellular body or DNA coding is the link to our existence. It is the original energy that determines that you are you.

We are connected to all of humanity through our DNA… 99% of our DNA is exactly the same as everyone else's. It is the final 1% that allows for differentiation. In our DNA lies the key to cellular memory, which holds the code for habits, beliefs and cultural indoctrination as a species. But in modern times, there are many things in our cellular programming that no longer serve us, and as we clear and balance our space, we allow ourselves to release automatic reactions to events and situations that are based on outmoded cellular hard-wiring… the code is actual undone! We clean our outer home – and we clean our inner home, as well.

The family tree records our lineage, our personal ancestry and the strong family ties that we were not only born into, but that we continue to cultivate. Our family group is like a tribe or a clan and it constitutes our ancestry. This ancestry can be compared to a root system, which absorbs unexpected life events, transfering endurance and strength to us. Within this family dynamic, we learn who we are and who we are not. It is within this structure where loving relations and a lifetime of support are reciprocated. The blood ties that bind too tightly through conditional love, blame, shame or guilt obstruct our energy creating blockages. Sadly, these rob us of joy.

Interestingly enough, the parts of the body associated with the Family Gua are the liver, gall bladder and the feet. The liver is where we hold onto anger, regret, resentment, shame, guilt, judgmental thoughts, negative emotions, and blame. These conditions create a root of bitterness and once this is planted, it can become part of our life pattern. Bitterness generates clouded and distorted perceptions that create major blockages in our health, wealth, peace of mind and heart. The only way to stop this vicious cycle is to forgive!

**The Art of Unconditional Love…** This Gua's mission is to connect us to our inner support system and tap into the strength, creativity, personal development and trust it offers. Healthy relationships with our immediate blood family and our best friends, co-workers, neighbors and community promotes an ongoing balance in our life. While in refining the art of unconditional love, it is essential to forgive others and ourselves. Taking responsibility for our life enables us to understand how to move on and be healed of our past. To forgive restores family relations; opening up additional heart space to more fully inhale the joys life has to offer. This process frees us to be fully present in the NOW.

The art of unconditional love found within forgiveness and gratitude transports us to a place of inner and outer peace, keeping our channels of balance and harmony open. Unconditional love permits healing to move us into places of clarity as we de-clutter our emotional and mental processes. It moves us into places beyond where we have ever been able to go before.

Set the intention of unconditional love by placing a bamboo plant in your family Gua. Bamboo is eternally green and is indicative of a strong character. During difficult times, it will bend, but not break; this is a symbol of adaptability. It also represents forward movement. It is associated with endurance, modesty, and fertility. Along with the plum and pine tree, the bamboo plant is one of the three friends of winter that signify the ideal scholar, purity of spirit and of course, flexibility. A healthy bamboo plant epitomizes a happy family image, growth, and prosperity.

Forgiveness enables us to heal those inner places where we are trapped in "should've, would've, could've." These patterns foster anger, guilt, and regret, when in truth, they no longer serve us. Practice the mantra of **"I release (name the person(s) or situations) and you may now go in peace"**. Forgiving past heartaches and less than excellent experiences releases us from yesterday's ghosts. In time, we will be able to see how valuable these experiences have been, as they become the soil where wisdom is seeded.

## Colorful Perceptions

The colors of green and blue are connected to this Gua. Green represents growth and nature. It calms the nervous system, promoting tranquility. Green promises hope and inspires expansion. Nature's ecology logically balances the environment so it isn't a surprise that the grass, trees and flowers live in harmony. The color green strengthens the heart, lungs and thymus glands as it rules the fourth chakra. Green is associated with renewal, eternal life, prosperity, beauty, fertility, family, learning and contentment.

Just as green is the color of hope; blue is the color of faith. Blue is also the color of the intellect, peace, meditation, spiritual understanding and tranquility. Blue is associated with the color of greater soul awareness, as it denotes compassion and is considered to be the mediator of truth. When one is true blue, they are deemed to be loyal. Frank Baum, author of *Wizard of Oz*, said, "Whenever I feel blue, I start breathing."

## Numerical Influences

The number Three is associated with the Family and Health Gua. This number inspires the past, present and the future to be considered as one, the trinity of birth, death, and rebirth. Some of three's key words are encouragement, artistic expression, creativity, strength, joy, laughter, sociability, optimism and growth. Divinity, mastery and enlightenment are also linked to the number three.

Living in a three-home opens the door to enthusiasm, as joy abounds in this home. The lively and hospitable energy supports expansiveness. The laughter reverberates where the opportunity for greater communication and pushing beyond limitation prevails. A three-home opens up positive thinking and assists its residents in living an empowered life. Although this home's entertainment calendar will be full, it will never exceed the host's ability to find their social balance. This home supports activity, comfort, nurturing, diversity, and spirituality.

Since the points of a triangle number three and this is the symbol of fire, seating arrangements in this shape or just having three chairs in a group will invite passionate discussions. It will spark lively debates and communal good humor. Something to consider, however, is that too many groupings of three will diminish your finances.

The expansive three energy moves continuously out and this can create tension. If you find this happening in your space, placing a small metal feature (three-legged frog is considered auspicious) in this location will reduce some of the pent-up energy.

## Elemental Persuasions... Friends And Foes

Placing objects with loving symbolism encourages the attainment of excellence. Again, we live with what we love and what we love shows up. This trigram teaches that even when life doesn't present itself in the manner we prefer, we can stay centered and not be shocked into regression. Each Gua has friends and foes. Enjoy knowing the difference and cultivate excellence through hearing only positive and supportive messages from you home.

### Friend

Wood - please refer to Chapter 7. Wood energy is upwardly mobile. It transforms a tiny seed into a tree. Think of the verticality of the tree as the classis shape of wood. Pillars, columns, stripes, or any upright pattern characterizes healing, creativity, strength, and personal development. Water in any form is a loyal friend to nurturing these processes. All items made of wood such as end tables, sofa tables, dining room table and chairs, cabinets, doors, credenzas, wooden head board and night stands; picture frames, statuaries and beloved family photos strengthen wood's presence. Any article in the colors of green or blue… or both. For instance, turquoise, since it is green and blue combined, enhance wood's energy.

Floral fabrics, artwork of floral arrangements, wooden objects such as a vase of flowers, and plants with coin shaped leaves, such as the Jade or Begonia plant. Indoor trees like a rubber plant's upright growth is symbolic of natures many gifts and her generous offerings that enrich life. Nothing is ever asked in return, her beauty and bounty are shared unconditionally.

In my visualization, trees (includes pillars and columns) represent the connection between heaven and earth. The tree shape must be replicated with any pillars or columns. Avoid squared-off columns. Wood energy is also found in fresh flowers (refer to Chapter 21), healthy vegetable plants, bamboo, and thunder hold the energy of Wood. The colors black and dark navy blue are also excellent in this Gua.

### Foe

In the controlling/counterproductive cycle of the elements, it was mentioned that metal (like the ax) cuts wood. Please keep all metal frames, metal trophies, metal statuaries, anything in white or gray, or round down to a bare minimum. When you are working with the map of energy, instead of using metal, round, or white objects, you can select a family ancestor who was also a mentor. You can even use a globe. Its round shape will be negated by its blue and green colors. Also, fire burns and consumes wood. Avoid red or orange… again, when you are anchoring the fame energy within an individual room, elect to use a certificate of honor in a wooden frame. There will be times when it is important to burn off some of the room's excessive wood and as you learn to hear what your rooms are saying, you will know when this is occurring.

### Geometric Shape & Symbolism

The shapes of pillars, columns, all things vertical (as in a tree) and stripes represent the Family Gua. Its action is quick growth, excitement, hard work, and strength. The expansion or branching out action is equated to development. Think of the tree and its uprightness. To enjoy excellent elemental Wood balance, make an effort to notice your posture. There are many exercises to help you attain an erect posture, which will easily support your body. And always remember to breathe.

Tree wisdom is **Symbolic** for every culture known to man. Because of its verticality, the tree is an excellent family icon. The tree's shape best represents the family's geometric energy. Metaphorically, a strong tree's root system prevents us from being blown away or uprooted when the storms of life rage on. Tree branches symbolize our reaching into the sky for inspiration. Another thought is how the tree's branches sway in the breeze, remaining flexible. Historically, the tree ranks as one of the most divinely creative emblems ever written about. Trees are symbolic of the link between heaven and earth. In countless folktales, a tree's branches represent knowledge. Proverbs 3:8 said, "Wisdom is like a tree of life to them who take hold of her."

In *The Uses Of Enchantment: The Meaning And Importance of Fairy Tales*, Bruno Bettelheim observed that the Brothers Grim thought the forest, "symbolized the place in which inner darkness is confronted and worked through; where uncertainty is resolved about who one is, and where one begins to understand who one wants to be." Bettelheim furthered his thoughts on the forest by saying, "Since ancient times the near impenetrable forest in which we get lost has symbolized the dark, hidden, near-impenetrable world of our unconscious. If we have lost the framework that gave structure to our past life, we must **now find our way to become ourselves**, and have entered this wilderness with an as-yet-undeveloped personality. When we succeed in finding our way out, we shall emerge with a much more highly developed humanity."

It is said that Merlin became most disconcerted with humanity and its ruthless spoils so he took to the forest for his sanctuary. There he found his compass once again as the cycle of nature restored him to his inner truth or the core of his being. Trees are alchemical and correlate to ecology, because their presence offers additional oxygen for the atmosphere. Their energy fields have been said to be healing and lend great comfort.

Write down the name of your favorite tree. In this section, please see the meaning of your specific tree(s). Why do you believe you resonate with its qualities?

## The medicine of the trees

**Alder:** Self-Guidance. It is a water-loving tree and grows by rivers, streams, ponds, and lakes. It is considered to be a gift, because its presence near the waterways always provides life-giving energy to the nearby land. This creates a centeredness and strength, inviting the inhabitants to enjoy firm footing. In early Venice, the Rialto Bridge was built on Alder piles. This wood must stay in the water, as on dry land it will split and quickly decay.

**Almond Tree:** Wedded Bliss, Good Luck. The almond blossoms denote fertility and a fortunate marriage. In myths and legends, almonds are objects of value and a sign of hope. They stand for life and immortality with divine approval. Almonds caution to be of commonsense and weigh all decisions carefully, wisely and intuitively.

**Apricot Tree:** Love and innocent charm. Its blossoms are associated with the widely popular plum blossoms and are a symbol of remaining beautiful during times of strain. It is a sign of spring's arrival indicating renewed hope.

**Apple Tree:** Youthful, faith and love. The apple was said to confer the gifts of prophecy. Although it is associated with the Tree of Knowledge and original sin, it is actually a gateway or a portal to hidden wisdom. There is truth to the adage, "An apple a day keeps the doctor away." An apple is excellent fiber, and pectin aids the stomach. In fairy tales, apples are closely connected to sages and magical transformations. For example, Snow White and the apple the Queen poisoned, due to her jealousy of the fairest beauty in the land. An apple encourages us to trust and be an open channel for worthiness.

**Ash Tree:** Grandeur and Sacredness. In mythical lore, it is considered the link between the inner and outer worlds as the heart of humanity began from an Ash tree. It is considered a tough specimen growing up to 150 ft. and living as long as 200 hundred years. It is considered the World Tree. Also thought of as the Shaman's inspired willpower, it holds the energy of the universal enchantment of abiding love and long-term friendship. It denotes faithful partnerships that are taken seriously. It is a tall, handsome tree and has a special affinity with lightning, so during a storm, do not stand under this or any tree. It symbolizes rebirth and forgiveness. The Ash enables us to recoup our true self and enjoy clarity.

**Beech Tree:** The Creative. The written word and innate wisdom is derived from the fact that the words Beech and book come from the same language roots. They denote ancient knowledge. Its forked branches provide the perfect divining rod to find water. In Siberia, the Beech tree is considered their World Tree. It is associated with creativity, wisdom, and the blessings of a magnificent lifetime marriage. The Beech is said to help one stay in excellent physical shape. In mythology, it was the messenger between Zeus and the Gods, because it could be trusted.

**Birch Tree:** Inspiration, new beginnings or journeys. Along with fertility, gracefulness and devotion are two of the Birch tree's attributes. In fact, the Birch tree was placed in households where couples wanted children and in stables to encourage the cows and horses to mate. The Birch draws protection and release to the person who holds it. It is used for a living May pole as it is strong. Folk stories tell of the Lady of the Woods, who is said to originate from the lovely Birch tree. She possesses elegance, lightness of being and her qualities bless all who see her with these same characteristics.

**Cedar Tree:** Poised and incorruptible. In Lebanon, the Cedar is both its national emblem and its Tree of Life. In the Bible, the Lebanon Cedar is mentioned 75 times. The cedar incense is considered the purest form and highly valued. The Cedar tree conveys good health and has a rare beauty that knows how to adapt to refinement. It symbolizes confidence, optimism, endurance (due to the fact that it is also part of the Evergreen family), and purification. It is said to be a sanctuary outside of time and space. In Lebanon, it is considered the Tree of Life.

**Chestnut Tree:** Of usual beauty. The energy of the Chestnut tree is symbolic of possessing a well-developed sense of justice, being honest, vivacious, optimistic, sensitive, and happily content with its lot in life. The Chestnut is not one to want to impress. Although its traits point to a well-balanced energy pattern, it is also associated with unruliness. This leads to a unique and unusual side.

**Cypress Tree:** Faithful. The Cypress is thought to be Turkey's most important sacred tree and is central to their Tree of Life. It is symbolic of being truthful, adaptable, strong, muscular, optimistic, and enjoys life to the fullest. It is associated with passionate lovers who enjoy one another. This pattern desires adequate financial success and appreciates acknowledgement… well, it expects acknowledgement for their many deeds of good will.

**Dogwood Tree:** Regeneration, eternal life, rebirth. Its beauty denotes when life is beginning her cycle of spring. The Dogwood's blossoms of pink and white are in the shape of a cross and have therefore been associated with rebirth through divine sacrifice. This delicate and refined blossom appears on exquisite Oriental artwork, usually accompanied with calligraphy. It is the state tree and flower of several states, Virginia being the most prominent.

**Elder Tree:** Completion, healing, prosperity. The name of this very sturdy tree means fire. The Elder is considered to be the mother of humankind and thus, one must ask the tree three times before they have permission to cut it down. It is considered to incur the wrath of the tree spirit if it is felled without this consent. Out of respect, the older generations know that they should tip their hats when passing this prominent tree. The Elder tree stands for self-sufficiency, high energy, enjoyment of mental and physical activities, thrives on transformation, spontaneity, and regeneration.

**Elm Tree:** High Minded. Folklore referred to it as the Elven tree, because the elves worked closely with this tall and proud tree. It was also associated with birth and death and its wood was used to make caskets. The Elm was the sacred holder of its people's memory of their culture. Its true magic lies in its ability to restore worthiness and self-value to a person who has fallen on times of failure. By turning the failure inside out, the tree encourages the person to see the benefits of his disappointments and turn them into stepping-stones. Bach Flowers Remedies treats for hopelessness with this herb.

**Fig Tree:** Practical talent and fortunate health. Its delicious fruit ripens in May and is a stable of the Middle East. This tree is mentioned more than any other tree in the Bible. "It was enjoyable to rest, mediate on God's word, and pray in the shade of a Fig tree." John 1:48. It is also mentioned that Jesus obliterated it for being barren… so lest we be eradicated, lets be productive! The Fig loves family, children, animals and all forms of life. Loving souls surround them, because their energy draws them. They do not tolerate arguments or criticism, because they appreciate peace and harmony. A Fig's energy might seem on the lazy side, but in reality, they are relaxed and allow things to come to them. They are sensible, intelligent, strong, have a good sense of humor and possess talents that produce a comfortable income.

**Fir Tree:** Mystifying. This tree appreciates beauty in people, art and landscape. Its cultivated tastes might make them seem aloof and are at times quite egotistical, but in truth, they deeply care about the people they call family. Fidelity is their strength and although they will cross paths with enemies who resent their sophistication, they also have a wide circle of friends. Their astonishing sense of style lends itself to their dignity. They are ambitious, talented, industrious and refined.

**Hawthorne Tree:** The union of nature's energy. Of all of the trees, the Hawthorne is greatly loved by the English. In many cultures, it enjoys the stature of renewal and is regarded as a symbol of marriage, love, and betrothal. It is customary for a wedding processional to include hawthorn bouquets. The Hawthorne wood is considered to be very lucky. On May Day, the Hawthorne ushers in the new birth of the season and the Beltane festival centers around the Hawthorne. The term 'bread and cheese' was aptly applied to the Hawthorne, because in the days of old, weary travelers could find sustenance by eating the leaves of this tree. When taken as an herbal tonic (per directions), the Hawthorne elixir removes blocked energy and assists the user to let go of fear. It remains a cardiac energizer and is a natural arterial blood pressure controller. Symbolically, it represents the heart energy and its characteristics are associated with trust, support and embracing a friend as if they were family.

**Hazelnut Tree:** Wisdom, extraordinary. This tree is called the poets tree, because of its intuitive and sensitive nature. The fruit of this tree is highly nutritious. It is known for its charm, honesty, popularity, compassionate nature, high energy, precise sense of judgment, and it is considered to be the power of life itself. The protectiveness of its presence inspires homeowners to plant it near by their homes. It is considered to have the best branches for divining rods and is associated with luck, fertility, and wishes. The tree itself is partnered with tolerance and high understanding.

**Maple Tree:** Independent. The independence of the Maple energy creates a unique expression that is full of imagination and originality. Since the tree is a fast growing species, learning quickly is associated with the Maple pattern. It is a beautiful tree, used in landscaping for its strikingly attractive red leaf. However, when these same beautiful leaves fall, it is a time of very high maintenance. The Maple tree is famous for providing delicious maple syrup and, even though not as well known, it also adds to the flavor of smoked bacon, turkey, and ham. Ice cream and cheese also derive extra taste from the Maple. Maple trees are a valuable wood and are used to make lovely furniture and cabinets. The Maple pattern loves to impress (thus the beautiful leaves) and they are very complex. It is associated with shyness, is reserved and sometimes a little nervous. As it matures, its self-directed nature usually overcomes these last tendencies.

**Oak Tree:** Endurance, strong, robust, and adaptable. Throughout history the mighty Oak has been considered a sacred tree. Its protective shield, stability and comforting essence have endeared it to all cultures. The Celts called the mighty oak tree the "Garden in the Forest" as it attracts the growth of various plant forms and is home to the birds, forest animals and insects. The English call it the "King of the Forest" and it is certain that its round was used for King Arthur's round table. Its beauty of grain and texture lends itself to lovely floors, cabinets and furniture of all types. We have oak floors in our home that are 130 years old. My husband continues to keep them in excellent condition as their warmth blesses us. The Oak is indicative of being healthy, sensible, grounded, and possessing the gifts of prophecy. It is said that the Oak is the first tree ever grown and the acorn is the first fruit ever eaten. There are over 400 species of Oak tree. The Oak is struck by lightning more than any other tree and is associated with the God of Thunder, Thor. In ancient times, the farmers revered the Oak, as it meant more rain for their crops.

**Olive Tree:** Wisdom, peace. King Solomon traded olive oil and its fruit has long been the standard of "gold" in the Mediterranean cultures. The words associated with the Olive tree are fruitfulness, purification, strength, victory, reward, warmth, empathy, longevity, and security. The Olive tree thrives in the sun, lives as long as 1,000-1,500 years, and its root system spreads out wide to absorb adequate moisture. Its oils have fueled lamps and when massaged into the skin, it protects and moisturizes. The Olive tree stands for meaningful conversations where tolerance and sophistication are enjoyed. It was the olive branch that the dove returned to Noah signifying that they were now out of harm's way and could leave the Ark. Thus, it also represents safety.

**Pine Tree:** Trustworthy, a symbol of royalty. Since the pine tree stays green all year long, it is easily the symbol for longevity, immortality and fertility. To celebrate the winter solstice, the Druids burned the Scotch Pine's wood in towering bon fires. In addition, they would attempt to invite the sun back by decorating pine trees. They adorned them with reflective objects and lights to represent the Divine Light. Our modern day Christmas tree owes its birth in this ritual. The pine tree is considered to be robust, a practical and good companion, enjoys a love of comfort and embodies fortitude. The Shamans forest of pine groves was considered sacred. Osiris was thought to be the tree spirit and upon his death, he was placed in a hollowed out pine tree. The pine tree lives up to 600 years and can grow to 100 feet.

**Peach:** True love and immortality. The Peach tree is regarded as an emblem of marriage. Whenever a single man or woman places a peace tree symbol in their bedroom, marriage will be imminent. Long lives with tranquility and prosperity are represented by the presence of a Peach tree. Its virtues include protection and to this day, many amulets, charms and seals are made from its wood. It is also known as the Fairy Fruit for its elixir of life-giving qualities via its fruit. It is used for New Year's celebration as it is regarded as a new beginning and is a favorite symbol for spring.

**Poplar Tree:** Lonely, standing alone. The pride of the Poplar tree can certainly lose itself in uncertainty and fear; however, just like us, its energy can be pulled forward by a nurturing and positive influence. In the Bach Flower remedies, this elixir is used to overcome and heal one's worries. There are three different types of Poplar trees… the Aspen, the Black and the White Poplar. This portal or doorway is a liaison to the realms of the natural world that are within us. When the veils are rent, we can step through and open our memory to inner truths. This door is said to reinstate our true self as an integral part of the whole self. In this state, we are able to see things as pure energy. The philosopher in us is able to prevail as it shields us. Once we learn to stay out of the fear energy, its fast-growing qualities promote excellence within us. It is also a tree that symbolizes good partnership.

**Rowan Tree:** Graceful beauty, peaceful. The Rowan tree has long been associated with the hidden knowledge of wisdom and discernment. Its qualities ushered in the ability to find healing and strength. Rowan characteristics are long in memory, passion, imagination, and are considered in some cultures to be the tree of the Goddess. Her charm imbues refinement and clarity of purpose. It is associated with sensitivity, protection and when meditated upon, it can be used to increase psychic powers.

**Walnut Tree:** Protection, unbounded aspirations. In my research of all the trees, this one was the most ambiguous. The references point to an intellectual energy with passionate characteristics. While on the other hand, it was viewed as hostile, unfriendly in that it doesn't like the mighty oak (jealousy?) and it can kill any vegetation growing near by. It is known to be full of these contrasts and all in all, is extremely uncompromising and stoic. If one were drawn to this energetic pattern, it would be wise to cultivate listening to your inner thoughts and nurture them along in a positive manner.

**Willow Tree:** Intuitive, empathic, fertile. The Willow is considered the Queen of the Water and the Alder is known as the King. *Wind in the Willows* inspired many poets and writers in that the willow is believed to bestow eloquence upon its visitors. Crisp communication is a gift that Orpheus the Greek received. His was so loved that Apollo gifted him with a lyre. His sweet music tamed the fierce forest creatures and enchanted Mt. Olympus' rocks and trees. Eventually, he taught the muses to play. Willow's dark side has been portrayed as death and sorrow. However, the place of death only opens the door for rebirth and in truth, sorrow hollows out more room for joy. Willow bark is the source of the aspirin tablet and is symbolic for removing pain. The love of travel is associated with the flexible willow as is the ability to envision greater horizons.

## I Ching Trigram

*Per Hanna Moog and Carol Anthony, "The Judgment: Shock brings success. Shock comes - Oh, Oh! Laughing words - ha, ha! The shock terrifies for a hundred miles, and he does not let fall the sacrificial spoon and chalice."*

In this hexagram, the Sage shows the cosmic purposes of shock. Cosmic chock is distinguished from the shocks that are delivered to the child by the collective ego during its conditioning process. Cosmic shock has either the purpose of warning a person that his attitude is arrogant, or to tell him the shock is a fate he has created. Shock can appear as a major event in a person's life, such as an accident, an injury, a shocking diagnosis, or the death of someone close. I can also be the shock of losing one's job after many years of faithful service. To the student of the Sage... the Judgment indicates the correct respond to shock: to not allow oneself to be throwing out of one's inner center or to be collapsed by fear, terror, or the idea of loss.

## Seasonal Cycle

Early spring is the time of year associated with the Family energetic pattern. After the plants have been wintering under the ground, they are ready to burst forth. As they shoot upwards, their green color is a welcome sight. This is a time of new beginnings and of upward growth. Again, the expansive energy of wood symbolizes creativity; healing and the circle of energies continue to move on.

## Energy Patterns For Individual Rooms specific to Family

Each room has an energetic pattern. See how the map of energy is a metaphor for your life. When your Family Gua falls in any of the following areas, this information helps you understand how to truly benefit from the room's strengths.

**Living or Great Room:** This is an exceptional room for the Family Gua as it offers a place for the family and friends to gather and deepen relationship. A family that spends time together has the opportunity to get to know one another. Life is cyclic and strong family relationships support us in times of uncertainty.

**Foyer**: Does Not Apply

**Stairs or Hallways:** Be certain that your stairway is not pouring out all of your resources if it lines up with the door. If this is the case, you will also find that you are easily drained. If there is room and it is safe to continue to use the stairs, place a jade plant in a black vase on the bottom step. If possible, place a crystal between the stairway and the front door, which would be your self-cultivation and knowledge Gua. The hallway and the stairways are perfect places to display a family photo gallery. Do not stair step any of the photos because it is preferable to hang them across the wall.

**Bathroom:** This is superb, because the water element of this room nurtures Wood. It is a place to have Jade or Bamboo plants. Create a spa like environment with greenery and use thick and thirsty green towels. When not in use, keep the toilet lid down. Place a plug in the shower and sink and unless you are draining your bathtub after use, keep this large area plugged too. When you go into a bathroom, you can feel the energy being pulled down, because this is the direction of water's natural flow. This is a great place to think of your ancestors and their eternal support.

**Home Office, Study, or Library:** The placement of an office, study or library in this section can be very productive. Wood is the energy of growth and creativity, so in abundance, place family photos, plants, antiques and wooden objects here. Do not let your back face the door, as this will burden you with backstabbing and gossip. Look forward and anticipate all of your most precious intentions to manifesting.

**Dining Room or Kitchen:** This is the heart of a family so it is a blessing to have this room in this place. This is where the family can gather and enjoy one another's company. Nurturing meals sustain us and in this Gua, they take on an added dimension. Our ancestors are probably hanging out in the invisible and are lending us an extra dose of energy. Relax into this space as it has a direct connection with your relatives. Set your table with your best crystal and china, place flowers on the table and keep all of your projects put away. Find another niche for these, because they will block your family energy, distracting you from being present. Check to see if your refrigerator and stove line up in front of one another. If so, this will create power struggles. If they do, simply place a green or blue dishcloth on the handle of the oven. Keep these areas spotless and never leave dishes in your sink. Otherwise, you will experience blockages in your family communications and this will lead to distant relations.

**Storage Areas:** Take inventory of what you are storing there. Is there a connection to the state of your family affairs and to these items… as in impasses? If this room is not a dedicated storage area such as a closet, then move everything out but the items appropriate to this room. If this a storage area or closet, hang a fully faceted crystal on a nine inch red ribbon and/or install a mirror in the very back of the closet and face it towards the door. Do not place it on the floor and lean it against a wall, as this will create a fun house effect. You do not want your family life to be on a shelf. Up the wattage on your light bulbs… let's get that energy lit up. As always, keep this area de-cluttered.

**Bedroom:** Our master bedroom is located in the Family Gua. At one time, it was sage green, but we had so much green in our home, we needed to calm down this room with another color. However, we still have the perfect amount of wood; for example, our tall, solid wood headboard, nightstands, dresser, corner shelving and chest of drawers are all made from a strong wood. In this room, we enjoy healthy plants. Over our bed hangs the first painting my parents purchased when they married in 1946. It depicts an elegant vase filled with a beautiful floral arrangement. We love it. It is safely supported so it will never surprise us in the middle of the night by falling on our heads. This is also the perfect place to have your antiques and/or vintage collectables.

### The Sage Meditation

Imagine yourself standing the middle of your home. You are facing the Family/Roots section of your house's floor plan. In your mind's eye, see your Family intentions and affirm great good thanks for all of the support you now enjoy. At this time, visualize a Sage wearing an emerald green robe with an embroidered golden tree located right over the heart. You now bow and greet the Sage. He/she is holding a silk pillow with an emerald stone on top. The Sage hands you the emerald, also known as 'The Healers Stone". You accept this stone and know deep within, your Family intentions will beautifully unfold. You thank the Sage, who is your friend for the cosmic help. Stand in the room's center and close your eyes. Become very still and take long, deep breaths. When you are centered, ask the Sage to reveal the heart of this room. Should you not hear anything, continue to practice and eventually, you will "hear" your answers? As you listen, you will feel led to remove the less than nurturing items from this Gua and you will do so with confidence. Adding the positive enhancements is an intuitive process. In fact, this Gua's teaching encourages you to trust the process. Give thanks for the Sage's support and bow to this energy, allowing the Sage to return to the ethers.

Be advised, there is always a map of energy within a map of energy. Now that you have brought this section of your home into alignment with strength, forgiveness and cultivating excellence, stand in the doorway and look into the room. If there is more than one room, map the energy separately according to each of the entrances. Line the bottom of your energy map up with the doorway and have a grand time Feng Shui-ing this room(s) accordingly. Make these changes with an open heart and a mind clear of clutter. If there is a question regarding where to place what, remember the dominant energy will always be the one of the larger Bagua. If this portion of your home is missing, respect the Family section's guidelines and honor the accoutrements. If this section of your home is missing, please refer to Chapter 10 for further insights.

Jewels to Re*Member

*Cultivate excellence, for hidden within you are the seeds of kindness, trust, strength, & forgiveness. Once you begin to develop these seeds, they will surely blossom on your Wisdom and Peace trees. - SJH*

# 19

-

# *Pure Abundance*

## Be Grateful

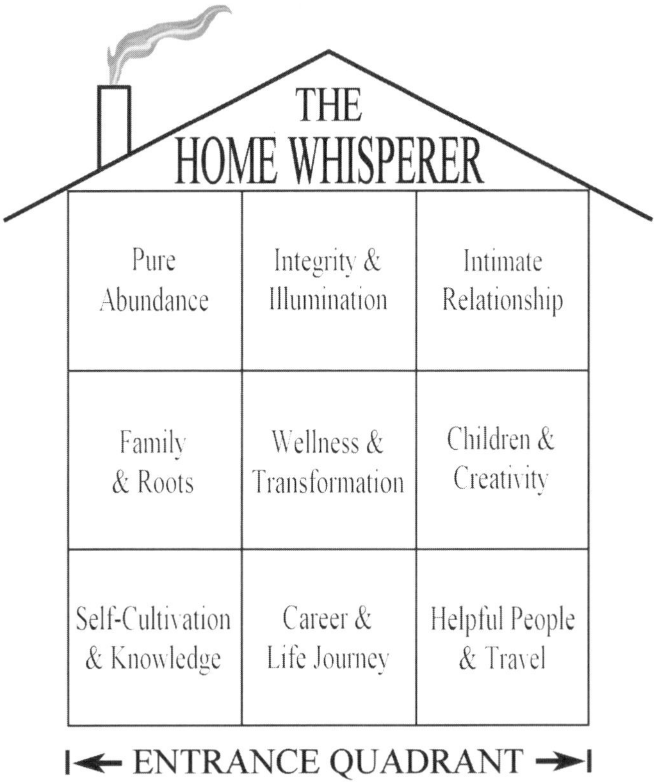


- **Location: Upper left quadrant of the Bagua Map**
- **Sacred Geometry:** The verticality of a rectangle
- **Numerical Influence:** Four
- **Color:** Purple, Blue & Red
- **Element:** Yin Wood-Eldest Daughter
- **I Ching Trigram:** Sun, Persistent Wind
- **Operative Words:** Gratitude, skills, talents, contentment, movement, action, planting seeds for future harvest, productivity, & perception
- **Gemstones:** Amethyst, Pietersite, gold, diamonds, & citrine
- **Chi Imagery:** Photos/artwork of wind or wood objects, aquariums, Bamboo plant, all living plants with rounded leaves such as Jade
- **Season:** Early summer
- **Directional Energy:** Upwards and out
- Affirmation: **I am abundant, bountiful, vibrant, & I am well.**
  I live an abundant life.
  I now benefit from great good prosperity.
  I give thanks that I easily receive money for ________.

I live in abundant harmony and balance.
I rejoice in the continuous flow of prosperity into my life.
I am grateful for my loving family; abundant friends and I enjoy excellent health.
I am creatively rich beyond measure!
I am One with Gratitude.

### Visualization:

*The Winds of Fortune gracefully waft through a well-tended garden. Glorious flowers in every color, shape, and size stir up the energies of growth, creativity, healing, and joy. The garden of your life is infused with this same Chi; it is replete with pure abundance. Tend it with loving care and learn how to be one with nature.*

The wind denotes circulation and movement. The activity of abundance blowing in and around your life already exists. In the Hebrew vocabulary, wind is synonymous with the words of breath and spirit. Think of the wind as breath and breathe in the pure abundance that forever surrounds you.

### Creating & Connecting with Pure Abundance

| True | Wealth | Good Fortune | Abundance | Prosperity | Blessing |
|---|---|---|---|---|---|
| | | | | | |
| Accurate | Affluence | Chance | Great Quantity | Abundance | Approval |
| Correct | Assets | Destiny | Large Measure | Affluence | Consent |
| Exact | Capital | Fate | Loads | Opulence | Favor |
| Factual | Means | Kismet | Plenty | Riches | Go-Ahead |
| Faithful | Possessions | Luck | Profusion | Richness | Lucky |
| Proper | Prosperity | Providence | Prolific | Success | Permission |
| Spot On | Riches | Wealth | Wealth | Wealth | Sanction |

The winds of change combined with the energy of Yin Wood generate penetrating insights, novel ideas, growth, creativity, trust, and flexibility. Since the wood energy moves upright, wealth should be moving upward, imbued with continual and prosperous growth.

Since 1995, I have facilitated countless Feng Shui workshops on abundance. Consistently, when the attendees get to the heart of these teachings, they are able to create exactly what they intended. Usually, the manifestation exceeds what they had hoped. Working with this Gua enables you to remember what you already know. Intuitively, you understand how to believe, achieve and receive pure abundance.

## Abundance's Mission

Hanna Moog and Carol K. Anthony are considered the voice of the I Ching. The following is an excerpt from their interpretation of #55 Abundance. ENJOY!

"Abundance refers to a variety of things:
Abundance of caring feelings
Abundance of prosperity and progress
Abundance in regard to life and its limitlessness
Abundance in the forms in which life takes place, whether they be visible or invisible
Abundance in caring, help and nourishment for all the needs of life
Abundance in our cosmic possessions
Abundance in help to bring us back into unity with the cosmic whole
Abundance of gifts, such as the gift of love
Abundance in cosmic patience with human
Abundance of space for creativity, such as for the expression of life
Abundance both of inner and outer space
Abundance of space for evolving our consciousness
Abundance in the Sage's teachings
Abundance of health"

## Becoming Abundant

Pure Abundance is truly a state of mind. When you *believe* yourself worthy to be prospered, wealth is an effortless process. Think of a well-tended garden where the flowers therein represent every one of your wishes coming true. Pure abundance blossoms in the ability to enjoy a well-rounded life of wellness, harmony, loving family relations, dear friends and spending your time in pursuits that are of great interest to you. Remember, you will reap what you sow, so see yourself sowing these seeds of pure abundance into the fertile soil of possibilities. Weed out disbelief, fear, frustration, and doubt. Water your garden with positive thoughts, action and BELIEF.

Being increased gets everyone's attention, as everybody is attracted to abundance. Numerous "How To Increase Your Wealth" programs have been initiated and are effectively taught by many leaders. To name only a few of these notables, Dr. Wayne Dyer, PhD., Anthony Robbins, Deepak Chopra, John Randolph, Joe Vitale - panel participants on The Secret DVD and CD. Indeed, the list is long and even though the messengers mentioned above are varied in their approach to the path of wealth, there is a common thread running through each of their teachings.

These teachers discovered that the path to pure abundance is hidden within one's own person. It begins at the thought level. Since Source or the Cosmos itself is unlimited, you are an unlimited being, a companion and a benefactor of this infinite supply. It is the wisdom of, "When you are *ready* to enjoy pure abundance, you will do so." - SJH

Because money is energy, manifesting it is a process of growth, development of skills/talents, planning, and creativity.

Notice the people with whom you associate. What is the quality or essence of collective consciousness are you presently associated with? Are the people in your life supportive? Do they reflect your code of honor, your values? Since the people in your life act as a mirror to who you are, look around and see exactly what kind of life you have created.

With everyone we meet, we are called upon to notice our reactions, pay attention to what our feelings are telling us about ourselves. Every response to another is based on perception, not fact, and if we pay attention, we can easily learn what we need to release or forgive in order to open to our willingness to receive.

Often, my client's first request is for increased income. At the root of this intention is actually a wish for contentment, peace and prosperity. As stated above, money is simply an energetic exchange. When you increase your attractor frequencies with belief and harmony, you unbridle the quality of life experiences already hovering around you. These offerings are hidden within your inner and outer home. They are simply waiting for you to call them forth. They are part of your energetic imprint.

In Chapter 5, you learned how to focus your intentions, consciously cultivate positive thoughts, words and deeds; you space-cleared your environment as detailed in Chapter 6. Step into the miraculous garden and be part of the pattern of pure abundant energy. Be upgraded!

## Gratitude

*"Gratitude is the memory of the heart." - French Proverb*

Count your blessings! Recognize how fully abundant you already are. Living in gratitude empowers you to move beyond the frequency of lack and step into the amazing energy of fullness. Regardless of how a situation seems to look in the physical, it has a purpose. Giving thanks for each and every experience-from the not so great to the amazing, enables you to refresh Source's flow of abundance into your life. Living in the mindset of appreciation connects you to wisdom, clarity, wellness, and happiness. A hidden component to living in pure abundance is being a good steward. And yes, it will be pressed down and multiplied back to you. This is the law of reciprocity and is a basic Universal law.

Abundance is created when you gratefully live in the NOW. The last syllable in abun-dance is the word "dance." Dancing is associated with movement and is considered an ancient and sacred way for beautifully transforming your inner and outer environment. Allow your dancing to be expressed through the beat of the music.

While dancing, let yourself be freed from all past circumstances that may have generated fear, doubt, guilt and shame. These energies block healing, contentment, and joy from appearing in your life. Glean the knowledge from these past events and move on. From this place, you are aware of creating an abundant tomorrow with today's positive thoughts. Live in gratitude, for this is where abundance resides… and dance, dance, and dance!

## Skills and Talents

Develop the skills and talents in your chosen field with the idea of creating the lifestyle of your choice. Skills and talents may take years to refine and yet, in a matter of moments, you can step into the miraculous.

The summer before my junior year at Texas Tech University, I applied for a summer job as a receptionist-secretary-bookkeeper... oh my, that was 1969. In today's vernacular, I would have been an Admin Assistant. Very interesting, no? It was a well paying position and was listed at a local employment agency. The employee counselor was none other than the business teacher from my high school alma mater... this was her summer job. She reviewed my application and determined I was a good candidate.

Since she would receive a fee from the firm, she had another form to complete. When she called to make my appointment, they asked that I rush right over. This firm had requested each applicant hand-write their name and a short sample sentence. Since time was of the issue, the agent/teacher filled out this information and I completed her form. The interview went wonderfully well and I was hired!!

Little did we know this firm had a graphologist on their payroll! Since my counselor taught high school business classes for over 30 years, she was the very best candidate. I had those skills, but my creativity was my passion. This firm was called Corporate Motivation and their mission was to train people how to use more than 10% of their brain. The courses they marketed were based on books such as Think and Grow Rich, Psycho-Cybernetics, Dale Carnegie's courses on speaking, Norma Vincent Peale's insights on positive thinking, and too many to name here. I was introduced to a world of setting intention and then putting action behind it.

Once I realized what had happened, I told them the reason I was hired. When the graphologist read my handwriting, he surmised I was highly intuitive. They determined I was supposed to be there and could help them help others to be the best they could be. They gave me a raise and I was so honored to help so many people find their life's purpose. Plus, I loved being paid to counsel others and to simply read. Applying these truths changed my life forever!

Reel/real magic is waiting for you, too. No, you will not have the same template that I co-created, but you already have what you require to be prosperous. Spend time in meditation and ask for it to be revealed. Align with your life's meaningful destiny and enjoy a greater sense of fulfillment.

Regardless of your income, become a philanthropist. In addition to donating whatever your financial means will afford, the giving of your time, talents, and skills is a valuable endowment. When you give of yourself, you will experience true wealth and pure abundance. Select a foundation or cause that mirrors your passion and volunteer to help.

Invest in your bank of pure abundance by reading stories of people who have had a profoundly positive impact on the world. Create an inner trust by studying their thought patterns and moral code. What made them tick? What made them so enthusiastic? What set them apart from the norm? Since everything is energy, can you see how connecting yourself to these great masters enables you to vibrate at a higher level? Believe in your skills and trust your abilities. This belief reveals deeper hidden talents and gifts. Who knew that my summer job at the movie theatre, at the age of 16, would set up such a powerful course for my life?

## Colorful Perceptions

The colors of purple, blue and red are associated to this Gua. Purple represents royalty and expresses the highest form of spiritual wisdom, intuitive insights, and prosperous energy. Think about the unlimited benefits of enjoying financial clarity and foresight. I strongly suggest that you elect to place purple in your pure abundant Gua. Even though mixing red and blue together create purple, why not set the noblest energetic pattern and utilize the color purple?

## Numerical Influences

The number four is associated with the Pure Abundance Gua. Since this number forms the symbol of the square, it inspires stability. Think of four corners of a foundation. It is also the number of security, completeness, safety, and solid work habits. It represents the four seasons, the four cardinal points on a compass… north, east, south and west. Consider the person who is dependable and has a strong work ethic. In time, this person will experience a greater financial resource, as reciprocity is a Universal law.

Living in a four home secures steady employment opportunities and ways to fulfill them. There will be a sense of deep security and confident growth. The winds of change will bless these residents as they move through their life's experiences more easily and effortlessly.

Placing two couches opposite one another creates a square. This invites an ease of tension and creates security. If your family numbers less than four, add enough chairs to equal four and produce a greater sense of being grounded. If you number is greater than four, replicate this number by creating a square centerpiece. Group four items together to draw in this safe and secure energy pattern.

### Elemental Persuasions - Friends and Foes

More than any of the other Guas within the abundance Gua, you can pull in extra financial support by anchoring each of all five of the elements in this section. For example, arrange a bamboo plant famous for prosperity in a red vase with rocks or gemstones of any kind generously inside to hold bamboo plant erect. Fill with water and place your arrangement on a square ceramic tile. You have created an environmental affirmation honoring all five elements. The Bamboo plant=Wood Element; the red vase=Fire; rocks or gemstones=Metal; Water in Vase=Water Element; and Square Ceramic Tile=Earth.

This treatment can be utilized in any room of the home. As you continue to study this book, you will find a host of examples to perfectly balance each element.

### Friends

An excellent example of wind and wood energy is found in a bamboo wind chime. Preferably, this enhancement has four chimes. The symbolism of the bamboo is considered one of great abundance, flexibility, being open to change, longevity, and positive growth.

In this Gua, place items in the colors of red, blue, and/or purple and objects made from wood such as photo frames, statuaries, live flowers and plants. Artwork or photos of flowers and trees are also affirmations of abundance. Items that speak of prosperity to you, such as coin collections or other objects of value, create abundant Chi and are a welcome enhancement. Since rabbits are known to multiply, add photos, figurines, or statuaries of them in your prosperity Gua. Place your Template of Alchemy-Vision Quest Map in your Pure Abundance Gua. It can go behind your door, but make sure the telephone repairman hasn't been summoned!

Behind my desk in the Pure Abundance Gua for my office, I have a large poster of the film "Secret Garden". My husband handcrafted a lovely wooden frame for its oversized dimensions. The poster reads, "The timeless tale of a special place where magic, hope, and love grow." Use belief to seed prosperity into the rich soil of your life. For surely, this is where the promise of magic, hope, and love blossoms.

## Foes

A cluttered area blocks prosperity as it prevents your winds of fortune from blowing in. Make sure this area is well organized and everything in it is in good working order. A client of mine had a beautiful antique clock in this Gua, but it did not work. She was forever experiencing off timing conditions and missed opportunities. Once she repaired the clock, she found herself in synch with greater abundance.

Unpaid Bills… when your bills arrive, instead of feeling depressed, see them as Paid In Full. You can purchase a rubber stamp with those very words imprinted on it. When your bills arrive, routinely and joyfully pay them. Whenever you can, pay a little more each month and soon, you will be able to stamp them Paid In Full. If you pay your bills online, do so with a smile on your face. I read where Louise Hay was forever thankful for her every bill. When I pay our bills, I write Thank You on the memo portion. Living in Gratitude pays off!

## Associated Trigram

Sun - Persistent Wind. It is essential that one understand the importance of stepping into our destiny of abundance. Hanna Moog and Carol K. Anthony describe this teaching in the Hexagram #42 INCREASE, Sun-Wind over Chen-Wood. It instructs as follows: "The Judgment: ***Increasing. It furthers one to undertake something. It furthers one to cross the great water.*** The harmonious activities of the cosmos are directed toward increasing all parts of the cosmic whole. Increasing the welfare of the whole is a cosmic principle that reveals the loving and caring nature of the cosmos. This understanding is at odds with the assumptions made by Western science that cosmic resources are limited, and that human effort is somehow necessary to overcome this shortfall. This is only true inasmuch as people have separated themselves from their original unity with the cosmos by adopting mistaken ideas and beliefs about its true nature. In assuming that Nature requires correction or improvement, humans have created a parallel reality that is characterized by lack. This hexagram is a statement that a person can reunite with the Cosmos and participate in its constant flow of gifts, if he "undertakes something," meaning, if he rids himself of the mistaken ideas and beliefs that slander the gift-giving nature of the cosmos."

This teaching aligns one with the infinite source of the cosmos… we are never alone and if we but ask, we have amazing benefactors working on our behalf.

## Geometric Shape and Symbolism

The Abundance Gua has two energetic patterns, the first being the distinct upright shape of the Wood element. Wood energy is also represented in the verticality of the tree, pillar, or column shapes. All plants and flowers are considered to be wood energy. This element nourishes, is rooted and grounded so that it is not blown over by a strong wind encouraging soul growth and awareness. Secondly, the wind's swirling motion is the alchemical energy generating abundance. Use wind chimes call forth the beneficial Chi.

For the Pure Abundance Gua, Flowering Wisdom symbolizes wealth and prosperity. The unique language and energetic pattern of flowers link mankind with heaven's perfect harmony and earth's complete balance. Each flower represents the finest expression of feminine beauty. The Orientals believed that for each woman living in this world, a flower bloomed in the next world. The Greeks long held true that asphodels blossomed in paradise. Flowers are universal symbols of vivacity and at the same time, graceful tenderness. When you are setting Pure Abundance intentions, the following flower energies can assist you. Knowing their meanings adds an extra zip in your frequency field.

## Flowering Wisdom

Allium - Global Awareness
Amaryllis - Sensuality
Aquilegia - Purity
Azalea - Modesty
Bluebell - Rare Beauty
Bougainvillea - Overcoming adversity
Buttercup - Clarity
California Poppy - Pure abundance

Columbine - Follow your bliss
Celandine - Infinite possibilities
Cerinthe - Creativity
Chrysanthemum - Auspiciousness
Corncockle - Spontaneity
Cranesbill - Expansion
Cyclamen - Truth
Crocus - Transformation
Dahlia - Compassion
Delphinium - Spiritual attunement
Dwarf Iris - Celestial perfection
Echinacea - Strength
Forget-Me-Not - Faithfulness
Foxglove - Healing
Gardenia - Strength
Geranium - Diligence
Gladiola-Paradise
Hellebore - Perfection
Hollyhocks - Code of honor
Honeysuckle - Catalyst for positive change
Hyacinth - Balm for the Soul
Hydranga - Achievement
Jasmine - Friendship
Lavender - Healing
Lilac - Virility
Lilies - Innocence and wisdom
Leucojum - Clarity
Lupine - Poise
Lychin - Enthusiasm
Mallow - Passion
Morning Glory - The Bright optimism of the dawn
Nasturtium - Flexibility
Nicotiana - Belief
Nigella - Calmness
Ox-Eyed Daisy - Bliss
Opium Poppy - Openness
Orchid - Endurance
Peony - Wealth
Primrose - Awakened Awareness
Pulsatilla - Release
Rose of Sharon - Beauty, peace of heart and mind
Roses - Love; the mystic center of one's being
Snap Dragons - Delightful surprises
Sunflowers - Radiance
Thistle - Keen perception
Tulip - Growth and rebirth
Verbena - Tenacity
Violet - Companionship; bringing in light and love
Wisteria - Beauty

The liver and the gall bladder are associated with this Gua. In Chinese medicine, the gall bladder is considered to be the decision-maker; where action is initiated. Joined with the liver who is considered the planner and when in balance, the virtues of focus and vision are present.

## Seasonal Cycle

Late Spring/Early Summer. The bulbs have come up and the trees are showing their fragrant buds. It is the time of year when you plant the seeds for a summer and fall harvest. Symbolically, what seeds can you plant? Study the long list of flowers on these pages and choose several that resonate the energy you want to attract into your life. No space for a garden? Consider container gardening. Living in gratitude, thinking positive thoughts, kindness and intention sow the seeds of promise into the fertile soil of *belief.* The blowing wind or movement combined with the Wood element holds the energy of new growth, expansiveness, creativity, action, productivity, flexibility, and vibrancy.

### Energy Patterns for Individual Rooms Specific to Pure Abundance

**Living or Great Room:** This room speaks of where you place your interest in life. It is an excellent position to create a private area for family and friends to feel safe and secure within its four walls. Displaying your special treasures in this room furthers the prosperous energy you are asking to come in. Play soothing music, enjoy lively and meaningful programming, play games, be involved in vigorous and stimulating conversations in this room; benefit from living an abundant life to its fullest.

**Foyer:** Does Not Apply, although the Abundance Gua will not be found in the entrance, take great care that your front door does not open into either of the following scenarios. Stairs that face the front door symbolically pours money right back out the front door. Back doors or large windows that are lined up with the front door encourage money to leave as fast as it came in. Create a meandering path of Chi into your home so that your well-earned finances not only stay around for a longer period of time, but they have the time to be multiplied.

**Stairs or Hallways:** Place large artwork at the top of the stairs such as Georgia O'Keefe's famous purple petunia flower painting. This draws the eye upwards. Please do not cascade pictures or artwork in a downward spiral along the wall next to the stairs. This moves the energy far too fast and symbolizes a great deal of money coming in, but going out as just as fast.

**Bathroom:** Many of my clients gasp upon discovering their abundance could be going down the drain in the bathroom. Take heart, this situation can be negated. When not in use, keep your sink and tub or shower drain covered. Financial leakage can occur, because water or money in this area moves downwards and away from the home. Before flushing, always close your toilet lid. To cancel out financial outflow, hang a mirror on the outside of this room's door. Add thick and thirsty towels in the color of purple to your décor. According to your lighting, add either silk or live ivy. Elegantly decorate the bathroom and think of this room as regenerating your finances and renewing them. Create a spa like atmosphere where you can relax in luxury.

**Home Office, Study, or Library:** This is an outstanding area for either or these rooms. Locate your desk in the Pure Abundance position of the room itself. Be sure that you keep your files de-cluttered and up to date. Clear your voice mail, e-mail and keep your bills paid. A gently flowing desktop fountain speaks of abundance and stimulates enhanced Chi. The bamboo plant example mentioned before is perfect for this room. My husband's office is situated in the

Pure Abundance Gua of our upstairs. Because he is more of an active person and does not spend that much time behind his desk, we hung a battery-operated swivel from the ceiling. From this we hooked a prosperity bell. It is continuously moving and this movement creates healthy and wealthy Chi.

**Kitchen:** Personally, our kitchen is located in the abundance Gua. Not only is our kitchen alive and well, but also it is the place where we gather. Our floor is rich with beautifully refinished 130-year-old oak panels. High gloss black counters and black appliances (symbolizing water that waters the wood), fresh fruit and plants are throughout this alchemical space. Even if we are dining out, I make it a point to turn on the gas burners for a few seconds.

**Dining Room:** From season to season, the centerpiece on our dining room table will vary, but it always consists of either a tall and upward growing bamboo plant, a purple cornucopia filled with fresh or vibrant waxed fruit, or fresh flowers. A potted plant is always appropriate, too, as it introduces the energy of earth where one's finances enjoy stability. Whatever you display on your dining room table, you are attracting the same to you.

**Storage Areas:** If this area is where your storage is located, hang a fully faceted Austrian crystal. You can also use the battery operated swivel method we applied to my husband's office. Install energy efficient bulbs and consider responsibly keeping the light on. Boost the Chi by placing an amethyst in this area. This room does represent storing your funds so be relieved that it may serve to help you save your money.

**Master Bedroom:** When the master bedroom is located in this Gua, it is important — true for all the bedrooms -- that you do not have a computer, television, or home office in this space. This energy will not tolerate being shared with work-oriented pursuits. This room is designated one of relaxation where you can dream luscious dreams and return to the world fully rested to pursue your passions. Dress your bed with luxurious linens in the colors of violet, purple, red, or lavender. Add in fresh flowers, play soft music, toss two purple accent pillows to plump up on the bed, and drape velvet, silk or any fabric that speaks to you of luxury, on the bed or dresser. To attract new money into your life, place nine Chinese coins in a purple pouch under your bed. For an added abundance enhancement, display an amethyst on your dresser or nightstand. Before going to sleep each night, give thanks for all of the blessings you enjoyed that day. It may be the sweetness of being surprised by seeing a cherished friend to receiving a well-earned bonus. As you slip into slumber, place a smile on your face because within the core of your being, you know that you are at peace, content, healthy, and filled with pure abundance.

**Child's Room:** Again, de-cluttering is essential. A messy child's room in this section will definitely block your abundance. Pitch in and help create organization. After this has been accomplished, it is a great opportunity to introduce financial awareness. Add a large piggy bank, jade plant (considered beneficial because the leaves are shaped like coins), a picture or replica of a ship with sails at full mast, coin collections, their kite hung from the ceiling (suggesting wind generated opulence), groupings of four meaningful items and of course, their very own treasure map.

**Guest Bedroom:** It is always suggested that an empty guest room have some sort of activity. A battery-operated swivel holding a prosperous wind chime will keep the Chi moving. Paint this room in a pleasant shade of violet. You can even create a hybrid room that will double up with this guest room. Hobbies such as scrap booking, sewing, or a game room will keep the Chi upbeat.

## Pure Abundance Celebration

Imagine standing at the entrance of your Pure Abundance Gua. If there are two or more rooms, include all of these rooms in your imagery. In your mind's eye, see your intentions for Pure Abundance. Visualize a Sage wearing a royal purple robe with embroidered golden flowers located right over the heart. You now bow and greet the Warrior. He/she is holding a silk pillow with an amethyst gemstone on top. The Sage hands you the Amethyst, also known as "The Wealth Stone", Violet-Lavender possesses an especially superior vibration and its mission is to heighten spiritual awareness. Per the Crystal Bible, "Double-lilac crystals take you into beta brain waves. They also stimulate and then calm the throat and heart chakras." You accept this sacred stone and know deep within, your Pure Abundance intentions are beautifully unfolding. Thank the Warrior, who is your friend, for this cosmic help.

Turn into the stillness, the quiet and take long, deliberate deep breaths. Become centered and notice how grounded you are. When comfortable with this state of awareness, ask the Sage to reveal this Gua's action of growth and creative path to you. As you listen, you will feel led to remove the items that no longer serve you and the objects that will nurture and support your desires. Bow to the Sage and express your deep gratitude for the valuable insights you have gained.

If you are not receiving the clarity promised in this process, look diagonally opposite this Gua to the Helpful People and Travel that is located in the front-right quadrant of your home. This is the assistant/helper area for Pure Abundance. Be certain this area is de-cluttered and properly balanced. You will learn more about how to work with this remarkable Gua later in the book. For now, walk around this area repeating your affirmations for wealth, peace, contentment, pure abundance.

## Flora Wisdom

*"BELIEVE in your infinite prosperity… only you can make this shift, so please do so" –SJH*

*"The Sun will not rise, or set, without my notice and thanks." - Winslow Homer*

*"If you have two loaves of bread, sell one and buy Hyacinth to feed your soul."*
*-Persian Proverb*

Home Whisperer Home Work~

1. Is this area of your home free of clutter Yes ___ or No ___. Name the specific areas that are yet to be cleared and de-cluttered and see them as completely refreshed.

2. Are your rooms organized so that you do not miss the many opportunities coming your way?

3. Are you ready to receive abundance? Yes ___ or No ___ If your answer is no, what is holding you back?

4. In your Pure Abundance Gua, select four items you chose to add to this area. What is their imagery/symbolism?
5. What room(s) is this prosperity area? Kitchen, bathroom… observe the room(s) at face value and literally translate their meaning. See Chapter 16.

6. Is your Template of Alchemy-Vision Quest Map up to date? When something on your map is manifested, draw stars and hearts around it and simply "Be" with the process. How can you be upgraded if you are an ingrate? No can do!

7. Our children's school colors were purple and gold. One of the sports cheers is to sing song the words, "Purple, purple, purple." Assess your prosperity Gua and make sure you can chant, "Purple, purple, purple!" Write this word on a piece of paper 40 times. This isn't a punishment it is merely imprinting the purple power into your auric field.

8. Create an abundance and/or gratitude affirmation poster or collage for this area of your home. Display it where it can be seen on a regular basis. Write an affirmation for abundance.

9. When placing your loving items in the space that serves you, practice using your intuition. Learn to hear what each object is saying to you by giving it your full attention. This is not a lengthy process it is only a thoughtful one. On a piece of paper, list your favorite items. Write a brief summary of how they are nurturing and boosting the Chi in your home and in turn, your life. In other words, what are they saying to you?

## *Jewels to Re*member*

*Amethyst - "The Wealth Stone": Violet-Lavender possesses an especially superior vibration. Its mission is to heighten spiritual awareness. Per the Crystal Bible, "Double-lilac crystals take you into beta brain waves. They also stimulate and then calm the throat and heart chakras. Violet flowers bring light and love into the environment." Place this stone in your bedroom and in your pure abundance Gua.*

*"Call forth the fortunate blessings. At this very moment, they are elegantly circulating around you. Within this powerful energy, give flight to dated thought forms, inner struggles, and worn out systems. Release old energies, as they no longer serve you. Once achieved, you can no longer forestall these winds of supreme good fortune to be discernible. They are gracefully waiting to blow and flow into your life." -SJH*

*"When they were youngsters, I told my children that Can't was not a word, action, or deed. The word Can't is actually a weed and must be pulled early on from the garden of life. In its place, plant the word Can. You will love its growth and beauty" - SJH*

# 20

-

## *Integrity & Illumination*

## Be Enlightened

## Transcendent Radiance & Clarity

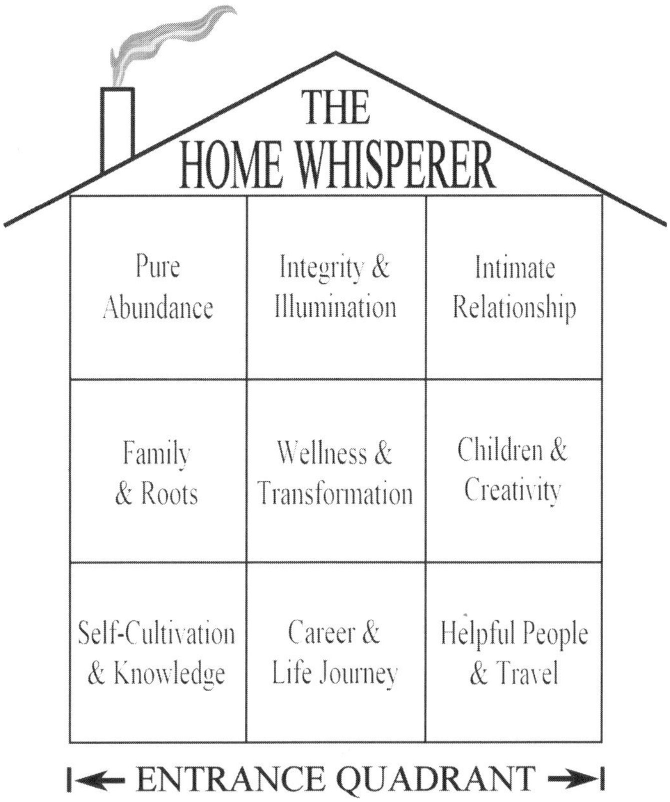


- **Location: Upper center of the Bagua Map**
- **Sacred Geometry:** Triangle
- **Numerical Influence:** Nine
- **Color:** Red
- **Element:** Yang Fire, Middle Daughter
- **I Ching Trigram:** Li, Clinging Fire
- **Operative Words:** Awareness, Illumination, Enthusiasm, Respect
- **Gemstones:** Ruby, Tiger's Eye, Sunstone, Fiery Opal, and Star Sapphire
- **Chi Imagery:** Photos/artwork of people or animals, the sun, fireplace, bright lights, the Phoenix, candles, and all items in the color of red
- **Season:** Summer
- **Directional Energy:** Up and outwards
- **Affirmation:** I live my life on purpose with passion and clarity.
  I live an honorable life.
  I now benefit from great good integrity.
  I give thanks that I easily receive recognition for my work.

I live in integrity, clarity, and enjoy respect.
I rejoice in the continuous awakenings in my life.
I am grateful for my loving friends and family.
I am clear, I am enthusiastic, I am passionate!
I am One with Clarity
I Live My Life on Purpose with Passion and Clarity.

## Visualization

*In the chambers of your heart, enthusiasm and passion faithfully are aglow. These twin flames ignite a state of awakened enlightenment.*

Passionate energy blazes a path that radiantly shines forth from within. Enthusiasm sets the energy to accomplish your heart's desires. Being true to one's higher goals brings forth illumination, which evolves into integrity. An integrous person creates the time and space to step into the spotlight and express the best of what truly lives inside.

Radiance fans the flames of the heart igniting one to seek out your heart's desires. An integrous person expresses the best of what truly lives inside of you. Being aglow with purposeful living you discover what Rilke poetically scripted, "You are the future, the red sky before the sunrise, over the field of time." You are a beloved child of the Universe. When you open the door to your higher calling, good standing in the community, and a life of infinite respect awaits you.

When you discover "Who you know yourself to be and what you are known for," the bountiful blessing of clarity is bestowed. The clarity of inner truth instructs a person on how to live in harmony. Living in harmony enables a person to utilize their talents to uplift the world, give of their gifts to make the world a better place in which to dwell.

Per the I Ching, the Cosmic Helpers gather round one who lives in a state of awakened enlightenment. Gifts are conferred and show up as "innovative ideas, inventions that change the world, talents and skills that are widely noticed and appreciated." Honor the Cosmic Helpers and you easily create integrity and illumination. From the inside out, fan the flames of your passion and clarity. BE ENLIGHTENED!

## Integrity

Integrity is a state of accountability. When you are centered in the inner home's values of wholeness and fulfillment, you are able to make decisions based on sound input. The high frequency of integrity creates a unity with Comic Consciousness. This accord enables you to live in the field of integrity. Integrity is alchemical and is fundamental to living in love, respect, poise, and wisdom.

## Illumination

Awakened enlightenment is the result of illumination. When you are fulfilled, you walk in contentment and joy. Within this realm of illumination, you respond to life and live far above a survival mode. You have stepped into your own joyous being of light where all fears have been transformed.

## The Heart

To work from the heart of compassion creates a sense of living within a global community. We experience a connectivity that enables us to confidently express our passion. When the heart is not centered or in balance, panic disorders, depression, even bipolar disorders can surface.

The fourth chakra is called Anahata and is located in the heart center. This center connects the energy of the lower chakras to the higher and more enlightened chakras. The process of enlightened awareness is when cosmic energy flows up from the lower charkas to and through this heart space. In acupuncture and in chakra teachings, it is deemed as the seat of the soul. In this sacred place, fear vanishes and in its place, compassion evolves. This heart space is believed to be the Tree of Life's central location where the emotions and the mind are in complete harmony… the balance of yin and yang.

Found within the Jewish Torah is the *Secret Chamber of the Heart*. It defines the heart's infinite energy and its mystical mystery.

"If someone should say to you, 'In the forbidden city of Imperishable,
In our body, there is a lotus. And in the lotus a tiny space
What does it contain that one should desire to know it?'
You must reply, 'As vast as this space without is the tiny space within your heart. Heaven and earth are found in it; fire and air, sun, and moon, lightning and the constellations. Whatever belongs to you here below, and all that doesn't, all this is gathered.'"

To be transformed through relationship, life experiences and connecting with all that is beautiful, the heart must be opened. Each of us is on a mission to serve others joyously from our heart. Let your sparks fly and your exuberant flames peak upward, and transform shines forth.

## Animal Totem Wisdom

The energy and wisdom of the animal kingdom serves to teach us who we are and guide us onto our highest path of service. Their medicine is of great power. The following are the symbolism passed down through the ages of these beautiful species.

| | | | |
|---|---|---|---|
| **Butterflies** | Transformation | **Owl** | Prevents being blindsided |
| **Bluebird** | Great happiness | **Peacock** | Visionary |
| **Cardinal** | Self-Love | **Antelope** | Flexibility |
| **Crane** | Longevity | **Bear** | Going within |
| **Dolphin** | Community | **Deer** | Gentleness |
| **Doves** | Peace | **Dogs** | Loyalty |
| **Dragonfly** | Standing in your light | **Elephant** | Strength |
| **Ducks** | Marital fidelity | **Elk** | Nobility |
| **Eagles** | Illumination | **Horse** | Freedom |
| **Heron** | Self-reliant | **Lion** | Passion |
| **Hummingbird** | Drinking in the nectar of Life | **Rabbit** | Regeneration |
| **Mockingbird** | Discovering your life path | | |

## Colorful Perceptions

Red – Think of Tiger Wood's power Sunday when he routinely wears the color of red. It certainly is an attention-getter as it makes you stand out. It is the color of setting one apart from the crowd.

Orange -- A mixture of enthusiastic red and optimistic yellow, orange represents unity. This color encourages harmony

## Numerical Influence

Nine symbolizes the three trinities (3 times 3 equals 9). Nine represents the higher principles of the sacred Triad. The Chaldeans believed 9 to be very special. They actually separated it out from the other numbers and kept it apart in their numerology. from the other numbers. Nine is considered thrice sacred and represents perfection, balance, and order. In Numerology, the positive characteristics of nine are fulfillment, self-less-ness, completion, universality, cosmic awareness, understanding, interrelatedness, forgiveness, compassion, idealism tolerance, generosity, benevolence, humanitarianism, emotionalism, and justice. Nine is also associated with accomplished artists and thinkers who are inspired by universal truths.

Living in a nine home affords the residents to reap the benefits of their past accomplishments. Sowing what one reaps or as Pearl Buck once said, "In order to reap the whirlwind, one must sow the wind." This home offers the occupant recognition for earlier interests and these are usually of the universal sort. This home attracts the compassionate and creates the prophetic. It's sympathetic ear listens to the needs of humanity and does something about them. This proactive wisdom serves mankind in the highest of fashion. Whether one is a visionary, a mentor, equal rights activist, or a full time caregiver, the common thread is empathy.

This home is about planting the healing seeds and harvesting their bounty. In the truth that we are all connected, the universal family will be more apparent in this home. This vibration personifies the law of attraction. The residents will find themselves being a shoulder for humanity's cry for help. Their mercy comes through to comfort and support those in need. The compassion and discernment of the nine vibrations are strong enough to stand in the gap for humanity. Generosity of self gifts mankind with their wisdom and refined insights. This altruism creates foresight that will be enlarged and allow old limitations or boundaries to be dissolved. This home may encourage old friends or past co-workers to look the residents up. When this occurs, it is purely an opportunity for the nine residents to spread their goodwill abroad via one person at a time. They take their role of humanitarian seriously and care deeply for the people they meet throughout life's journey. They are able to separate the individual from the mass cause they are passionate about. After all, it is the individual who makes up the need to make this world a better place.

### Elemental Persuasion

Yang Fire ~ Middle Daughter Fire is the element of Integrity and it burns away that which is not essential and molds into its purest form. Fire is a mediator of transformation. In the process, the smoke from this transmuting fire swirls upwards to the skies symbolically creating communication with the cosmic realms. It is about living in perfect balance with the King and Queen within one's own temple…one's inner truth. Inner truth opens the door to enlightenment and this Comic illumination enables you to express the best of your self in harmony and balance.

### Associated I Ching Trigram

Li ~ Clinging Fire: In the Hexagram #30 Attaining Clarity, per Hanna Moog and Carol Anthony, "The Sage shows the theme of this hexagrams to be the Cosmic Principle op Clarity as the characteristic feature of the Cosmic Logic. Like all Cosmic principles that form harmony, clarity, and Cosmic Logic are attained through a combination of thinking and feeling. They cannot be attained through mental effort alone. Clarity is attained through connecting with our inner truth, with the help of the Sage."

## Friends

Candles-even when they are not aglow, they are a powerful chatzkie. I have red candles in this area and I dot them with the oils of myrtle or spruce for added clarity. A fireplace in this area is wonderful. Also, Photos/artwork of people or animals, the sun, Lanterns; Anything that has a triangle in its pattern…hey, the star literally has five triangles and YOU ARE THE STAR so symbolically, this item in any form is perfect. I have a star handing above my mirror and I love the inspiration it gifts me. A pyramid is also an excellent item. We have a friend who loves Egypt and collects pyramids-yes, he loves the Lexor in Las Vegas too… he has his collection in his integrity area and he enjoys esteem and respect. Bright lights and all items in the color of red are terrific enhancements too.

For those of you whom are rebuilding a damaged reputation, adopt the Phoenix. This bird has appeared in numerous cultures as the bird of regeneration and upgrading one's life into new and more vital interest. The Jewish folklore believes the Phoenix bird was the only animal not to be banished from the Garden of Eden. It symbolizes the rising sun…new beginnings. The Phoenix is also considered the symbolism of rebirth and possesses life-giving powers. Phoenix surrenders to fire and steps out of it cleansed and endowed with a new life.

## Foes

For obvious reasons, water is not a friend of fire. However, if your bathroom is located in this area you can balance it by adding beautiful red towels to your décor. Items with a strong earthy appeal are also helpful. Almond soap, ceramic vases in the colors of butterscotch, terracotta or sable brown ground the space and absorbs the watery influences. Silken ivy plants in green pottery soak up the water too. Avoid the colors of navy and black in this area.

Paintings or photos of folks who are in a less than excellent circumstance convey lack of empowerment. This Gua is all about being empowered.

## Seasonal Cycle

Summer - The noonday sun

## Energy Patterns for Individual Rooms

**Foyer** - Non-applicable

**Living or Great Room** - One of my clients loved red. In their living room, they painted the back wall a rich red. They are successful realtors and by boosting this area, they reputation soars as respected and highly regarded business folks. Place nine candles on a wooden tray in this room. This represents the energy of passion and illumination. In full view, place a photo of your family in this room in a luxurious red wooden frame. If possible, have a fireplace in this room. Home Depot and Loews each have wonderful after market fireplaces. This is the best addition you could ever make to a room located in this Gua.

**Stairs or Hallways** - This is the perfect place to display a family photo gallery. Resist the urge to hang your photos in a stair step fashion. This particular pattern denotes water energy. Paint one of your walls in an earth tone.

**Bathroom** - Since this room denotes a watery space, this Gua is challenged. It is possible to create an environment that down plays these natural influences. Paint the walls an earth tone and select red or amethyst colored towels and bath mats. Conical or triangular tiles along the wall direct the eyes upward. Candles are the perfect chatzkie for this room and uplifting toward paintings of lovely butterflies to symbolize transformation and the joyful dance of life. Stand in your beauty.

**Home Office, Study, or Library** - This is considered a power area so any of these rooms in this Gua are empowered. A home office sets the stage for respect and integrity in your community. A study or library affords you the time to study and clarify exactly how, what, and with whom you choose to spend your precious time.

**Kitchen** - Since the kitchen is considered the heart of the home and this Gua represents the heart, it is an excellent placement. Often this is the location for a bulletin board that shows off the family's interests. Openly display the children's artwork showcase along with the adult's accomplishments .

**Dining Room** - a beautiful Chinese fan on the wall denotes expansion. A centerpiece of fresh flowers represents a wood energy that feed the flames of transformation. Integrity serves you best when you make sound decisions so choose to eat healthy food in this room.

**Storage Areas**-If this area is where your storage is located, hang a fully faceted Austrian crystal. Paint your shelving red.

**Master Bedroom**: When the master bedroom is located in this outgoing Gua, it conflicts with the idea of rest and relaxation. By concentrating on fire's transformational energies, think of your dream life and the insights you gain. Keep a journal by your bed and write down your dreams. Express yourself highest self through writing poetry.

**Child's Room** - Again, de-cluttering is essential. A messy child's room in this section will definitely block your abundance. Pitch in and help create organization. Display trophies and certificates of appreciation or perfect attendance

## Sage Meditation

Imagine standing at the entrance of your this Gua. If there are two or more rooms, include all of these rooms in your imagery. In your mind's eye, see your intentions for integrity, illumination-fame and recognition. Visualize a Sage wearing a red silken robe with a golden triangle located right over the heart. You now bow and greet the enlightened one. He/she is bestowing a Tiger Eye gemstone to you. You accept this sacred stone and know that your integrity and illumination intentions are beautifully unfolding. Thank the Sage, who is your friend, for this cosmic help.

Mentally, stand in the Gua's center and become very still. While taking long and deliberate deep breaths, become centered and grounded. When comfortable with this state of awareness, ask the Sage to reveal this Gua's action of growth and creative path to you. As you listen, you will feel led to remove the items that no longer serve you and the objects that will nurture and support your desires. Bow to the Sage and express your deep gratitude for the valuable insights you have gained.

If you are not receiving the clarity promised in this process, look diagonally opposite this Gua, which is the Career//Life Journey. This is the assistant/helper area for this Gua. Be certain this area is de-cluttered and properly balanced. Walk around this area repeating your affirmations for clarity, respect, integrity, and awakened enlightenment.

## A Jewel to Re*Member

*"Fame or integrity: which is more important? Money or happiness: which is more valuable? Success or failure: which is more destructive? If you look to others for fulfillment, you will never truly be fulfilled. If your happiness depends on money, you will never be happy with yourself. Be content with what you have; rejoice in the way things are. When you realize there is nothing lacking, the whole world belongs to you."*

*- Lao Tzu*

# 21

# -

# A Vitally Rich Intimate Relationship

## Be Receptive

## Being Present: Developing Trust~ Receptivity ~ Well-Being ~ Balance, Harmony

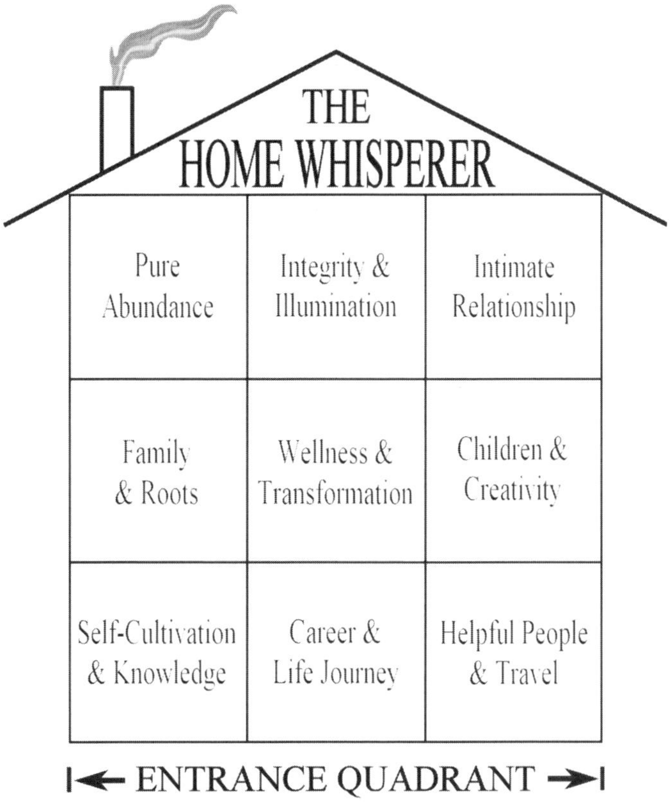


- **Location: Upper right of the Bagua Map**
- **Sacred Geometry:** Heart
- **Numerical Influence:** Two
- **Color:** Red, Pink, White, & Yellow
- **Element:** Yin, Earth-Mother
- **I Ching Trigram:** K'un, Receptive Earth
- **Operative Words:** Commitment, Trust, Loyalty, & Respect
- **Gemstones:** Rose Quartz, Diamond, Gold, & Pearl
- **Chi Imagery:** Photos/artwork of 2 happy people and a heart
- **Season:** Late Summer
- **Directional Energy:** Towards one another
- **Affirmation:** I am love, I am harmony, I am joy, I am loved
  I have a beautiful life and I am a beloved child of the Universe.
  I trust the process.

I Fill My Home and Each Room With The Vibration Of Joyous Love So That All Who Enter, Myself Included Are Nurtured!

Throughout history, the feminine principle of divine mother has risen within each culture to personify the Code of the Yin mission. As all symbolism is but an outward representation of things with inner meaning, the Goddess initiative encompasses the Great Mother. She is a soft yielding energy of being receptive, protective, wise, nurturing and kind. The Chinese goddess of mercy is Quan Yin. Her name means padma-pani -- born of the lotus. In Christianity, Virgin Mother grace. Tara, in her many forms, has been found on cave walls dated by 30,000 years. She is the oldest and the most revered of all goddess deities. In Tibet, she is called the faithful one, star of heaven. In Finland, she is Tar the goddess of wisdom. In the Cheyenne tradition, she is known as Star Woman and the Druids looked to her as their mother goddess, Tara. In all of these traditions, she is known as the great mother of healing and compassion.

### Visualization:

*The Great Mother Earth ushers in the code of the Yin Mission. This is the feminine mystery gracefully unfolding. Within this energy are receptivity, security, comfort, and stability. Held inside this sustainable is the supportive process where trust is nurtured deep within your heart. To know that you are unconditionally loved connects you to being centered and grounded. Accept this precious gift from Mother Earth.*

### Self-Love

This is the alchemical process of learning to love your self intimately. In turn, you are opening your heart so that you may love another. When you respect self, wholeness is experienced through every part of your being. Living in complete harmony in the core of your being develops trust, long-term commitments, devotion, and cultivates unconditional love. In addition to being open hearted, forgiveness, adaptability, romance, kindness, & happiness will find their way into your life. It is a connection to true and lasting love and this bond continually serves you.

This connection flows from inside your heart center to the outer world. Develop a rich inner life and celebrate yourself. Since you are forever in relationship - if not with someone who can be seen - you are always linked with the Cosmic Consciousness, allow your unique existence to exemplify the delicate and joyous balance of giving and receiving. This rightful action makes the world a better place to live…one person at a time.

Intimate relationship also represents a compelling and nurturing bond that includes not only your significant other such as spouse or long-term companion, but also encompasses friendships, professional associations such as business partnerships, colleagues, co-workers, clients, employers, and employees. It also includes your friends and neighbors.

## The Lovers

Carl Jung developed an archetypal system explaining various aspects of self. The archetype of the lovers is about having a profound appreciation of something (from cooking, traveling, gardening, sewing or collecting fine wines) or to someone. This infinite relationship gives purpose or organization to our life. It is an organic love affair inspiring devotion. When fully engaged, we are able to go beyond ourselves and live in passion and true commitment.

Embracing the inner and outer space of unconditional love creates a sanctuary within your heart. This loving flow of support connects you to the joys and many benefits of lasting love within and for yourself. This openness heartened embodies self-confidence in your energetic pattern and enhances other aspects of your endeavors. Love is the greatest transformational energy available.

Your personal bedroom is a wonderful place to usher in a greater ability to receive and give love. Regardless of where your bedroom is located in your home, create a haven within its walls. This room represents true internal shelter symbolizing your inner self. When the bedroom is in balance you can relax into complete safety and enjoy complete rejuvenation. Play soothing music and dress your bed in sensuous and high thread count sheets. Choose warm and inviting colors such as raspberry, lavender, terracotta, crimson, sable brown, apricot, or creamy vanilla as they beckon deep relaxation. This room is a retreat and bodes well for deep rest. Caring for this room supports the art of visionary dreams that reveal your highest vision of what life should look like for you. Consecutively, this calm and quiet space is the link to potentially express your true self in your waking life. Creating a serene atmosphere bridges the gap between the inner and outer you.

Dim the glare of bright lights as this lends itself to a clinical setting. Soft and well-placed lighting cozies a room. This ambiance creates a nurturing Yin atmosphere where the bliss of a romantic mood thrives. Remove your computer, television, any and all clutter, exercise equipment (a treadmill is symbolic of moving and going nowhere all at once!) and the desk you do business from. There will usually be another place for these items. However if you temporarily must have them in your personal haven, please drape it with a fabric. This reduces the possibility for the item to call your name and even preside over the room.

Survey the room and remove all objects that are less than nurturing or are holding a single energy. For example, a client of mine shares a home with her sister. In the sister's bedroom and over her bed, she had a large painting of a single beautiful Native American Indian woman. Her head was titled down and away from the viewer. This painting expressed a strong energy of loneliness and isolation. In fact, when the sister removed this painting, her depression lifted and she was light hearted once again. Unfortunately, she was so attached to the painting that within months she re-hung it. Once again the sister distanced herself from life itself.

To further balance the bedroom, flank your bed with nightstands that are in scale to the bed. Place a romantic lamp on each stand and items in groups of two. Such as two red candles-represents passion, two mandarin ducks-symbolizing long term relationship, two rose quartz gemstone-signifies true love and/or two pink silk roses.

Regardless of which room finds its way to your home's actual relationship Gua, display nurturing articles of two in this location. This is the alchemical process of learning to love your self intimately. In turn, you are opening your heart so that you may love another. When you respect self, wholeness is experienced from within every part of your being. Living in complete harmony from within the core of your being develops the ability to trust, make long-term commitments, be devoted, and cultivate unconditional love.

*"Strive with diligence to be a lamp unto yourself." - Buddha.* Stand in your own brilliant light and simply Be Love. To encourage balance, calmness, and auspicious living, spritz your bedroom and relationship qua with lavender essential oils, rose or ylang ylang.

## Aromatherapy

This is the medicine of the past and of the future. It holds the true essence in the apothecary jar for 'healing thyself'. The aromatics are found within flower essences, herbal compounds, berries, flower tops, grasses, resins, rinds, rhizomes, woods, tree roots & barks, seeds, and leaves. They are utilized in the form of distillers, diffusers, elixirs, and tinctures. Essential oils have an alchemical effect on the body, mind and heart. In Robert Beck's book, *The Body Electric*, he has proven the body has an electrical frequency. Each frequency has a measurable rate of electrical energy that is constant between any two frequencies. Essential oils have a very high frequency lending itself to the healing process. As are most remedies, results can vary from individual to individual.

Cloaked in mysticism and magic, beginning with the Egyptian culture as early as 3,500 BC, essential oils have played a role in history. Perfume was a highly appreciated product and as the Egyptians perfected it, they also developed topical oils that aided in tranquility, restoring beauty, and treating health challenges. The Egyptians were forever looking for immortality and in the process they developed their advanced embalming techniques. When these properties were studied, traces of cedar wood, nutmegs, clove, cinnamon, frankincense, and myrrh were discovered.

In 2697 B.C., the Yellow Emperor Classic Book of Internal Medicine was written containing over 300 different plants. It is the oldest surviving book and is still in use today. The Chinese culture was the first to use aromatics as a healing property. These herbs and flowers were used to promote wellness and longevity. Although there were many manuscripts throughout history with regard to many cultures, the Chinese left us with the better-preserved version.

Persia from 529 A.D. until our modern history, have contributed the most impressive products to date. From this country, the legendary man named Al-Razi (also known as Alcenni) lived from 865 to 925. He wrote over 237 books on aromatics and medicine. Picking up where left off, was Ibn Sina (980-1037). In that time, he was called The Prince of Medicine. He wrote a 14 volume medical encyclopedia that contained the wisdom of Hypocrites and all of the knowledge available during that time He is credited with improving the distillation process and the first person to successfully steam Rose oil.

During the same time in history, aromatics were being cultivated in India. Ayurvedic practitioners developed medicinal blends made the popular rose, juniper, frankincense, lavender, and lemon. Concurrently, and following a chronological time line, Hypocrites, a Greek physician, the "Father of Medicine, was the first person to take a holistic/aromatic approach as the choice of remedy. During his lifetime he developed over 200 compounds and is credited with being the founder of aromatherapy, as we know it today.

The Romans were appreciative of the power of essential oils for their fragrance and cosmetic value. Cleopatra is famous for her search for immortal beauty. In roughly 48 B.C., Caesar returned to Rome with Cleopatra after taking over Egypt. To prove his victory, he threw bottles of perfume out to the crowd. Through out history, the acquisition of these oils and spices led to establishing highly successful trade routes with India and Arabia. In fact, oils and spices are the reason trade routes were ever founded.

When Rome withdrew from Europe, the aromatic arts were not cultivated as widely. However as the Dark Ages evolved, secretly within the monasteries the monks became wise in the art of herbal remedy. They kept their gardens blossoming with herbs and flowers to distill into aromatic cures. Their concoctions remained a secret, as the monks were deeply mysterious in their application. Their widely guarded formulas have survived and have since been revealed. They are still in use today.

Over 3,000 years ago, the Aztec and Mayan civilizations used aromatics for smudging, wellness, and fragrances. For centuries, North American Native Americans have traditionally used aromatherapy in their sweat lodges, prayer ceremonies and in their medicinal practices.

By the mid-nineteenth century, European chemists and perfumeries were enjoying great good success. They had separated the essential oils into perfumes and began decantering them into jeweled encrusted bottles. This was a popular purchase and considered to be fashionable.

In 1930, Edward Bach, a pathologist and bacteriologist discovered a greater breadth of nature's medicinal properties. Through dedication to his research, he developed 38 remedies for mental and emotional cures.

In 1937, French chemist Guttefosse coined the term aromatherapy. He discovered Lavender's healing properties after suffering a burn in his lab. His book published in 1964, titled Aromatherapie was translated into English and gave credibility to the art and science. The English version of this book is titled Guttefosse's Aromatherapy and continues to be extensively referenced in today's world.

Throughout history, the, Egyptians, Arabians, Babylonians, Grecians, French, Romans, Greeks, Italians, South Americans, Native Americans, Persians, Spanish, Chinese, East Indians, Germans, Austrians, Hebrew, and finally Americans have discovered the magic and healing aromatics.

Spritzing an essential oil permeates a room with a healing ambiance by ridding it of residential negative energies. Essential oils reset and rejuvenate a home's energetic pattern. The following are for you to consider when you set your intention. Allow them to be your assistant in creating a fresh energetic blueprint. These are not to be ingested. Most of these oils are to be avoided if pregnant.

| | | | |
|---|---|---|---|
| **Angelica Root** | Restorative | **Marjoram Wild** | Purifying |
| **Anise** | Relaxation; promotes emotional balance | **Melissa** | Strengthens and revives the vitality of the home |
| **Amyris** | Calming | **Myrrh** | Meditative and inspirational |
| **Balsam Peru** | Anchoring | **Myrtle** | Clarifying |
| **Basil** | Clears the mind and improves memory | **Neroli** | Releases tension |
| **Bay** | Calming | **Nutmeg** | Regenerating |
| **Bergamot** | Confidence builder | **Orange** | Refreshing and regenerating |
| **Cardamom Seed** | Exotic | **Ormeis** | Nurturing |
| **Carrot Seed** | Replenishing | **Palmarose** | Refreshes and clears the home |
| **Cassia** | Energizing | **Patchouli** | Sensuous |
| **Cedar** | Strengthening | **Pettigrain** | Relaxing |
| **Cedarwood** | Soothes & relieves nervous tension of a home | **Pine** | Stimulating |
| **Chamomile** | Calming | **Peppermint** | Clears and cleans the air |
| **Cinnamon Leaf** | Vitalizing | **Rose** | Romantic |
| **Citronella** | Purifying | **Rose Geranium** | Sensuality |
| **Clary Sage** | Centering | **Rose Ott** | Creative |
| **Clove Bud** | Comforting | **Rosemary** | Promotes study |
| **Cypress** | Balance | **Rosewood** | Eases anxiety of a home |

| | | | |
|---|---|---|---|
| **Eucalyptus** | Cleansing and toning | **Sage** | Toning |
| **Fennel** | Supportive | **Sandalwood** | Sumptuous |
| **Frankincense** | Meditation | **Spearmint** | Stimulating; beneficial for stagnant air |
| **Geranium** | Mood lifter | **Spruce** | Clarifying |
| **Ginger** | Cheerful | **Tangerine** | Cheerfulness |
| **Hyssop** | Refreshing | **Tea Tree** | Powerfully rousing - a little goes a long way |
| **Jasmine** | Romantic | **Thyme** | Energizer |
| **Juniper** | Cleansing | **Vanilla** | Comforting |
| **Lavender** | Healing | **Vetiver** | Deeply relaxing, boosts self-worth |
| **Lemon** | Refreshing and mental clarity | **Wintergreen** | Bracing |
| **Lemongrass** | Cleansing | **Ylang Ylang** | Euphoric |
| **Lime** | Equalizing | | |
| **Mandarin Orange** | Uplifting | | |
| **Marjoram** | Helps relieve stress in the environment | | |

This Gua's mission is to appreciate the sweetness in life and create balance, harmony, sensuousness, trust and receptivity. Aromatherapy is a yummy way to introduce this beneficial element into your home and life. Enjoy the energies of such a variety of scents.

## Colorful Perceptions

The colors associated with this Gua are white, red, pink and yellow. **White** represents innocence and purity. It is often thought of as the divine white light gifting clarity and truth. In actuality, white is not a color at all. However, it is associated with kindness, wholeness, truth, and completion.

**Red** is the color of power. Tiger Woods always wears red on the Sunday of a golf tournament. It is indicative of passion, warmth, zeal, life force and vitality. Red represents enthusiasm and is the color associated with the root chakra.

When red and white are mixed together, **pink** is created. This tender loving energy communicates that everything is going to be okay. It is the color of love, acceptance, and protection. Pink calms down feelings of anxiety, is analogous with order, relaxation and deep contentment. Wear pink if you are ever feeling lonely or unloved.

**Yellow** is the color of the root chakra is a cheery color with lots of joy, happiness, and it inspires an uplifting mood. When used in signage, yellow promotes friendliness. When used in a meeting or conference room, it creates a sense of community. Yellow denotes a sunny disposition, intellectualism, and clarity. To encourage kindness, wear yellow.

## Numerical Influences

The number two is associated with the Intimate Relationship Gua. Couples come in pairs and so does the energy of this section. This is the dance of gentle yin and dynamic yang. The deepening of the mystical self begins when you begin to look beneath the surface. The balance of polarities is found in the number two components. Two is considered a kind, empathetic, diplomatic and cooperative number.

## Elemental Persuasion

Earth's delicious energy. I am considered an Earth muffin. I love to nurture and connect with my family and friends on a deep level. Over the years, I have learned to balance my giving with my receiving because then, I can be of more service. We of this energy know only too well the sweetness of life. Her joys, her long term vision for generational wealth… yes, I have already added our great, great grandchildren to benefit from the family fortune. It would be heartless to do otherwise. I have always been able to trust the process to know that regardless of what things may "look" like, there is wisdom and joy behind its veneer.

Earth's physics act as a shock absorber, an insulator of unexpected turns of events. When one is grounded, safety and comfort are present with any situation. With this energy, clarity is more easily attained to see a challenge through. Earth is life affirming.

The energy of earth encourages you to know true stability. Due to its movement towards the middle of a vortex, its organizing property holds things in order. Earth energy strikes a chord to your safety, sensuality, and your ability to be grounded. Living in time with Mother Earth's heartbeat slows us down long enough to recognize the jewels showing up in our lives on a daily basis. We often fly so fast, we miss these gifts.

## Sacred Geometric Shape & Symbolism

The heart is a profound symbol reminding us of the compassion and empathy we are to extol upon our fellow sojourners. The icon itself emits a sense of love, kindness and wisdom. Folklore has it that the back and wings of a dove of peace form the heart's shape. The dove was associated with Aphrodite's, the Greek goddess of love. It refers to the heart of spiritual, emotional, and soulful joy. The heart space represents sincerity and the complete knowing you ARE LOVE.

## I Ching - Love

"Life leads the thoughtful person
on a path of many windings.
Now the course is checked, now it runs straight again.
Here winged thoughts may pour freely forth in words,
There the heavy burden of knowledge
must be shut away in silence.
But when two people are at one in their inmost hearts,
They shatter even the strength of iron or of bronze.
And when two people understand each other
in their inmost hearts,
Their words are sweet and strong
like the fragrance of orchids."

- I Ching ~Translation by Richard Wilhelm 1873-1930

### Friends

Grouping items into two's support the Intimate Relationship Gua. As discussed early, this promotes the balance of the polarities. These items can anything that is meaningful to you. To enhance the Intimate Relationship of your home, choose one or more of the following to display in your home: Two Dolphins = commitment, love of life, and are highly social. Two Cranes = wisdom, rejuvenation and longevity. Two Mandarin Ducks = respect, fidelity because they are lifetime mates. Two pink candles stand for kindness found within a passionate relationship. Two pieces of rose quartz enhance the energy of true love. Two red silk or live roses and place two white, red or pink velvet or satin pillows on the bed.

### Foes

In the counterproductive cycle, wood energy covers earth and water dams it. Excessive plants and items representing water are to be avoided. The exception is a tranquil water feature depicting two loving items such as birds, angels, children, or animals.

### Gemstones

Rose Quartz, Diamond, Rhodochrosite, Pink Opal, Gold, Pink Tourmaline, Danburite, & Pearl. Photos/artwork of happy people, and a heart; all items made from the earth such as bricks, ceramic, pottery, or sand. This can be an earthen vase or clay container, items in the colors of white, red, pink or yellow.

### Associated Trigram

Receptive Earth embraces the feminine power of the goddess. It is the matriarchal society represented by the wise mother, the loving wife, the caring daughter, and the thoughtful aunt. It is the collective consciousness of affection. Per Hanna Moog and Carol Anthony, from Hexagram #7, the I Ching, "*The Judgment*: Modesty creates success. The superior man carries things through. Modesty, the Sage informs us, is one of the three fundamental Cosmic Virtues that all aspects of the Cosmic Whole are endowed with. The other two virtues are equality and uniqueness. Together, they give each aspect of the Cosmos its dignity. It is due to these basic virtues that a single force is able to rule the functioning of the whole: the force of mutual attraction of complementary aspects. Another name for this force is love."

### Seasonal Cycle

Early fall or, as it is popularly referred to, Indian summer. When the heat of summer has somewhat reduced and the harvest is ready to be gathered. It is a time of great abundance, nourishment, and stability.

### Energy Patterns for the Individual Rooms

There is a template that creates itself within this flow of energy. When a room falls into a certain Gua, it takes on significance beyond itself. This is so with the earth energy as it prepares you to go beyond self.

**Living or Great Room:** Since this private space is now quite visible to the world, create a corner with two chairs of the same proportions nestled together. Around this intimate space within your highly public room, place an exotic metal table such as those found in import stores. Place photos of you and your special someone. If you choose to be single at the time, place a photo of an anonymous couple—make certain they are a happy pair- in a metal frame. Poetry books, books on passionate and long lasting love along with two candles, two roses, two dolphin or crane figurines certainly ground the energy of intimacy.

**Foyer:** Does Not Apply

**Stairs or Hallways:** Paint these walls in an earth shade and celebrate this space by displaying photos of two people in happy modes. Stairways will create a faster moving energy than earth likes to have, however placing a large pottery (to scale for the stair treads) on the bottom step slows the energy down.

**Bathroom:** Located in this Gua, this room is highly supportive when you display earthen objects such as pottery or ceramic ware. Choose towels in rich earthy hues and even consider painting as accent wall in an earth tone. Square ceramic tile with thick sable brown bathmats anchor this energy and create a sanctuary of renewal.

**Home Office, Study, or Library:** The challenge for any of these rooms is that it takes time away from your relationship. Working can suffice for love and reading about love can be sufficient for being in an actual relationship. Honor any of these rooms by placing earthen statuary of a couple in a supportive pose. Have photos of happy couples on the wall. Think in terms of two!

**Dining Room or Kitchen:** Since this is the heart of a home, it is an excellent placement. Family can gather and enjoy one another's company. Nurturing meals sustain you.

**Storage Areas:** Even in a closet or storage area, there exist the opportunity to honor your relationship desires. Write a list of the qualities you desire or appreciate in your mate or mate to be. Frame these characteristics and hang these noble attributes in the privacy of this space.

**Bedroom:** Please refer to the personal bedroom in this chapter.

John Ogden said, "For it is love's prerogative to give, and give, and give." 'Tis true, but so is being receptive. Reframing that quote, "love's prerogative is also learning to receive, receive, and receive." An intimate relationship expresses the balance of giving and receiving. It goes beyond one's self. The commitment you make to something even greater than self is brought forth by dedication, loyalty, stability, supportiveness, and kindness. They each convey the heart of an intimate relationship. It is living in trust and being willing to follow the Highest Good.

The art of creating a loving relationship with your home develops the awareness of soul. You are always in partnership with your dwelling. Since home is where the heart is the inner heart supports and sustains every facet of your life too. In your outer home, love is literally instilled within each and every room. The soul of your inner and outer home brings joy, happiness, and a sense of belonging to your life. Both the inner/outer take very good care of you so in turn, BE thoughtful of them.

As you create an inner/outer home of increased beauty and joy, you also create the ability to love more. From this place you can give; give, and give and know the joy and balance necessary to receive, receive and receive. A deep sense of security, serenity, well-being, and bliss fills your life. This intimate relationship nurtures not only you, but also everyone who graces your home with their presence. Your generous inner and outer sanctuary provides all that you will ever wish for.

In this loving environment your thoughts are gentle as your dwell in comfort and safety. All of your extended kindnesses are mirrored back to you through loving friends and family. The energy of reciprocity is set into motion and if you choose a significant other to share this bountiful love, set intention for a richly romantic, trustworthy, and reciprocating love. As Nicolas Sparks encouraged, "But love… is more than three words mumbled before bedtime, love is sustained by action, a pattern of devotion in the things we do for each other everyday." BE LOVE!

### The Sage- Meditation

Imagine yourself standing in the middle of your home. Turn your attention to the Intimate Relationship Gua. In your mind's eye, see your intentions and affirm great good thanks for all of the support you now enjoy. At this time, visualize a Sage wearing a pink robe with an embroidered golden heart located right over the heart. You now bow and greet the Sage. He/she is handing a silk pillow holding two pieces of rose quartz, known as the pure love gemstones, to you. You accept these stone and know deep within that your intentions will beautifully unfold. You thank the Sage, who is your friend, for the cosmic help. Become very still and take long, deep breaths. When you are centered, ask the Sage to reveal the heart of this Gua. Should you not hear anything, continue to practice and eventually, you will "hear" your answers. While listening, you will feel led to remove the less than nurturing items from this Gua and you will do so with confidence. Adding the positive enhancements is an intuitive process. In fact, this Gua's teaching encourages you to trust the process. Give thanks for the Sage's support bowing & allowing the Sage to return to the ethers.

Please recall that there is a map of energy within a map of energy. Now that you have brought this section(s) of your home into alignment with trust, commitment, bliss, loyalty, receptivity, and love. Stand in the doorway of the room(s) and look into the room(s). If there is more than one room, map the energy separately according to each of the entrances. Line the bottom of your energy map up with the doorway and have a grand time Feng Shui-ing this room(s) accordingly. Make these changes with an open heart and a mind clear of clutter. If there is a question regarding where to place what item, remember the dominant energy will always be the one of the larger Bagua. In this portion of your home is missing, respect the Family section's guidelines and honor the accoutrements.

If this section of your home is missing, please refer to Chapter 10 for further insights.

## A Jewel to Re*Member

*"When the one man loves the one woman and the one woman loves the one man, the very angels desert heaven and come and sit in that house and sing for joy." -Brahma Sutra*

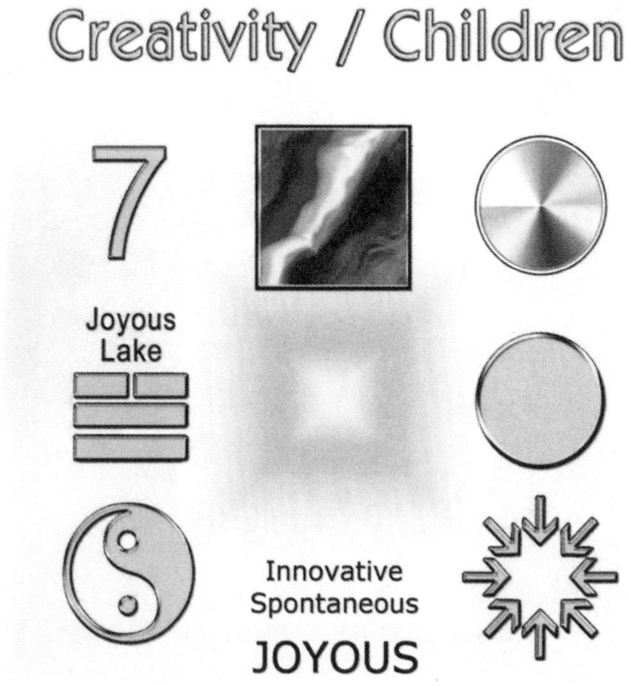


*22*

-

# *Children & Creativity*

Be Joyous

## Meet Your Personal Muse

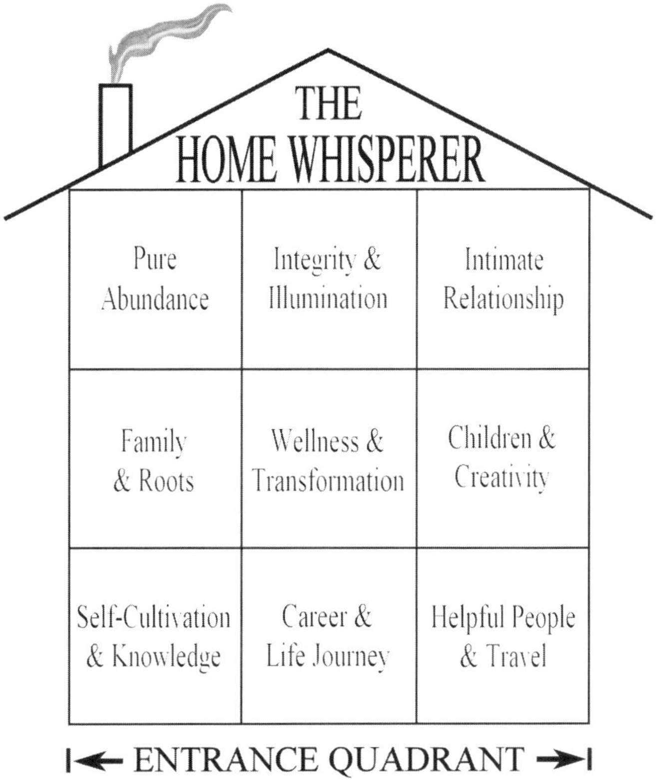


- **Location: Right center of the Bagua Map**
- **Sacred Geometry:** A Circle
- **Numerical Influence:** Seven
- **Color:** White, Pastels & Gold
- **Element:** Yin Metal, Youngest Daughter
- **I Ching Trigram:** Tui, Joyous Lake
- **Operative Words:** Focus, creativity, playfulness, refinement, joy, keeping correct within, communicative, charming, graceful
- **Gemstones:** Celestite, Crystal Quartz, & Pink Opal, & Pink Calcite
- **Chi Imagery:** Photos/artwork children's artwork, photos or sketches of children, children books, children's' games, DVDs, coloring books, crayons, water colors, bottle of bubbles, hobbies such as scrapbooking and quilting are excellent in this area; light bulbs - yes, this symbolizes bringing in those creative ideas so that you can experience the proverbial "light coming on"; music - my husband has his Wurlitzer replica in this area - things in an arch or a circular form, gemstones, crystals, metal wind chimes, white elephant = fertility, rainbows, grouping of seven items together such as seven stones or

seven metal rings, wedding rings or any kind of ring, metal figurines or statuaries, metal frames for photos, metal art, a thunderbolt or dorje, labyrinth, mandala, and last but not least, a Tibetan bell

- **Season:** Fall
- **Directional Energy:** Condensing and Contracting
- **Affirmation:** I easily live a life of inspiration.
  I enjoy childlike wonder.
  I follow my bliss.
  I create a life that I love
  Creativity is easy and simple for me
  I am resourceful, imaginative, inspired, and creative
  I live in balance and spontaneously

## Visualization

*Our precious inner child lovingly stands between the parents. The Mother Earth of the Intimate Relationship Gua and Father Sky from Helpful People and Travel. We are supported, inspired, encouraged, joyous, grounded... confidently expressing and living Cosmic Truth.*

Ingenious creativity flows easily within an inspired and orderly environment. In this space, call forth your muse and delight within your rich imagination. This muse is unlike the fleeting butterfly because she stays with you throughout the entire creative process. Inspiration and clarity transform your lofty ideas that dwell in the ethers, into the solid matter of the world. Whether it is a well-told story, elegantly written article, magnificent sculpture that speaks to the soul, or a hauntingly magical melody, this muse comes from deep inside you and your connection with cosmic consciousness. This extraordinary muse is a permanent source for genius-the genie from within. Beauty, creativity, encouragement, and imagination reveal themselves as your closest friends. Your heavenly support staff is wafting round you beckoning you to join them on a satin road paved by your inner most talents.

## Children

The symbolism of Children can literally be either one's off springs, the full circle of child rearing, or a creative endeavor; the projects one is bringing into the world by way of being the birth parent. And yes, the creative process can sometimes feel like labor pains. Bring it forth via your inner child and delight in the process of playfully happy creativity.

This Gua is associated with the I Ching trigram JOYOUS LAKE. When the mind realizes its cosmic connection with wholeness it becomes free of fear. Releasing this illusion creates a child-like trust unfolding peacefulness. Joy bubbles up from the wellspring within and once you experience this timeless knowing, you are forever aware of true harmony.

Once we get really clear about who we are, we are free to create with the highest ideas of the cosmos. Pure clarity can only be accomplished through connecting with our inner truth… the hidden treasures of our inner home.

### Inner Child

Before we have current memory and prior to learning a language pattern, we each come into our life journey with a memory or a knowing what perfect wholeness and cosmic harmony look, taste, sound, smells, and feels like. These treasures are stored within the mitochondria of each cell the body. To access our inner truth, we must be as a little child. If our precious child was not given the necessary support early in life to live fully and richly, it is time to work through the forgiveness teachings of the Family Tree Wisdom. Let go of all of your past hurts, tears, and fears. If an uncle, parent, or family friend was abusive to you in any way, recognize that he/she was your greatest teacher and you can move through the blockages. Allow your inner child to heal and be whole.

Call upon the Sage and the cosmic helpers to bring this child out to play. Boost your Inner Child and Creativity Gua with the items suggested in the Friends section of this chapter. Plus, purchase crayons and a beautiful coloring book. For one of my granddaughters, I bought the *Finding Nemo* coloring book. This story is about a father fish who goes to the ends of the ocean of find his son, Nemo. The colors are bright, the story line is heart warming and the activity is always fun.

Go to a park and swing, ride your bike, have a picnic, play Jacks, and/or play the games of Candy Land or Chutes & Ladders. Have fun watching animated kid-flicks, such as *Little Mermaid, Aladdin, Brother Bear*, or *Lion King*. Feel like a kid again and rent these timeless videos. The best way to your inner truth is through the heart of your inner child.

Being able to live in a place of sustainable joy creates healing. Healing yourself via the inner child enables you shine your radiant light on others and in turn, they are inspired to be whole. A term that perfectly expresses this truth and how we are to one another is Namaste'. It means, "I honor the place in you in which the entire universe dwells. I honor the place in you, which is of Divine Love of Truth, of Light, and of Peace. When you are in that place within you and I am in that place in me, we are one." Now, this is bliss!

## Joy

The juicy delightfulness of the Inner Child and Creativity makes us smile from inside out. The essence of joy is described as exultant ecstasy. The juiciness and delightfulness of the Inner Child and Creativity makes us smile from inside out. The essence of joy is described as exultant ecstasy. Open up your life and allow joy/ecstasy and exultation to come in. The hidden quality of joy is that it cannot be manufactured. It has to come bubbling up from inside. In order to do that, it must be as liquid to the core of your being. Find time to create, taste, smell, hear, and wear joy. Develop the ability to live in JOY. Joy sends a message of wellness to each and every one of our cells, our joints become more limber, and we are easily made flexible and willing to move forward. Elation, happiness, and pleasure…become one and embody the delightful qualities of joy.

Even the title of Alice Walker's book, *Possessing the Secret of Joy* speaks to the deeper part of my being. Her rich characters come alive and draw you in. This is a must read for anyone who appreciates gifted storytelling. Reading this book enables you to sink into JOY. Alice Walker is truly one of the best authors of our time and for time immortal.

## Gemstones

Since the Stone Age gemstones/crystals have been a powerful influence on all civilizations throughout time. They hold within them the earth's DNA. Each unique stone is a vast storehouse of evolution, revealing universal mysteries. In the Bible, gemstones are referenced hundreds of times and are used in the Breastplate of Aaron. In Exodus; it describes the Hebrew High Priest's stones. The early Egyptian, Chinese, Mayan, Aztec, Native Southern and Northern Americans, African, Celtic, and Atlantean cultures were advanced in gemstone knowledge.

Gemstones communicate a distinctive vibration or energetic pattern. They have long been acknowledged as a method of creating greater well-being and a remarkable means of increasing one's life force or Chi. Gemstones are noted to enhance one's personal life path, augment clarity, enlarge one's perception, boost personal creativity, and promote compassion. A crystal or gemstone takes on the outward appearance of its inner qualities. Crystal and semiprecious stones emit electromagnetic waves and have healing properties.

Through studying their abilities, you can tap into the stone's potent energies. Please note that a gemstone can be a rock or a mineral. It is the naturally occurring crystalline form and was created as the earth was formed, as sap dried and petrified, volcanic ash was purified under heat pressure, and even from mineral deposits in the ocean. The earth has three basic layers: the core, the mantle, and the crust. Just like us, the core consists of an inner and outer core, and the mantle is made up of an upper and lower mantle, while in between is a transition zone.

The following descriptions are *just a few* of a gemstone's properties and energetic patterns. Each gemstone mentioned has many more attributes and I encourage you to do an in-depth study of the stones that draw you. They provide balance, harmony, joy, stability, insight, confidence, and strength - again this is only a tiny list of their infinite range of abilities and blessings.

**Adamite**: Inner strength and the courage to navigate unknown paths.
**Agate**: Grounding and stability
**Amazonite**: Personal Truth
**Angel Wing Agate**: Focus
**Black Agate**: Enhance communication
**Blue Lace Agate**: Inner attunement
**Holly Blue Agate**: Spirituality
**Iris Agate**: Opens one to inner truth
**Moss Agate**: To perceive beauty
**Plume Agate**: Rebirthing process
**Purple Sage Agate**: To speak only words of enlightened awareness
**Rose Agate**: Poise
**Amber**: Devoted to connecting with the perfect cosmic consciousness. It brings forth our intentional desires into the manifested NOW.
**Alexandrite**: Regeneration and rebirth of the inner and outer selves.
**Amethyst**: It is said to attract abundance and true enrichment into our lives via deep contentment.
**Ametrine**: To access the higher states of awareness calling forth peace
**Andulusite**: Clarity
**Angelite**: Protection and it symbolizes peace unto the world, dispels anger, and restores our universal connectivity.
**Aquamarine**: Courage, release of fears
**Aventurine**: Growth; decisiveness
**Azeztulite**: For clarity; this stone invites in alternate realities
**Azurite**: Insight
**Beryl**: Intuition
**Bloodstone**: Great Bravery
**Butlerite**: Considered the stone of inner travel to aide in self-discovery
**Calcite**: Humanity's Teacher, spontaneity
**Caledonite**: Assists with public speaking
**Carnelian**: Encourages stability within one's home, prompts action
**Cat's Eye**: Enhances awareness

**Celestite**: The perfect gift stone to bestow upon a friend with the blessings of love and esteem.

**Chalcedony**: Benevolence, good will, and encourages generosity

**Chinese Writing Rock**: For beautiful and lucid dreaming.

**Chrysocolla**: Sacred Sounds

**Chrysanthemum Stone**: To live in the Now and to be inspired. To positively express Divine Love through our thoughts, words, and deeds.

**Citrine**: The merchant's stone so place it by your card service machine or your cash register. It also encourages living in a state of wealth.

**Copper**: Stimulates initiative and optimism.

**Coral**: Inner Peace, intuition, and imagination

**Black Coral**: Dispels the fear of the Darkness

**Blue Coral**: Improves Communication

**Pink Coral**: Continuity, maintaining awareness

**Red Coral**: Attunement to Wisdom

**White Coral**: Connecting with the Ethereal and communicating Cosmic consciousness' messages to humanity

**Danburite**: Stand in the bright light of Self

**Diamond**: Brings forth purity in love and trust in intimate relationship

**Dioptase**: Forgiveness

**Emerald**: The Healer's Stone…spontaneous correctness

**Fluorite**: Enhances Focus and is known as a stone for discernment, health, intellect, and wellness.

**Blue Fluorite**: Excellent for organized bookkeeping and clear communications and sequential thought processes.

**Chinese Fluorite**: Protection

**Colorless Fluorite**: Aligns the Chakras

**Green Fluorite**: Eliminates negativity within a physical environment

**Purple Fluorite**: Psychic and spiritual growth

**Yellow Fluorite**: Enhances Creativity

**Garnet**: The stone of health and wealth

**Geode**: Assists in decision-making

**Gold**: Allows Beauty to come from within

**Granite**: Purportedly to bring forth an increase in $$$

**Hematite**: Enables the body to remain cool; it is known as the "Stone of the Mind" it manifests the Light.

**Howelite**: Disperses self-criticism

**Ivory**: Purity

**Jade**: Cherish one's desires of the heart and smooth the progress of the manifestation of these dreams. This stone provides confidence.

**Jasper**: The nurturing stone…enhances being grounded.

**Bat Cave Jasper**: the bliss of living…to flow and to be centered.

**Red Jasper**: Dream recall

**Rose Jasper**: Protection

**Royal Plum Jasper**: Stability

**Jet**: Calming

**Kyanite**: Aligns all of the charkas automatically and instantaneously

**Lapis Lazuli**: Aids in discoveries the hidden mysteries stored within our cellular structure and opens the door to complete awareness.

**Larimar**: Nurturing

**Lazulite**: Insight how to let go of unnecessary worry

**Lepidolite**: Acceptance

**Lodestone**: Gratitude for every one of life's experiences

**Malachite**: Transformation

**Marble**: Logical thinking

**Mica**: Self-Reflection

**Moldavite**: Transformation

**Moonstone**: A stone for wishes and intention setting, delivers insight and reflects the cycles in one's life

**Obsidian**: Protection

- **Apache Tear Obsidian**: Comfort in times of grief
- **Black Obsidian**: Stimulates Creativity
- **Blue Obsidian**: Telepathic properties
- **Gold Sheen Obsidian**: To speak from the heart.
- **Green Obsidian**: Communion with Source
- **Purple Obsidian**: Stimulates clairvoyance
- **Rainbow Obsidian**: The stone of enjoyment
- **Red Obsidian**: Vitality, embracing change
- **Silver Sheen Obsidian**: A mirror to soul

**Opal**: True and spontaneous action

- **Andrean Opal**: Protection during spiritual journeys; divination
- **Black Opal**: Grounding
- **Blue Opal**: Creativity and ingenuity; provides inner knowledge

- **Fire Opal**: Brilliance and clarity
- **Golden Opal**: To release limitations
- **Green Opal**: Promote relaxation, problem-solving in a dream state
- **Pink Opal**: Renewal; guides one along life's journey, opens up awareness through enlightenment
- **Red Opal**: Encourages positive results in one's endeavors
- **White Opal**: Promotes business acumen

**Petrified** Wood: Fresh beginnings; eliminates worries

**Phenacite**: Initiation

**Piertersite**: A vision stone - high state of awareness

**Pyrite**: Keeps out negative vibrations, prevention stone

**Quartz**: Brings the energy of the stars to the soul-is an amplifier stone

- **Blue Quartz**: Assists in connecting with others without fear
- **Golden Quartz**: Healing
- **Green Quartz**: Inspires creativity
- **Pink Quartz**: Love
- **Rainbow Quartz**: Universal Love
- **Smokey Quartz**: Grounding
- **Tibetan Quartz**: Aides in reading the Akashic records

**Rhodochrosite**: The child within; using this stone in meditation brings forth the golden circle awareness and creates JOY.

**Rhodonite**: Living into one's greatest potentiality; stone of love, calming, confidence in one's life path. Good for the heart chakra

**Ruby**: Life Force; stone of nobility

**Rose Quartz**: Love

**Sapphire**: Joy and peace of mind…opens one up to beauty and intuition

- **Black Sapphire**: Aides in job searches; encourages self-confidence
- **Blue Sapphire**: Strength in multi-tasking
- **Green Sapphire**: Encourages fidelity
- **Indigo Sapphire**: Broadening one's horizons; strengthens one's ability to follow through with responsibilities and see them as joyful, promotes alertness and attentiveness

**Seraphinite**: Higher spiritual vibration

**Sodalite**: Life Journey

**Selenite**: Divine Self

**Sugilite**: A Dream Stone

**Sunstone**: Brings forth leadership qualities and draws in abundance
**Tiger's Eye**: Clarity, intuition and balance.
**Topaz**: Intention; success in all paths

- **Blue Topaz**: Enhances communication skills; being one with the Universe's perfection
- **Golden Topaz**: Just like a battery, this stone re-charges your energy
- Rutilated Topaz: Enchantment, brings light and love to one's life path

**Tourmaline**: Promotes understanding, an excellent stone for balancing each and every chakra. Encourages balance and alignment

- **Black Tourmaline**: Purification
- **Blue Tourmaline**: Activates the Throat Chakra; to live in harmony within one's home and workplace; to be of service
- **Brown Tourmaline**: Grounded; brings inner peace and alignment
- **Colorless Tourmaline**: Healing; aides in becoming service oriented
- **Green Tourmaline**: Compassion
- **Neon Tourmaline**: Through meditation, communication with other Worlds is made available… highly powerful.
- **Orange Tourmaline**: Emotional stability
- **Pink Tourmaline**: Trust in Love and Humanity's Enlightenment
- **Yellow Tourmaline**: Activates creativity and motivation in career Advancement. Stimulates spiritual awareness.

**Turquoise**: Healing; Wholeness
**Zincite**: Promotes group intention and removes energy blockages/phobias

## Colorful Perceptions

**White**: Purity as in the pearl of great wisdom or Mother of Pearl.

**Pastels**: The softness of metal plays itself through the pastel of a sunset where cotton candy pink and golden taffeta swirl across the sky

**Gold**: This anointing of godliness denotes illumination.

**Amber**: The Harvest as in Amber waves of grain

## Numerical Influences

Seven-The number seven holds the most sacred essence of all the numbers. Its energetic pattern embodies the three, which is the triangle and the four which is the circle… Three + Four = Seven. Seven is held to a higher standard as it represents the intellect and philosophy.

## Elemental Persuasion

Yin Metal-The energy of the mind… it refines and defines our efforts from the average into the elegant. Breath is considered a metal influence is to breathe in from the heavens the joy of creativity, improvement, beauty, sophistication, and clarity.

## Associated Trigram

Number 58…The Joyous per Hanna Moog and Carol Anthony,

*"The Judgment: The Joyful. Success. Perseverance is favorable."* The trigram Tui, doubled in this hexagram, has been traditionally associated with two images: the still water of the lake and the stagnant water of the swamp. Here, the Sage pointed to "still water" as representing the conditions that bring about true joy, and "stagnant water" as the conditions that pervert it. The still water thus represents the Cosmic Principle of Joy.

Defined further, the still water of the lake represents the liquidity and stillness of the mind that make insight possible. Liquidity means not fixed in one's views, while stillness is the absence of ego-emotions and preconceived ideas. Liquidity and stillness make a person receptive to the light than enables instant communication with the Sage through mind-flashes. A mind-flash occurs when the liquid light transforms Cosmic Consciousness (which exists as a feeling) into words or images that express the Cosmic Truth needed in the moment. It is to be noted that mind-flashes are but one of the myriad ways in which the Sage is able to communicate."

## Sacred Geometry Symbolism

The Circle has been of great importance as it literally changed history. The Mesopotamians invented the wheel for their chariots in 3200BC. Since then, everything from the automobile wheel to computer disk is made in a circle or wheel shape. It shifted how we moved from place to place and through mobility, lightened our toil in the fields. Evidence of the wheel's importance shows up as follows: the full circle of collective community, the circle of communication, and the circle of love. The wheel of fortune is associated with luck or chance, King Arthur and his round table, the circle dance, the Buddhist wheel of dharma, Tibetan prayer wheel, the Native American medicine wheel and their dream catchers, the Rose window is a series of side by side circles upon circles, and of course, Stonehenge is a circle. From the Bible in Ezekiel, "*Now as I looked . . . I saw a wheel upon the earth beside the living creatures . . . their construction being as it were a wheel within a wheel . . . The four wheels had rims and they had spokes, and their rims were full of eyes round about. And when the living creatures went, the wheels went beside them, and when the living creatures rose from the earth, the wheels rose. Wherever the spirit would go, they went, and the wheels rose along with them; for the spirit of the living creatures was in the wheels.*"

The Rainbow - Half of a circle is an arch. The rainbow is an arch and symbolizes a bridge connecting heaven and earth as paradise. It reminds us of the peace at the end of the rainbow and the pot of gold. It represents a celestial wonder and divine benevolence.

## Friend

In addition to the items at the beginning of the chapter, the Bell is an excellent chatzkie. Think of the myriad of ways a bell is used in our lives. The doorbell alerts us that we have visitors or a delivery. The cash register bell… yes, there are still some merchants who still use registers and not the computers, symbolizes added wealth. A horn can be considered a bell of sorts and useful to warn or be warned.

The bell in reference to this Gua is the Tibetan or Balinese bells. I have a Tibetan bell given to me by Denise Linn at one of the Western School of Feng Shui advanced trainings. I have it on my desk and whenever I feel stuck, I ring this bell. It disperses the energy beautifully. Upon ringing it, I can literally feel its tonal cleansing that sends ripples through the air. Harmony is once again vibrating throughout my home office and throughout my being. I pause and breathe in the cleared air. Inspiration, innovation, and joy once again whisper to me.

*"The world is so full of a number of things, I'm sure we should all be happy as kings"*
*- Robert Louis Stevenson*

Robert Louis Stevenson wrote a treasure trove of books, such as *Treasure Island* and *Kidnapped*, *The Strange Case of Dr. Jekyll and Mr. Hyde* (he actually dreamed this story and within ten weeks, it was finished). In addition to these better-known novels, he wrote beautiful poetry from a child's eyes. As a child, *A Child's Garden of Verses* was one of my favorite books. Poems such as The Swing, My Shadow, "I have a little shadow that goes in and out with me, and what can be the use of him is more than I can see." The Wind as it spoke, "I saw you toss the kites on high, and blow the birds about the sky; and all around I heard you pass, like ladies' skirts across the grass." The Land of Nod, The Sun's Travels, The Lamplighter, The Moon, Good Night, My Bed is a Boat, Shadow March, In Port.

I pay homage to the boy who wrote of the mysteries of dreamland and places where treasures are sure to be found. Allow your inner child to drink in his effortless words that will surely transport you into the rich and inspired field of imagination.

## Foe

Since metal is forged and melted in a refinery by way of fiery furnaces, fire is metal enemy. For this area, avoid large prints or color in red or bright orange. Keep your candles to a minimum and if you have a choice, do not have a fireplace here. If you do, hang a large (to scale) mirror over the mantel and place crystal objects on that very mantel. Steer clear of items in a pyramid, triangle, or conical shape.

## Seasonal Cycle

Autumn - A time of Harvest

## HINTS from the Home Whisperer

Please reference the Bagua pattern at the first of this chapter. Notice that diagonally across from the Inner Child & Creativity Gua is the Family/Roots Gua. In order for creativity to emerge, it is supported by the strength of our family… our actual family, our co-workers, our community, and/or our tribe.

The lungs are associated with the Inner Child and Creativity Gua. To breathe in life's pleasures deeply and fully expands the lungs. When we are open to expressing our creativity, we can breathe in life's joys.

## Energetic Patterns for Individual Rooms

**The Foyer**: Does Not Apply

**The Living or Great Room**: What a great media room this Gua is. Your television, music, DVD station…even X-Box works well here! Gather the family round the game (round of course) table and play games. Monopoly, Rummy, Trivia Pursuit, and Scrabble are great ways to be mindful… literally because you have to think! Have fun while exercising your brain too.

**The Hallway or Stairway**: Place the artwork of young children, either your own or your grandchildren's, niece's or nephew's… hey, you can even ask the neighbor's child to draw something that inspires them. Take a photo of a swing at a nearby park… well, be careful you don't look weird taking photos of children. "Stranger danger" should not have to apply to you! At any rate, a nice photo of a swing with you in it works too, then print Robert Louis

Stevenson's (he's the man!) poem, *The Swing*'s verse onto it. "How do you like to go up in a swing, Up in the air so blue? Oh, I do think it the pleasantest thing, Ever a child can do." Place your childlike prints in a horizontal fashion so that earth supports this fast moving energy area.

**The Kitchen**: The art of cooking certainly embodies the art of creativity, too. If you ever watch the Food Channel, you will know what I am talking about. Anyone who loves to cook will enjoy having a kitchen in this Gua. Our son and daughter-in-law have this floor plan and they are always coming up with yummy recipes. They eat healthy… even baby Gavin (at the time of this writing, he is 20 months) loves to eat all sorts of fruit, vegetables and whole grain breads. Their daughters Abigail, now 9, and Gabrielle, now 8, also enjoy beautiful and healthy foods. Their favorite television channel is the Food Network, go figure!!

**The Bath**: Metal is a container for water and since this area is considered a water room, release and rejuvenate in a safe and secure energy. Be cognizant to use round white or an earth colored bath mat by the sink and the bathtub. Paint the walls in an almond, yellow, linen, or even a light brown… an accent wall of sable brown enriches this room and creates warmth. Metal bath accessories and a metal bowl with radiant gemstones is always a nice touch too.

**The Master Bedroom**: Now this is what I am talking about… get creative! Dream creative dreams; decorate with pastels and mother of pearl. Display your silver hairbrush on a metal tray and show off your exquisite jewelry case out on your dresser. Have twin amethysts on your bedside tables as these denote fidelity and enrichment.

**Guest or Child's Room**: Oh how perfect… if it is a guest room and is not used much, consider creating a hybrid room where you can enjoy your hobbies and crafts. If a child occupies this room, honor his or her interests by creating a thematic room. Soft little ballerina shoes dancing from the ceiling and a framed photo of The Nutcracker Suite against a soft pastel wall (neither over the bed) inspires your little dancer. If baseball is your son's past time, there are a host of symbols to delight him. Safely air out the room so that their lungs can breathe.

**Garage or Storage**: Many garages and storage areas have room for craft stations or even a small workshop. Think creatively and use this space for more than your car or out of season clothing.

## The Sage Meditation

Stand in the middle of your home and face towards the Inner Child & Creativity Gua. Looking toward this area, face this Gua's entrance(s). Think about your intentions for this area. Visualize a Sage wearing a white silken robe with a circle located right over the heart. You now bow and greet the enlightened one. Continue to stand in the middle of your home and stay very still. While taking long and deliberate deep breaths, become centered and grounded. When comfortable with this state of awareness, ask the Sage to reveal this Gua's creative path to you.

As you listen, you will feel led to remove the items that no longer serve you and the objects that will nurture and support your desires. You receive valuable insight and along with this gift, the Sage bestows an exquisite Rhodochrosite gemstone to you. You accept this sacred stone and are at peace that your intentions for this area are unfolding beautifully. Thank the Sage, who is your friend, for this cosmic help, and when you express your gratitude, the Sage returns to the ethers.

If you are not receiving the clarity promised in this process, look opposite this Gua, which is the Family/Roots area. This is the assistant/helper area for this Gua. Be certain this area is de-cluttered and properly balanced. Walk around this area repeating your affirmations for creativity, innovation, inspiration, and playfulness.

## A Jewel to Re*Member

Proverbs Chapter 8:21-32 "That I may enrich them and may fill their treasures full… when he established the heavens I was there; when he set a compass upon the face of the deep, I was there." It was put forth that we have the ability to create, rejoice, and to live in wisdom yet at the same time be childlike. We are timeless, ageless, unbounded, and we are infinite. We are creating our tomorrows today with our words, our thoughts, and our deeds.

# 23

-

## *Helpful People & Travel*

Be Inspired

## Living in Synchronicity ~ Travel/Moving Forward ~ The Father Energy, Refinement

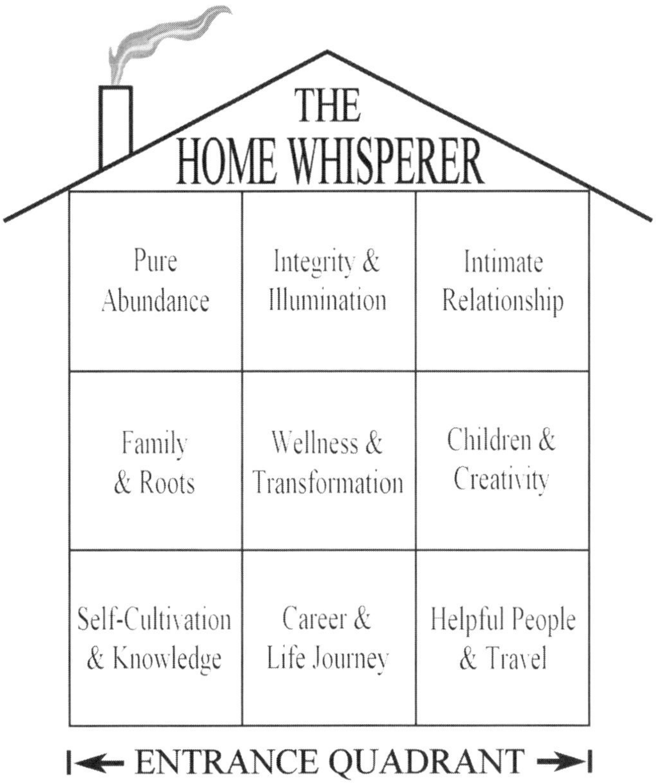


- **Location:** Right lower corner of the Bagua Map
- **Sacred Geometry:** Elliptical-such as the Angel's halo
- **Numerical Influence:** Six
- **Color:** Black, Silver, & White
- **Element:** Yang Metal-Father
- **I Ching Trigram:** Ch'ien-Creative Heaven
- **Operative Words:** Blessings, synchronicity, angelic, father, heavenly, inspiration, refine, mentor, golden rule, compassion, & community
- **Gemstones:** Angelite, Azurite, Lazulite, Pietersite, Celestite, & Silver
- **Chi Imagery:** Angels, globes, metal bells, photos/artwork of mentors, windchimes, crystals, dolphins, Quan Yin, fairies, and silver boxes
- **Season:** Late Fall
- **Directional Energy:** Inward moving, condensing and contracting
- **Affirmation:** I live in synchronicity.

I vibrate with complete kindness.
I Live in synchronicity and vibrate in complete kindness.
I listen to my soulplay and trust its voice.
I am guided and walk in synchronicity.
I call upon the cosmic helpers for all of my needs.

### Visualization

*The cosmic helper's silver ribbon wrapped itself around the Earth. With each swirl, the love of the Father radiated back to the Earth, blessing the people with Universal awareness and intuition. They spoke the language of soulplay. Peace was made manifest within the Earth and within the people's hearts and minds.*

### Angels & Our Guides

Angelic energy and our guides are synonymous with the values of the Helpful People and Travel Gua. Historically, every culture has a version of an angel. Depicted as divine messengers of God, they inspire us to expand our ability to do the highest of good and be the most compassionate person we can possibly be. It holds the potentiality of having angels/cosmic helper's show up before we even ask, and when we do ask for their assistance, it is generously given. Inspiration lines the silver cloak of Helpful People wisdom and enables us to be the helper for one another. There is an old saying that the only way a person can get into heaven is on the arm of someone he or she has helped.

*"We are each angels with only one wing, and we can fly by embracing one another."*
*- Lucretious*

It may very well be that your experience of transformation taught you the necessary wisdom needed for another to reconnect with his or her heavenly self. Sharing the knowledge reproduces the benefits six times over - it is the Law of Reciprocity. Plus, it is a relief to know that all you went through had a purpose.

### The Heavenly Father/Creator Energy

Know that you are not a stray soul; you are a beloved child of the Universe!! Within each of us lies the archetype of the Heavenly Father. It enables us to feel watched over, protected, and safe. From this energy, we are directed, have the ability to be organized, take action, and symbolically, we experience having a loving heavenly father from the inside out. Call forth the help of the heavenly energies via the father, the cosmic helpers and the creative energy therein. They whisper the language of soulplay in your heart.

## Mystical Mentors

This Gua honors our mentors in life who may blissfully reside in this space. Mother Teresa, Jesus, Dr. Wayne Dyer, Ph.D., Deepak Chopra, Buddha, Gandhi, Paramahansa Yogananda, Einstein, Louise Hay, and Oprah - just to name a few - honored the call to create peace and refine harmony in the world through their works, talents, and skills. These pioneers of belief faced times of great challenge and criticism. In retrospect, they paved the way for higher, more enlightened awareness. Just as they did, listen to your heart. Hear how life is calling you to make a difference.

Confucius reminded his people to always welcome the guests from afar as one never knew when the reciprocity of a stranger's kindness would be returned. Giving favor was a natural way of life along the famous China trading routes. They were indicative of wide spread travel and the fortunes brought by way of them increased the people.

This energy reminds us to refine our intentions, create beauty and live in clarity and order. The elegance of this field serves to improve life and see the big picture. It holds the clear sightedness of a visionary and the guidance of gifted leadership.

## Living in Synchronicity

When you experience life in synergy and serendipitous occurrences, you are walking in synchronicity's energetic field. Carl Jung, a Swiss psychologist, brought the actual term of synchronicity to light. He described the process of "temporally coincidental occurrences of causal events." Living in synchronicity is being in the right place at the right time.

Ayn Rand, a Russian immigrant and the noted author of such revolutionary works as *Atlas Shrugged* and *The Fountainhead,* has written about the 2nd day she was in Hollywood. She was standing in front of the Cecil B. DeMille's studio when he drove up and took notice of the young screenwriter. He offered her a ride and then a job on the film *The King of Kings.* During the next week at the studio, she met an actor, Frank O'Connor, whom she later married. They were together until his death fifty years later.

On that fateful day, the doors of heaven opened up for her. She was provided a fatherly hand via Cecil B. DeMille, and this synchronistic moment paved the way for her to express her far-reaching visions. Of course, Ms. Rand was ready for this situation. She was a graduate of a prestigious screenwriting school, spoke several languages, believed in the value of how she lived her life and she had great discipline. She personified the definition of luck, which is, as they say, "When preparation meets opportunity!"

Live your life fully and trustingly in the field of synchronicity. Pay attention to its impact on your life and the lives of those around you. Know that you are in the right place at the right time. Listen to the whispers of your soulplay.

A quick story to share: For my mother-in-law's birthday, I wanted to gift her something unique. We live in a resort community in the Arizona Mountains so shopping is a delightful experience. The numerous charming boutiques offer all sorts of surprises to be found. As I mindfully drove down our main street, my soulplay strongly impressed upon me to stop at one of our antique shoppes. I faithfully listened to my cosmic helper's voice and the minute I walked in the door, I saw the birthday's treasure.

On the wall was a 1947 calendar with a Norman Rockwell-ish sketch of a woman who was identical to how my mother-in-law looked in that year. She was holding a baby. This was indeed special, but the heart of the gift was expanded. My husband and sister-in-law were born eleven months apart—in 1947. Needless to say, she loved the gift and it was an honor to her for the wonderful mother she is. Trust your soulplay voice and walk in synchronicity.

## The Art of Travel

The Travel portion of this tandem reflects moving forward and actual travel from one location to another. To move from one state of mind to the next requires movement. Positive development along life's path is essential to grow. As we have learned, Helpful People and Travel offers the bliss of living in synchronicity. In this same vein, travel yields the virtue of knowing you are in the right place at the right time. The richness of travel gifts the sojourner with a higher education or deeper pleasures.

The Art of Travel enables you to move forward, to change your everyday scenery and "trade up" by embracing change. As you take to the open road, be prepared for swift transformations to take place. Travel light and travel wise, for these renewing experiences will refresh every part of your being. Allow thoughts and plans of travel to swirl around you.

The consideration of travel can be just as much fun as the trip itself. Pouring over travel brochures, selecting the time of your departure and return, coupling your journey with a birthday or anniversary to create special memories or simply traveling for a vacation all have special significance in the Art of Travel.

Ask the question, "Why do we travel?" To me, travel is an adventure where I experience the new and unexpected. I love to immerse myself in other cultures. Exploring historical sites where previous civilizations once thrived opens our mind to fresh visual and auditory experiences. These rich occurrences expand our awareness and teach us more about ourselves.

The neoteric sights and sounds or uniqueness of a place refines our tastes and delights our senses.

When planning a special trip, there are many ways to go. Traveling by land, sea or air will move you from point A to point B, but it is in the travel itself where you will truly unravel the mystery of self. The alchemical experience of travel possesses the ability to transform one's deeper self. The Art of Travel requires you to be flexible, be kind, be open, and be adventurous. To perfect the Art of Travel, always expect the best of circumstances to unfold. Do your homework and know where to mine the area's richest treasures. And remember to leave yourself some free time. This is where the unexpected nuggets reveal themselves.

Your private vehicle, train, or bus can take you places. For those who love the ocean, visiting Hawaii or any island could be just the place for you. Or a cruise might be on your horizon. Where one sails at night, explores foreign ports by day, has the convenience of only unpacking once and you can enjoy all of your meals, exercise, socializing and entertainment on board. After flying into a departure location, you can float away to Alaska, the islands of Hawaii, the Mediterranean, Europe, Africa, India, or South America.

Traveling by airplane can test your manners and strengthen your ability to cope. However, it is wonderful to cover great distances in so little time. Flight delays are an opportunity to catch up on your reading or if you have your laptop computer; you will not skip a beat.

Become a tourist in your own region and tap the Chamber of Commerce's rich system of information. Enjoy the Art of Travel in your surrounding splendor by hiking, biking, horseback riding, golfing, or roll back time by spending the day antiquing. Take in a movie where reel magic suspends your reality by transporting you to the past, present or future via the silver screen. Visit your local library where amazing books take you to far away places, expanding your universe via "arm-chair" travel.

Dream, develop and expand your personal Art of Travel by way of books, movies, boats, cars, planes or trains. Cultivate these pursuits, for surely they will enrich your travels, refining and defining your unique Journey of Life.

## Blessings

Blessings are a form of angelic, fatherly, heavenly, synchronistic, answers to our deepest and most secret desires of the heart. The matrix of a blessing extends itself from the thought level out into the universe and back again into our real time and space through several codes.

First of all, think POSTIVELY and RELEASE your desires to the heavens, removing all attachment. It is a quantum law that when we change our thoughts, our outer experience of temporal reality also shifts as it all begins at the thought level. Secondly, it is essential to *believe*, as belief really works! Know that you are a beloved child of the Father-Mother-God and worthy of receiving blessings. Thirdly, celebrate your synchronistic manifestations. Fourth, notice the needs of another and secretly fulfill that desire... this can be as small as sending a card to uplift their spirits or sending money to meet some of their financial needs... be the INSTRUMENT OF A BLESSING. Fifth, understand that ENERGY or the desire of your heart in its most basic form is the material of the Cosmos and it also exists within you.

This creates the attractor energy to pull it to you like a magnet. This energy literally broadcasts the energy of quantum physics. It begins at the thought level so continue to believe, think positive thoughts, release, celebrate, be an instrument of blessings and create attractor energy by all of the above.

## Colorful Perceptions

The colors of black, silver, and white are associated with Helpful People and Travel. Black symbolizes the endless opportunities existing for each of us. Black is the absorption of all colors. It possesses depth, sophistication, elegance, mystery, and harmony.

White: Purity, white light of awareness and clarity White is not actually a color as it is the reflection of all other colors. It represents purity, sharing, reverence, peace, and humility.

Silver: Many Feng Shui books denote the color gray for this area. To me, silver has always been my choice. Silver's luminosity is a mirror to our soul. Silver removes negativity, promotes popularity, and is a balancing agent. Carrying a silver nugget or wearing silver is said to bring great advantage, such as refining one's communication abilities and adding elegance to one's sphere. The magical properties of silver are furthered by placing a silver box, silver envelopes, silver purses, silver containers, or a silver folder in the Helpful People and Travel Gua in your home or on your desk. This exercise aides you in the following ways:

**Wishes/Intentions?** Write down your wishes and place them in one of the above vessels. Simply ask the Cosmic Helpers assistance. In turn, they deliver your request directly to the Universe. Know that if these wishes/prayers are for your highest good, they will be manifested and show up in perfect and divine order in your life.

**Creative Projects?** Do you have endeavors on the forefront that requires originality and innovation? Ah-ha! You have come to right place. Write an invitation to your muse, asking for divine inspiration, inventive ideas and novel concepts to come to you. Place these requests in the silver container. They will pour forth by your giving thanks and being joyous in the process.

**Challenging People?** If you know a person who is not a happy camper and just being around them is an energy drain, place their name in the container of your choice. See them as happy, delightful, and contented. Yes, it may be a stretch. This is a person who needs your help and when you clean up people pollution, you are furthering the world.

**Selling A Home?** if you are selling your home, place your realtors' card in this place.

**New Job?** Place this desire in the magic silver holder and allow the Universe to be your agent of change. Press the Cosmos into service and get ready to receive. Re*member, it is important to do the work as we know the definition of luck is when preparation meets opportunity. Silver also represents higher spiritual truths, travel, reliability, intelligence, and friendship.

## Numerical Influence

The number six holds the energy of beauty, charm, art, and spiritual awareness. The talents of a visionary are evident in this pattern as are service, understanding, synchronicity, inner truth, harmony, inspiration, community, generosity, philanthropic deeds, and volunteerism. This Gua supports outgoing authority, leadership qualities, and an eye for detailed work lending itself to highly analytical abilities.

**Living in a six home** is dedicated to the energy of compassion and comfort. The harmony afforded in this home creates an opportunity for balance. However, the deep sensitivities of the residents of this home might become sequestered. This can be avoided by keeping one's activity in the world flowing. The reclusive energies are usually spent in meditation or reading to enlighten the residents, within and without. A healthy balance is attained through generosity and receiving.

A six home creates synergy where you will find synchronicity is a daily occurrence. The support of a six home engenders intimate marriages and close friendships. When a family resides in a six home, the loving nature of the home stimulates open communication and caring relationships. Inspiration and compassion set the stage for innovative ways to make the world a better place.

A six home is an excellent place for budding artist, poets, and writers. The energy is conducive to getting in touch with the rhythm of thc universe. The beauty and serenity of a six home nourishes one deep within. This kind of nurturing enables one to give and successfully teach those who have not yet discovered how they too can prosper… mentally, physically and spiritually. Mentors, counselors, philanthropist, anyone wishing to express and experience beauty and art will flourish in a six home.

## Elemental Persuasion

This masculine yang metal energy is focused on mental activities and the processes of refinement. This inward moving energy contracts and condenses. Metal unifies energies in concert and pulls them together.

## Friends

You will love the energy of angelic, Quan Yin, faeries, and/or Buddha figurines. Not only can you consider these chatzkies for your noble home's Helpful People and Travel, but the front right hand side of your desk is an excellent location to call forth your blessings and helpful folks/networking opportunities. Glass garden globes and actual globes of the world are excellent symbols for moving forward. Metal bells, Dolphins, photos/artwork of mentors such as Dr. Wayne Dyer, PhD, Deepak Chopra, Gandhi, Mother Teresa and even a photo of your earthly father is excellent in this Gua.

Metal or ceramic hands - when my daughter was five; she gifted me with an exquisite pair of ceramic hands that she painted a soft white with pale silver cuffs. I love these and have always had them where I could enjoy their sweetness. In addition to the above objects, a metal wind chime, and crystals of any shape or size.

Blessings stones are rocks of any kind that have rings around them. These rings are indicative of it being a sacred stone and hold the wishes of its bearer to fulfill. At a very young age, I collected ringed and heart rocks. I love finding these ringed stones along our walking paths. You can even write your affirmation or intention on them. During your prayer/meditation time, they are wonderful to hold. Remember the energy of gemstones such as Angelite, Azurite, Lazulite, Pietersite, Celestite, & Silver are powerfully supportive to this Gua's inner and outer inspiration.

Several years ago, I was dreaming of a beautiful silver box and one day, our daughter gave the same dream box to me. I use this small box to drop my client's business cards and I write the names of everyone with whom I am collaborating to place in this special box. If your home is for sale and you have it listed, place your realtor's card in a silver box in your Helpful People and Travel Gua. In our 7 Streams of Energy business, we have a silver cardholder for our patrons and for their businesses to prosper. It sets intention for us to be their helpful person and a liaison to their greater wellness.

For my business to expand, workshop intentions for the highest idea of energy to be presented, and for all my co-creative processes, I have a large silver envelope that I use to inspire and move these projects forward. Within this magical envelope, I have placed business plans for investment consideration, ideas for an invention, and even postcards of exotic and interesting places we plan to visit.

### Foes

In the counterproductive cycle of the elements, fire is the strongest foe of metal's energy. It is best to keep the colors of red or orange to a bare minimum along with shapes of triangular, conical, or pyramidal configurations.

### Associated Trigram

Ch'ien - Per Hannah Moog and Carol Anthony's I Ching interpretation, "The Judgment; the cosmic consciousness is great through its interpenetration of all things; it discerns what feels harmonious and brings it into form through transformation. …The words, 'it discerns what feels harmonious' refer to the conscious response of the Cosmos to everything that happens. The cosmic consciousness is a *feeling* consciousness that also thinks. The conscious response is a thinking response that is expressed in the cosmic words, "Yes" and "No." It says 'yes' to what feels in harmony with its unity and what benefits all of its part. It says 'no' to what feels harmful to its unity (discord) and retreats from it. Thus, as a whole, the Cosmic Consciousness is a system of harmonics with self-defined parameters."

The phase "… and brings it into form through transformation" refers to the fact that the cosmic consciousness employs transformation rather than changes as its primary way of operating. Through transformation, it brings into form what feels harmonious. The result of this is Nature.

"Penetrating" also refers to the way cosmic evolution is carried out as far as humans are concerned. It occurs through the invisible penetration of harmonious thought and feeling from one person to everyone around him. In order to know what feels harmonious, every person possesses a cosmic memory of what cosmic harmony feels like. This memory is located in every body cell. It is meant to guide human thinking and help humans find the correct words and names for things - words that express their essence. When feelings of Yes and No come from a person's inner truth into his fully conscious mind, and are then acted upon by saying the inner Yes or No to them, they penetrate without effort or intention to the inner truth of those around him."

### Sacred Geometry

Elliptical - such as the Angel's halo is the shape of this Gua.

## Symbolism

The Cosmic Helpers of Transformation thrive in the Helpful People/Travel energy. Please refer to the Glossary section to refresh this valuable teaching

## Seasonal Cycle

Early Autumn… consider the harvest, the time of year when the color of amber dresses the oak trees, and golden-yellow topaz adorns the ash trees. In fact, the Ash is the perfect symbolism for community. They grow underground in the network of a strong root system.

## Energy Patterns for Individual Rooms Specific to Helpful People and Travel

**Living or Great Room**: This is an excellent room for this Gua, as it usually doubles as the family's media room. Please be mindful and keep your television exposure in balance and always know that YOU make the program choices, not the media. The silver, black and white surfaces of the televisions, DVD & CD players, the surround sound that sometimes accompanies these devices and the stories they bring into the home are avenues to greater awareness. As described in the Art of Travel, "reel" magic is always a delightful experience. Choose your viewing selectively and if it is of the highest expression, so will be the energy in your home.

**Foyer**: If your foyer is located in Gua, it is the perfect place to serve as a transition from the outside world and the inside world. Second to the Career/Life Journey Gua, and symbolically, this is the ideal placement for a foyer. Placing a mirror in this room is symbolic of doubling your aspirations to serve. A mural, portrait, or painting of an angel is appropriate for this area.

**Stairs or Hallways:** This could be viewed as a stairway to heaven. Please make sure you have a large painting at the top of the stairs to bring the energy up and not have it flowing out into the street. If the stairway is even with the front door, place a circular rung with a mandala pattern on it in between the two. This mat circulates the energy around the home slowing it down so that your resources are not pouring away from you.

A hallway will create lots of change in this area. Introduce red items to burn off the tendency for circumstances to move too fast. Hanging a fully faceted Austrian crystal on a 9" inch red ribbon from the ceiling or on the bottom rung of the stairs will also pool the energy, yet keep it flowing back into the home.

**Bathroom**: Bathrooms are symbolic of release and elimination with regard to letting go of those things that no longer serve you, and renewal in the form of healing. Silver accents best suite this room, where you can lounge in a long soak in the bathtub. Music and fragrance wafting through the air reminds you of a spa like environment where you can keep your head in the clouds and simply relax. Have angelic photos or figurines in full view.

**Home Office, Study, or Library:** Again, this is an excellent placement for these rooms. The energy of community from any of these patterns is supportive. The Home Office will realize additional networking opportunities for the resident. The Study/Library is a place to learn.

**Dining Room**: Being of service in the community comes home to the dining room that showcases a wealth of hospitality. Host dinner parties in this room and make it come alive with your friends and fellow neighbors. Have a potluck where everyone brings a dish from their family's home country… albeit generations past. Display items from your travels and when traveling, purchase souvenirs specifically for entertaining. Allow the conversation to flow filling the room with cheer and hearty laughter.

**Kitchen**: Display your post cards and play places you have yet to visit on a Vision Quest board. Use the side of your fridge and every time you notice your distant travels to be, do something to activate that wish. Pull up the area's history, locate it on a map, do a map quest and post it. Traveling by train, plane or car? Find magnets in these symbols and apply them to your fridge too. Find an angel of traveling mercy and put her in the group.

**Storage Areas**: Place a battery-operated mobile of angels in this area. Activating this otherwise stagnant Gua will boost your social activities. I have several angels in mine to liven up the place.

**Master Bedroom**: This is a haven of celestial energy just waiting for you to go to sleep and dream. Keep a dream journal by your bed and upon waking recall your dream visits and dream visitors. On the wall, have dreamy photos of other worlds and angelic realms being displayed. For an added enhancement, place elegant small silver and small black pillows upon your bed Use silver frames and a silver vase to hold.

**Bedroom:** Many of my clients have their guest bedrooms located in this area. My first question is always, "How often do you have guests in this room?" Frequently, we will double this space up as a craft room or create a hybrid space in this area. In any event, the goal is to keep the energy moving.

## Seasonal Cycle

Late fall

## The Sage Meditation

Stand in the middle of your home and face towards the Helpful People and Travel Gua. Looking toward this area, face this Gua's entrance(s). Think about your intentions for this area. Visualize a Sage wearing a silver silken robe with a located right over the heart emerging. You now bow and greet the enlightened one. Continue to stand in the middle of your home and stay very still. While taking long and deliberate deep breaths, become centered and grounded. When comfortable with this state of awareness, ask the Sage to reveal this Gua's inspirational path to you. As you listen, you will feel led to remove the items that no longer serve you and the objects that will nurture and support your desires. You receive valuable insight and along with this gift, the Sage bestows an exquisite Celestite gemstone to you. You accept this sacred stone and are at peace that your intentions for this area are unfolding beautifully. Thank the Sage, who is your friend, for this cosmic help and when you express your gratitude, the Sage returns to the ethers.

If you are not receiving the clarity promised in this process, look diagonally opposite this Gua, which is the Family/Roots. This is the assistant/helper area for this Gua. Be certain this area is de-cluttered and properly balanced. Walk around this area repeating your affirmations for inspirational, synchronicity, moving forward, and travel.

## Jewels to Re*Member

*Create a helpful and productive community circle whose abilities complement and harmonize with your own. Build healthy alliances that support one another meeting your neighbors' needs. Redefine what community should look life. Stretch across past boundaries and into the global market. Extend yourself beyond all limitations.*

*The Cosmic realm is but a breath away. Celestial helpers wait to be called forth and pressed into service. Re*member their mission is to help you. Ask, ask, ask... there are cosmic helpers for banking, shopping, exercising, traveling, hair, health, wisdom, family fun, joy, abundance, insights, intimate relationship, creativity, innovation, inspiration, and synchronicity. These are only a few... there are thousands of Cosmic Helpers. They are in the unseen world and they faithfully are standing by your side. Call them forth.*

# 24

–

# *Career & Life Journey*

## Believe

## Courageously Navigating the Waters of Life – the Flow

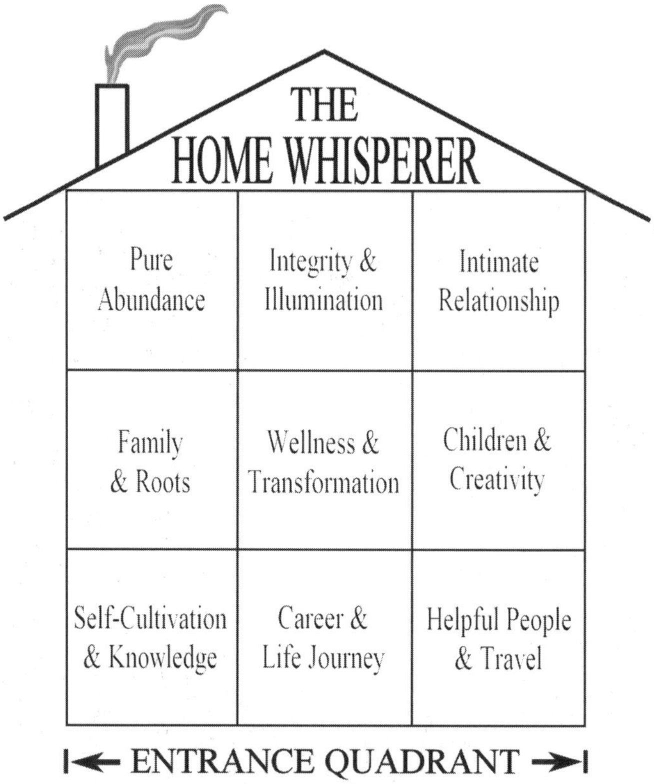


- **Location:** Bottom center of the Bagua Map
- **Sacred Geometry**: Curvilinear
- **Numerical Influence**: One
- **Color:** Black, Deep Blues
- **Element:** Water-Middle Son
- **I Ching Trigram:** Kan, Deep Water
- **Operative Words:** Motivation, Flow, Alignment, Courage, & Trust
- **Gemstones:** Black Spinel, Jet, Obsidian, Pearl, Black Onyx, and Adamite
- **Chi Imagery:** Photos or artwork of bodies of water, all objects in the colors of black or deep blue, aquarium, pond, and/or a water fountain
- **Season:** Winter
- **Directional Energy:** Downward and diagonal
- **Affirmation:** I trust every phase of life. I am in the flow.
  I am a joyous, fulfilled, successful and centered person…I believe in myself and with an open heart, and I completely accept success. I am valuable.
  My life is in perfect & harmonious balance. I honor my skills by fully expressing my

talents in the career of my choice.
I have placed myself in the flow of an infinite stream of success.
My career easily flows and I experience the waters of fortunate blessings
I Appreciate Myself-I Attract Honest and Trustworthy people into my life
My home resonates with renewal and rejuvenation. It blesses all who visit with a deep calm and tranquility.

Merging your private dreams into your public responsibilities expresses the depth of your being without comprising the desires of your heart. Working and playing in the flow creates fresh days filled with abundant opportunities. The promise of one's life path is to experience the intertwining of fulfillment and purpose. The curvilinear energy symbolic of water is associated with this Gua. It represents life's infinite possibilities. Navigating the uncharted waters of your career/life journey with courage and sincerity reveals your true inner self. Think of water's mystical, meditative and flowing qualities. The imagery enables one to connect with the highest order of courage. Life can be riddled with ups and downs just as rivers run from high to low and like the ebb and flow of the ocean. Such is life but when you are centered deep within, you experience calm and serenity. Serenity holds a space for you to delve deep within core of your being. In this profound place, the ambiguity of your true purpose is revealed.

As Ranier Marie Rilke's great poetic insight revealed, *"There is only one journey. Going inside yourself."* Turning within to reflect on your life choices strengthens your inner connection to the mysteries of the greater web of life. Working and playing in the flow creates fresh days filled with abundant opportunities for continual renewal. The Career/Life Journey symbolizes the waters of rejuvenation and release to bring wholeness to your life journey. This alignment acts as a bridge across the great abyss or the dark night of your soul carrying you into positive transformations. When motivation, authenticity, peaceful, and meaningful experiences are yours, clearly you are on your perfect path.

Flowing within the center of your being is a connection to the mysterious waters in the greater web of life. Invite positive Chi by creating a winding path leading up to front center of your home. You can easily do so by planting flowers in this wavy pattern or by placing flat garden stones in a meandering configuration. Say "thank you" to life and refresh yourself in the deep realization and manifestation of living your highest purpose. BELIEVE!

Throughout the course of our lives, we fully experience the expansiveness of the ocean, the streaming of a river, the calmness of a lake, and the majesty of a waterfall. Deeply lodged within each experience is the opportunity to connect you with your destiny. In this place, you are refreshed and rejuvenated. You are perpetually linked with Cosmic Consciousness and when venturing out in right action, you are less likely to experience life's shadowy waters where indecision confronts you. Reflection yields clarity and by working through challenges, you discover your true gifts. Your talents are sometimes hidden within the cloak of adversity. So say Yes, Yes, Yes to turning an obstacle into a steppingstone.

The Lotus is the symbol of renewal and grows in muddy water. The Lotus flower closes at night and sinks under the murky water, at dawn it rises and opens fully once again. Untouched by the muddy waters, the lotus rises above the surface to bloom beautifully, thus it represents victory over adversity. It also symbolizes the purity of heart and mind. It is the path and search for enlightenment. The Lotus flower is one of the most ancient of terrestrial symbols. Be like the lotus and regardless of the waters you find your self in even hot water, look within for your gift and you can transform yourself!

If fear attempts to rob you of your destiny, know that there is a lifeline. Within this chasm lies the opportunity to shape of your future. For it is only from these subterranean recesses (the emotional waters of uncertainty) where potentiality unfolds. At some point in time, everyone has passed through these very same shadowy waters. These choppy currents such as illness, a death of a loved one, weariness, doubt, and depression will challenge every fiber of your being. Again, summon courage calling on your ability to believe in the best outcome. *Fear knocked, faith answered and no one was there.*

## Numerical Influences

*One* is the number associated with Career/Life Journey. It represents individuality, originality, fresh new beginnings, purpose, advancement, innovation, confidence, and following your feelings and intuition. It embodies the entrepreneurial spirit to embark on the journey of heart and follow your dreams. This energy supports your highest and most secretive aspirations. The number one enables you to confidently and creatively work through all challenges and be healed of any past isolation you may have experienced. It encourages determination, leadership and to go with the flow.

**Living in a "one" home** is conducive to a person who is self-employed or the driven person who can succeed by doing most of the work alone. A one home is nurturing of self and if by any chance there are several strong individuals at this address, they will learn to creatively work with this strong energy. The number of one encourages purpose, direction, and taking the initiative to see things through.

## Colorful Perceptions

Black, navy blue, and/or very deep and dark tones are associated with the Career/Life Journey Gua. Black is symbolic of the mystery of life, spirituality, intellectual depths, wisdom and continuity. Blue is the agent of truth representing clarity of communication or it can be indicative of having the blues. As aforementioned, there will be watery depths in your life when you may experience emptiness in your careers/life journey. These times call out for courage and motivation. To find happiness, look within. By designing a supportive home, you can safely go within to reflect and meditate. This process allows you to find and experience the fulfillment you are looking for. It begins with you. Creating flow inspires you to be more creative, arouses resourcefulness, births courage that develops into additional confidence. Confidence lives side by side with knowing. This ability renews and transforms your genuine self. Be the true you not the blue you. Express your genuine self. The definition of the word genuine is "to be original". Since there is not another you in circulation, convey who you are, freely express your ideas knowing you are gift to the world.

## Elemental Persuasions

Water is associated with this Gua. Also, connected is the moon and all nighttime activities such as dream work.

**Dreams**: Historically the significance of dreams is symbolic and/or metaphoric. They are intended to reveal deeper insight or an overview of a pressing situation or upcoming circumstance. This is a spiritual connection to greater awareness and the experience may capitulate you towards greater wisdom. These nighttime visions are indeed mystical experiences.

Prior to going to sleep, ask the dream weavers to send you soul awareness through insightful dreaming. If you have a project that is taxing, bring it up on your mind's screen and give thanks that it is being resolved. If you have a special desire of the heart, see it on a large movie theatre screen. You can feel as though you are in the audience watching it all come to pass. Smile as you slip into a wonderful night of deep rest.

Upon waking each morning, take a few moments to reflect on your dream activity and then jot down your thoughts in a dedicated Dream Journal. This process will be the beginning of your dream symbols and their meanings. It is important that your archetypal symbols line up with YOUR point of reference. Dream books often draw from older energies and might have some negative connotations. For example, for as early as I can recall, dreaming of a carrot always meant unexpected windfalls for me. However, some Dream books have said that carrots mean something different. This is a personal journey and although many of your interpretations will line up with universal symbolism, there are many that will have greater personal relevance.

## Keep Dreaming!

To insure that your dream messages are remembered, create a personal sanctuary… a private retreat in your bedroom. This dreamy space is where comfort should reign supreme. Within these walls, your bed has a clear view of the bedroom door….not your home's front door. Make sure you do not have your bed on the common wall of your bathroom. If your bed has a view of the bathroom, keep the bathroom door closed. Surround yourself with tranquil objects allowing this room to transport you into the portal of sweet dreams.

It is best to have a tall headboard to support your nighttime journey. Avoid all dead plants (always a good rule of thumb) in this room and be certain that you have a wreath of energetically brilliant silk flowers on your wall. A wreath promotes unity. Two nightstands of equal proportions should flank the bed and each stand can have a lamp. Remove all exercise equipment. Plus, this is not the best place for a desk. Please do not bring work to bed with you. Instead, drift off to sleep with thoughts of many blessings on your mind. Make it a habit to name at least ten things to give thanks for that happened that day.

It is essential for you to make the time for reflection. All of the answers you seek in your life journey can be found within. The mystery is unveiled in the watery depths of dreams, meditation, and journaling.

## Geometric Shape & It's Symbolism

The curvilinear or wavy line represents this Gua. Think of its free-form movement and consider all of the patterns therein. The asymmetrical line is symbolic of flowing. Look at the magic square and notice the water's icon; you can doodle this curvy line and not grow tired. This icon placed on business card logos, in signage and of course actual curved items placed at your front door, bring in blessings and encourage them stay for a long while. To create a wavy path to your front door, plant or simply place flowers or paving stones in this wavy pattern.

## Personalized Enhancements

Programming your environment with the intelligent property of NO FEAR creates an atmosphere where courage can develop. Courage is where success and enterprise live. *"With courage, you will dare to take risks, have the strength to be compassionate, and the wisdom to be humble. Courage is the foundation of integrity." ~ Unknown*

Surround yourself with any of the following objects and increases you Career/Journey Chi. Blue or black or very dark items, swimming pools, aquariums, gold fish bowls, fountains, mirrors, crystal or glass; photos of lakes, streams, oceans, waterfalls; items with your company logo; items or fabric that flows… like paisley! Affirmations or quotes with key words.

## Associated Tri-Gram

K'an means Deep Water. It represents independence, self-reliance, hard working and endurance. Finding yourself in the abyss is the perfect opportunity to be in touch with your inner self. Life awareness is sometimes gained from a place of discomfort. It is not designed to be a place to linger so please know that with courage, you will get to the other side of all challenges. Moving through these dark waters protects you from the danger. Your courage, confidence and capacity for making decisions from the inner depths of your being permits you to 'follow your bliss'. When Joseph Campbell coined that phrase it was out of his desire for everyone to know that when you make the decision to do what you love, clarity and even the money will absolutely follow. This is the Universal Law.

The I Ching states, *"One is faced with a danger that has to be overcome. Weakness and impatience can do nothing. Only a strong person can stand up to his fate, for his inner security enables him to endure to the end. It is only when we have the courage to face things exactly as they are that a light will develop out of events, by which the path to success may be recognized."*

The calm of your deep inner waters nurtures and relaxes you. Think of the relaxation as a bubbling brook, lake, stream or the ocean offers. Imagine yourself in one of these surroundings. Taste the salt in the sea breeze, hear the water in the brook wash over the rocks and as you dangle your feet in the water, feel it splash you, or sit on the dock at the lake and watch the sun rise. Immerse self in nature's calm.

As you are drinking in the renewal of the water, envision being suddenly whirled out of your serene setting. Oh my, you just became distracted and you are now running from appointment to appointment, balancing your cell phone with the steering wheel of your car and thinking about the work you have to do on the upcoming project. Whoa! What happened? Until you slow down and let your dreams, intentions and the desires of your heart catch up with you, you will not be aware of them when they do show up. Slowing down does not mean to become less productive, oh contraire, it simply means for you to become more organized allowing this system to support you and your dreams.

Distractions can be interpreted as holding up your progress, but remember, nothing can keep you from your "good". Even though it might seem you are being sidetracked, this is life's way of balancing your life. If you have to reach the ocean by way of the stream and then the lake, you will get there. Stay in the flow and in the know.

Every day make an appointment with yourself and observe your day. Reflect on its activities, evaluate the direction you are flowing and take the time to redirect any activity that is taking you away from your purpose. Core vales and the alignment process are essential to being in the flow.

## Seasonal Cycle

The season associated with Career/Journey is winter. In this place, we are encouraged to evaluate our past and move into the future with courage. Truly, our potentiality lies in the unbridled awareness that we create our life path through our belief systems, and in turn, our possibilities are just like the ocean they are vast.

This is the time of year to be mindful of regrouping and reflection. New Year's Resolutions are in order. Align your New Year's resolutions with your core beliefs. As much as possible, withdraw from the outside and take the time to restore, rejuvenate, rest and renew your soul and your body. It is a time of homecoming where you can plan to live into life's richest possibilities--they are achievable. This is a time of healing and from this space, you discover how to embrace life's transitions and life's flow.

## Energetic Pattern for Individual Rooms Specific to Career/Life Journey

Each room has an energetic pattern. See how the Bagua is a metaphor for your home. When your Career Bagua falls in any of the following areas, the following information helps you to understand how to truly benefit from the room's strengths.

**Living Room or Great Room:** This is an excellent room for the Career Gua as it offers a place for you to show case your authentic self. Who you truly are! Even if you are quite and reserved, your Yin–like approach to living will be evident and your guests will respect your privacy. If you are an outgoing personality, your inclusiveness will also be greatly appreciated and respected. This is the room to place a metal turtle, the long time symbol of abundance and stability in one's career. The turtle reminds you that the path is certain and steady so enjoy it and be consistent. Be true to yourself.

**Foyer:** This is the place to let the universe know that you are willing to do what it takes to grow and increase your lot, be a positive force in the world, create abundance, flow freely and enjoy life. Turn on your porch light, locate a fountain (to scale) flowing in here, place a mirror in this room, and be certain that your greeter is of a welcoming sort. You can also place red silk geraniums in this space…geraniums are actually considered a water element and red in of course is highly energizing. Place a bamboo flute over the inside of your doorway with red tassels and the musical end pointed to the heavens. This symbolizes inviting in the richest of life's experiences…family joys, rewarding relationships, and of course, the free flowing and nurturing waters of life itself.

**Stairs or Hallways:** Be certain that your stairway is not pouring out all of your resources if it lines up with the door. If this is the case, you will also find that you are easily drained. If there is room and it is safe to continue to use the stairs, place a jade plant in pottery on the bottom rung of the stairs. If possible, place a crystal between the stairway and the front door. Although a major project, it is preferred to turn the stairway into another room by engineering a small diversion for the bottom two stairs. An erected half-wall/screen serves to display your greeter.

**Bathroom:** This is excellent as the water element of this room will support and serve you in your quest for career/life journey excellence. When not in use, keep the toilet lid down. Place a plug in the shower and sink and unless you are draining your bathtub after use, keep this large area plugged too. When you go into a bathroom, you can feel the energy being pulled down because this is the direction of water's natural flow.

**Home Office, Study, or Library:** The placement of an office, study or library **will** enhance your greatest aspirations for career/life journey fulfillment and the opportunity for advancement. Do not let your back face the door, as this will burden you with backstabbing and gossip. Look forward and anticipate all of your most precious intentions that are sure to manifest.

**Dining Room or Kitchen:** This is rare, but it does happen…side note, this is why I prefer Essential Feng Shui because there is always a solution. Take the time to enjoy your meal planning, shopping and preparation. Relax in this space as it has a direct connection with your work habits. Eating in a hurry is likely to have you rushing through important steps at work. You are more suspect to overlook important details that could be an issue. Set your table with your best crystal and china, place flowers on the table and remove your projects. Find another niche for these because candles floating in an elegant bowl are better suited here, as they will softly light the room. Check to see if your refrigerator and stove line up in front of one another. If so, this will create power struggles. If they do, simply place a yellow dishcloth on the handle of the oven. Keep these areas spotless and never leave dishes in your sink. Otherwise, you will experience back-ups in your deadlines, blockages in your payroll and stymied increases in your pay raises. Oh yes, you will not be appreciated for the wonderful job you are doing!

**Storage Areas:** Take inventory of what you are storing there. Is there a connection to the state of your career to these items…as in boring? If this room is not a dedicated storage area such as a closet, then move everything out but the items appropriate to this room. If this a storage area or closet, hang a fully faceted crystal on a nine inch red ribbon and/or install a mirror in the very back of the closet and face it towards the door. Please do not place it on the floor and lean it against a wall, as this will create a fun house effect. You do not want your career to be distorted. Up the wattage on your light bulbs…let's get that energy lit up. As always, keep this area de-cluttered.

**Bedroom:** Please see the information listed in this chapter under dreams.

**Outside:** To keep the flow, hang wind chimes, install water fountains (always to the left of the door looking outside), display beautiful and well- tended flowers…think of what dead flowers must be saying to your career. A clean entrance is a must. Let the winds of fortune blow your way and the waters of life nurture and prosper you.

The Sage- Meditation

Stand in the center of your home and face your Career/Life Journey Gua. Think of your Career/Life Path intentions and affirm great good thanks for this area giving you all of the support you have enjoyed. Now visualize a Sage wearing a black robe with an embroidered golden wavy line located right over the heart. You now bow and greet the Sage. You know deep within that each of your precious intentions will unfold in the life's journey, its current, its beautiful flow. Allow this Sage to be your friend. Once you are comfortable with this idea, please allow the Sage to present your with the pearls of wisdom. When you "receive" them, rest in the knowledge that anything and everything are possible.

Remember the ripple effect? Dropping a stone into a pond changes the entire eco-system of this environment. Around the stone's entry, rings begin to ripple out. This effect is an excellent teaching for your life journey. When you take responsibility for your Career/Life purpose and ask yourself why you are doing what you are doing.

See yourself in the middle of that pond and notice your journey's ripple effects. Experience the success and you are capable of creating through your present career. If you wish to change this career, consider your many options. At night just prior to falling asleep, give thanks for the impeccable career that gives freedom and expression of your talents and skills, where you will be appreciated, is in alignment with your values and offers a business or art culture of growth, integrity and abundance.

Simply make a choice to be a positive power in the world. Live with what you love in a clutter-free environment and take excellent care of yourself. Drinking the right amount of water every day enables your body and your mind to stay in the flow. Get the rest you require, as a stressed-out person is not having fun. Weariness will cloud even the sunniest disposition. Make it a habit to notice the beauty in the world, focus on the positive and stay in the NOW. Live in the mindset that everything you lend your hand to holds purpose. Be in the flow.

## Dream Big Dreams

Only speak in positive and present terminology such as, "I enjoy great good success instead of "I *will* enjoy great good success" Imprint your mind and subconscious with these orders. With a large smile on your face, repeat these journey mile markers daily and necessary out loud.

In your notebook, write down your Intentions for your Life Journey/Career. It is essential for your intentions to be written in your own personal handwriting. Remove all fears or doubts and allow yourself to dream without limitations.

*Jewels to Re*Member*

*"Hard things are put in our way, not to stop us, But to bring out our courage and strength." ~ Anonymous*

# 25

-

# *Self-Cultivation & Knowledge*

## Be Still

## Discern the Wisdom Within the Quiet

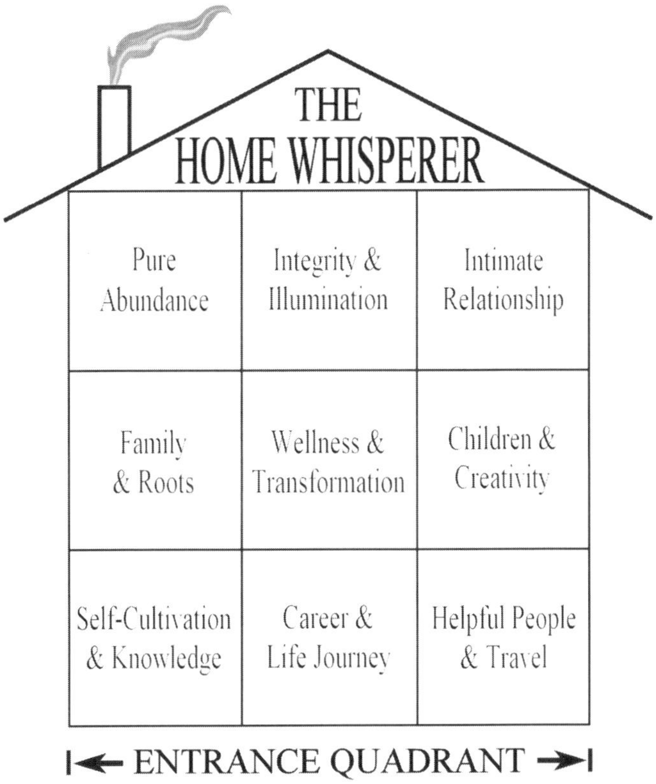


- **Location:** Lower left corner of the Bagua Map
- **Sacred Geometry:** Horizontal Rectangle
- **Numerical Influence:** Eight
- **Color:** Royal Blue, Green, & Black
- **Element:** Yang Earth/Cultivating Wood
- **I Ching Trigram:** Ken, the Still Mountain
- **Operative Words:** Inner Peace, Tranquility, Meditation, and Wisdom.
- **Gemstones:** Lapis Lazuli, Butlerlite, Blue Topaz, Feldspar, & Lazurite
- **Chi Imagery:** CD's/books on study subjects, photos/artwork of a mountain or wise people you look up to, mandala, & Yin/Yang.
- **Season:** Early Spring
- **Directional Energy:** Downward
- **Affirmation:** I rejoice and live in peace, freedom, and joy. My path is enlightened with clarity and wisdom.

  I rejoice and live in freedom, and joy.
  My path is enlightened with clarity and wisdom.

I live in the wisdom of my being and I am at peace.
I am calm in the sacred time of meditation and I listen.
I am the Lotus, I am Peace, I am Wisdom

Visualization

*Being still and the ability to hear the "quiet" embodies the Universal Consciousness's highest idea of wisdom. In this stillness, a lotus opens up in our heart and in turn, we are within her center. Her petals flower into full bloom. We are one with peace.*

The art of meditation is at the heart of Self-Cultivation and Knowledge. It begs the questions, "How much time do you spend in the Quiet?" – and – "Are you able to hear, truly hear the inspirations from beyond this time and space?" This organic process begins at the first stage of development. The application of study refines your knowledge of the cosmic web of life. Learning offers new growth. Meditation and education offers a clear communication with higher universal forces. Stillness is a place of alert readiness. Cultivating the art of contemplation inspires inner truth to reveal itself. During challenging times, this tranquility will support your every action.

During your time with this all-knowing silence, be still and listen, really listen to what the Cosmos is trying to share. Open your mind and ask the Sage within for assistance to receive insight and wisdom. Gift yourself the sacred time and space to reconnect with your True Self.

This True Self knows the importance and value of self-cultivation and knowledge, self-discovery, self-education, self-fulfillment, self-respect, a healthy sense of self, self-awareness, and self-love. This Self is waiting for you to call and she will faithfully answer.

Meditation promotes peace, tranquility, grounding, and noble heartedness. Wisdom is fostered from within and the process enables you to deepen your relationship and know your True Self. From this place, you are able to trust your inner 'knowings' and act accordingly. Your opinions have value and you matter!

In times of antiquity, the emperor of the dynasty sought to improve his court by adding scholars. Every year, a test was given to the oldest son of local commoners' families. Since the Self-Cultivation and Knowledge area is located in the front left hand side of your home, while facing inside towards your home, it is where these young boys improved learning skills and enhanced their self-mastery. If a son passed these rigorous tests held in the capitol, the entire family was brought into the court to live. In today's world, this is remains an excellent location for a study/library, an altar, meditation room, or simply a room to reflect on the beauty and joys of life. Be secure in your oneness with ALL THAT IS.

## The Art of Peace

Paramahansa Yogananda shared the following insights/affirmations on peace. Be still and Be One with his wisdom and truly feel the words resonating within you. For true peace is only found within.

"Peace flows through my heart, and blows through me as a zephyr.
Peace fills me like a fragrance.
Peace runs through me like rays.
Peace stabs the heart of noise and worries.
Peace burns through my disquietude.
Peace, like a globe of fire expands and fills my omnipresence.
Peace, like an ocean, rolls on in all space.
Peace, like red blood vitalizes the veins of my thoughts.
Peace like a boundless aureole encircles my body of infinity.
Peace-flames blow through the pores of my flesh, and through all space.
The perfume of peace flows over the gardens of blossoms.
The wine of peace runs perpetually through the wine press of all hearts.
Peace is the breath of stones, stars, and ages.
Peace is the ambrosial wine of Spirit flowing from the cask of silence,
Which I quaff with my countless mouths of atoms."

Invite peace into your life by turning off the television or radio… remove white noise and listen to the quiet. In addition, for dedicated meditation, please consider creating a beautiful altar. This ritual blesses you. The time you spend in prayer/meditation takes you beyond linear time and actually adds back to you more time to live in the field of synchronicity and peace. I have experienced this phenomenon. When I call the Cosmic Helpers to work with me regarding pressing responsibilities, health questions, or even what to prepare for a sumptuous meal, I am given the perfect answers/insights.

I have a room dedicated to meditation/prayer, but if you do not have the space available there are many ways to create an altar. The trays used for serving meals in bed are perfect, as are TV trays. Place a fresh flower in a vase atop this tray, if you have one – add a meditation scarf and/or a symbol of your highest ideal of life. This could be a feather-messenger from the heavens to your heart, a bell for creativity, Quan Yin figurine for compassion, or a candle that represents your passion. I have gemstones on my altar that have specific energies/frequencies such as a piece of Lapis Lazuli that stimulates enlightenment and contacts spirit guardians. It enhances dream work. Since I meditate early in the morning, this is a time to drift and I often recall my previous night's dreams during this time. I allow them to be positively "downloaded," and then I move through them in peace and contentment.

## The Chakra System

Auras or the colors of red, orange, yellow, green, blue, indigo, and violet emanate from all matter and are connected to the charkas system. Chakra is from the Sanskrit word and means "wheel of light. When I first began this study, I was drawn to it because I have seen auras for many years. It was interesting to see how they corresponded with the information I had intuitively received over the years.

The colors are created by the spinning vortexes of energy within our bodies. There are seven energy centers that run up the spine. They begin at the pelvis area and continue up to the top of your head. Beside the color that is associated with each chakra, there is a musical or tonal note that clearly influences the specific energy for that particular chakra. They each have a unique energetic field and vibrate accordingly. Our bodies are open to color and absorb it. When we think about these colors, vibration, and the organs each chakra is connected to, we can improve our well-being.

Chakras were first mentioned 50,000 years in the Egyptian civilization. Throughout history, cultures have discovered this system and used it for balancing, restoring energy to the body, and to improve a person's health. In reference to Feng Shui, the chakra system has the following teachings:

**First Chakra:** Kundalini -Family/Roots (Belief Systems received from parents, grandparents), located at the base of the spine, color-red, tone is C, and influences the sexual organs, bladder, prostate, colon. Gemstone: Ruby

Second Chakra: Spleen –Pure Abundance (Fulfillment), located in the middle of the pelvis, color orange, tone is D. Influences the intestines spleen, and hips. Gemstone: Aquamarine.

**Third Chakra:** Solar Plexus -Integrity/Illumination (Sense of Worth-We are sensitive to the opinion of others), located in the solar plexus, color is yellow, tone is E, and it influences the stomach, liver, gall bladder, and adrenals. Topaz or Peridot

**Fourth Chakra:** Heart –The Unity & the Intimate Relationship, (The Healers such as Buddha, Jesus, Yogananda, Mother Teresa), the center of the chest, color is green, tone is F, and influences the heart, lungs, ribs and upper digestive track. The ability to attract or draw to yourself; what is desired is expressly related to enrichment. Since money is energy and green is associated with money, when you give from the heart, you will never lack. The brighter the auric field, the greater the ability to attract and sustain is at play. IN fact, true abundance and energy are mutually equal. Gemstone: The healing stone is the Emerald

**Fifth Chakra:** Throat –Inner Child/Creativity, (Expression to speak or to teach, spiritual leaders, divine rulers signifies the ability to speak Truth). It is located in the back of the neck and the throat area, color is blue, tone is G and it influences thyroid, teeth, and lower jaw. Gemstone: Sapphire and Lapis Lazuli.

**Sixth Chakra:** Third Eye Helpful People and Travel (Inspiration, intuition, and insight. To make a difference, the move forward; Mentors, Spiritual Friends), located between the brows, color is indigo. Tone is A; Pituitary Gland, nose, ears, eyes, the brain. Gemstone: Alexandrite

**Seventh Chakra:** Crown - Career/Life Journey (Encourages us to release and be aligned with the Courage to Trust-this is area of saints and prophets). Top of the Head, color is violet, tone is B, and influences the brains-innovative ideas. Gemstone: Amethyst

**Eighth Chakra (Transpersonal, 18" above the crown of the head):** Self-Cultivation and Knowledge. Meditation/being able to make spontaneously truthful choices. Not usually shown on the traditional Chakra system, however it is the influence of cultivating wisdom and enlightenment./ The It shines from the etheric body and reflects our perfect emotional, physical, and spiritual body, it is the pattern of Wholeness. Gemstone: Diamond

## Colorful Perceptions

Royal Blue - The agent of truth representing clarity of communications. There are watery depths in your life when you may experience emptiness. These times call for faith; the royal blue is majestic. Blue as stated in the Family Gua (Chapter 19) is associated with the intellect, peace, meditation, spiritual understanding and tranquility. Blue is also the color of greater soul awareness as it denotes compassion and is considered the mediator of Truth. In the marketing field, blue is utilized to create value in all products. Since blue doesn't create an emotional response as the more charged colors evoke, it is never used to market food items.

Green - The color green is considered to be peaceful and is associated with ecology. It is hopeful and possesses strength. It inspires creativity, mature growth, renewal, eternal life, prosperity, beauty, learning and contentment.

Black - This color represents the mysterious and the infinite. As shared in the Career/Life Journey Gua, this color is symbolic of the deeper issues of life, spirituality, intellectual depths, wisdom and continuity.

## Numerical Influences

Turned on its side, the figure eight becomes the sign of Infinity. Truly, meditating creates infinite resources to flow into your life. It stands to reason that this number also represents self-empowerment and Cosmic Consciousness. More than any other number, the eight is a financial and materially broadening energy. The focus gained through meditation enables one to attract enrichment via fulfilling life experiences. Tiger Woods has stated that his mother's Buddhist loyalty has given him the gift and the ability to be focused.

The vibration of eight encourages on being thoughtful and encompassing one's spouse and family's needs. Wisdom in spending and investing is always important while attracting and wisely investing great gains. The understanding of "KNOW THYSELF" is most applicable here. And of course, the timeless adage, "To thine own self be true."

Eight represents the Cultivation of Knowledge, Financial Gain, Self-empowerment, Perspicacity, Wealth, Achievement, Gifts, Compensation, Dividends, Benefits, Profit, Global Conscious Awareness, Abundance, and Infinity. Eight is associated with large corporations, which takes the symbolism of a mountain to new level. Balancing the finite with the infinite and matter with spirit creates an aptitude for successful business. Skillful planning and developing a wise inner self yields abundance in spiritual and material matters. Cultivating the art of contemplation reveals the paths one should take and inspires naturally accurate actions. This practice enables you to discover the hidden treasures of your inner and outer home via transcendental awareness. You will learn about the jewels of yourself and your surroundings.

**Living in an eight home** can be compared to hitting the lottery. As you cultivate self-mastery and financial acumen, and as you apply discipline, your worldly possessions will be plentiful. Even before financial comfort is evident, the flow of many friends and family in and around you will always be present. Omnitude is the operative word in an eight home. Balancing financial responsibilities and being sensitive to the cares of others is extremely important in an eight home. The fullness of life pours forth for the residents of an eight home. As they develop greater skills and higher education, leadership and recognition of their many accomplishments is supported. Where integrity is present, honor and prestige will follow. Organization is essential in an eight home. By paying homage to the clutter-free life style, the residents avoid self-imposed blockages. The eight home residents will not sit on their laurels, as they know the importance and responsibilities of opulence and abundance. Through managerial excellence and keeping their priorities clear, great good success can be acquired in this energy field.

## Elemental Persuasions

In Essential Feng Shui tm, this is considered a wood energy... the growth/cultivation of inner truth. Through my own experience, I resonate with this teaching. The increase of the inner self through meditation is an organic process developing a wood-or new experience of awareness. Plus, its season is spring and this refers to a wood pattern.

Other Feng Shui disciplines teach the earth element as a support system in this section. It is derived from the trigram of Still Mountain. Use your own understandings in this Gua to better develop your insights. I will say that I will never place water in this Gua so there is a part of me that says to also honor the earth element.

### Friends

Photos of meditative or Zen gardens. Books, books, books, and more books on subjects you are studying, simply interested in or would like to see in your life. CDs or DVDs on the topic of meditation. A copy of The Secret is an excellent chatzkie for this Gua. Photos/artwork of a mountain, a yogi, a knowledgeable person whom you admire, and/or a mandala, items in the colors of black, blue or green are perfect here as are scrolls with prayers or even a prayer shawl or a meditation scarf draped over your altar. Gentle music. Lapis Lazuli gemstone - it is said that King Solomon wore a ring with this stone. I worked with a general manager of a large radio station and this stone came up for him to acquire. That weekend, he and his wife attended a gemstone show and he won the door prize. Yes, it was a gorgeous Lapis Lazuli ring from Afghanistan. Just a reminder… set you intentions and BELIEVE!! Other stones are Blue Topaz, Feldspar, & Lazurite.

### Foes

White noise breaks the nervous system down and creates spiritual and mental clutter. Daily newspapers and some monthly magazines are full of negative chatter. They will work to hide your treasure and keep it hidden. Any items that slow down your ability to process your highest ideal of life, such as junk food - sugar will rob your treasure chest. Unwise choices are certainly a foe to your inner peace. If you have a presentation to give and the night before, you choose to stay up too late watching a horror movie… well, you might not be at your very best the next day. Choose to take care of yourself by eating healthy food, getting plenty of exercise and thinking wonderfully positive thoughts!

### Sacred Geometry

Horizontal Rectangle represents concentration to go beyond the language. Language wraps an experience into the material whereas meditation looses it to timelessness, the intuitive. At this level, spiritual mysteries are unraveled and the significance of visualizations is revealed. The horizontal bar symbolizes an altar where you can better understand your life's callings. It also represents the still mountain.

### Associated I Ching Trigram

Ken ~ The Still Mountain. Per Hanna Moog and Carol Anderson's translation, "Not expecting/not projecting," the Sage informs us, is a person's natural state of mind. It means residing in one's center, where discernment springs spontaneously from the feeling of what is harmonious and what is discordant. Such a state is in harmony with the Cosmos and draws its help in all situations."

### Seasonal Cycle

Early spring is the time of year associated with Self-Cultivation and Knowledge. As the bulbs are beginning to appear, early spring reminds us of our inner wisdom that, although seemingly dormant, is ever present. The knowledge within each cell of your body has memory. This memory possesses infinite wisdom and all you have to do is listen.

### Energy Patterns for the Individual Rooms

There is a template that creates itself within this flow of energy. When a room falls into a certain Gua, it takes on significance beyond itself. This is so with the earth energy as it prepares you to go beyond self.

**Foyer:** This entrance calls to your inner home treasures to come. Place a greeter in this room to welcome guests into your sacred space. I have seen a life sized Quan Yin in this Gua and it spoke the language of beauty and grace.

**Living or Great Room:** Should one of these public rooms be located in this intimately private Gua, you can create privacy by arranging a reading corner. Place an overstuffed black, green or blue chair in a corner with books of your interest nearby. I even have noise reducers that I wear if I want to be totally engrossed in my reading. To discover your home's hidden treasure of wisdom, inner peace, and calm, look within.

**Stairs or Hallways:** Paint these walls in a quite shade and within this space display photos of your mentors. Stairways will create a faster moving energy than most areas so setting a plant in a royal blue ceramic vessel (to scale for the stair treads) on the bottom step slows the energy down.

**Bathroom:** Located in this Gua, this room is highly supportive when you display photos of Zen or meditation gardens. My bathroom doubles as my second meditation room. During my bath, I release old energy patterns by soaking in a salt or aroma-therapeutic bath. I prefer pampering my mind, body and spirit with Hugo's Vegan soaps. They are exquisite! Create a place of renewal and hear what spirit is saying.

**Home Office, Study, or Library**: If an office is located in this Gua, the challenge exists of a nagging voice that says, "Instead of meditating, you should be working!" You can still that voice by creating sacred time within your work routine. If a library is in this Gua… hurray! This is perfect as you can curl up on a comfortable couch or comfy chair and read away. Anything you must learn will have a greater chance in this room. Honor any of these rooms by placing a photo of your mentor.

**Dining Room or Kitchen:** Nurturing and healthy meals strengthen, bless, and sustain you in the best of possible ways.

**Storage Areas:** Even in a closet or storage area, there exists the opportunity to honor your teachers and mentors, and it can even be a room to place your altar. Place a fully faceted Austrian crystal here.

**Bedroom:** Relax, renew, release, and rejoice in the quiet of a bedroom. Use all of the ideas suggested in the Intimate Relationship area, but add a chair in the corner of this room to meditate or read in. Recent clients of mine created a reading nook in their once - harried bedroom. They placed meditative icons, a framed photo of their wedding date written in Mayan, they removed everything that spoke too loudly, and the transformation in their lives was profound.

## The Sage- Meditation

Stand in the middle of your home and face your Self-Cultivation and Knowledge gua(s). Affirm great thanks for the inner peace that you now enjoy. At this time, visualize a Sage wearing a royal blue robe with an embroidered infinity symbol located right over the heart. You now bow and greet the Sage. The Sage hands a silk pillow with a beautiful Lapis Lazuli ring atop. You accept this ring and place it on your finger… it fits perfectly. You thank the Sage, who is your friend for the cosmic help. Walk into the room's center and close your eyes. Become very still and take long, deep breaths. Continue to Be Still. Give thanks for the Sage's support. Bow and allow the Sage to return to the ethers.

Please recall that there is a map of energy within a map of energy. Now that you have brought this section(s) of your home into alignment with trust, commitment, bliss, loyalty, receptivity, and love. Stand in the doorway of the room(s) and look into the room(s). If there is more than one room, map the energy separately according to each of the entrances. Line the bottom of your energy map up with the doorway and have a grand time Feng Shui-ing this room(s) accordingly. Make these changes with an open heart and a mind clear of clutter. If there is a question regarding where to place what item, remember the dominant energy will always be the one of the larger Bagua.

*"What you are now is the result of what you were. What you will be tomorrow will be the result of what you are now. The consequences of an oppressed mind will follow you like the cart follows the ox that pulls it. The consequences of a purified mind will follow you like your own shadow. No one can do more for you than your own purified mind. No parent, no relative, no friend, No One. A well-disciplined mind brings happiness." - A Buddhist Saying*

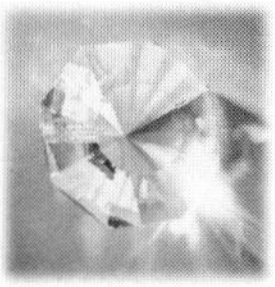

A Jewel to Re*Member

*"Happiness is when what you think, what you say, and what you do are in harmony."*
*- Mahatma Gandhi*

*"Anyone who has a library and a garden want for nothing." -Cicero*

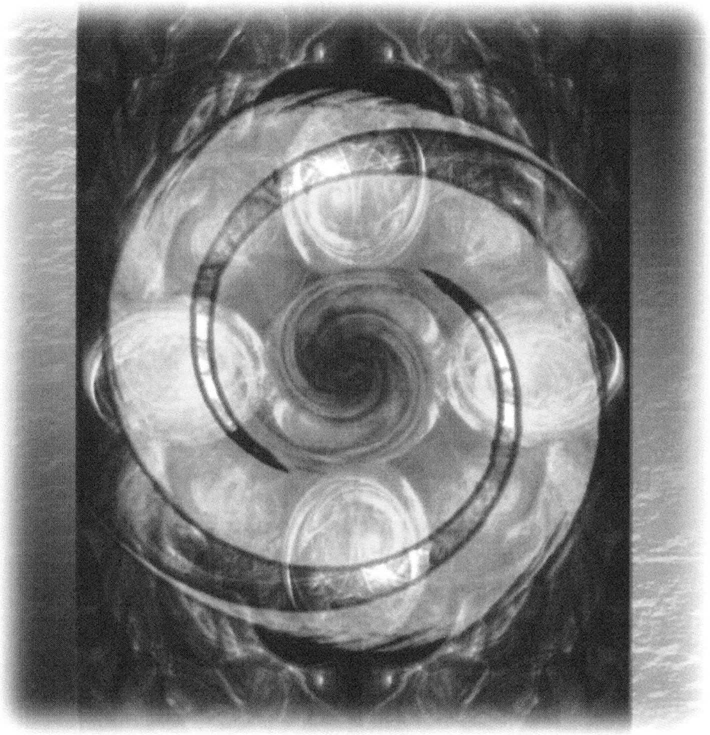

# 26

-

# *Unity/Chi*

## Be Well – Be Transformed

*"Your purpose here on the Earth is to give the gifts that your soul desires to give; those that create harmony, cooperation, sharing, and reverence for life, no matter what form they take."*
*~ Unknown*

## Dancing the Dance

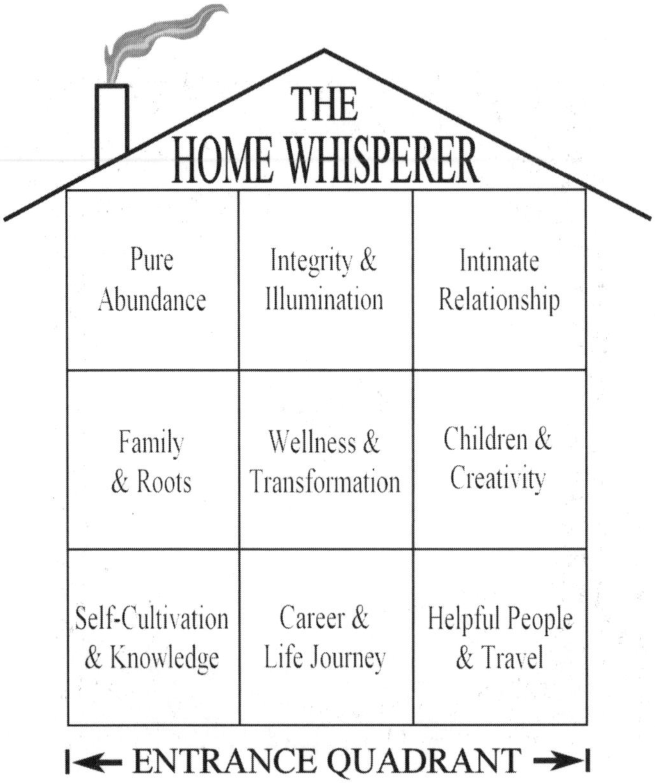


- **Location**: Center of the Bagua Map
- **Sacred Geometry**: Square
- **Numerical Influence**: Five
- **Color:** Brown, Orange, Harvest Gold
- **Element**: Earth
- **I Ching Trigram**: This is the hub. It is symbolized by the Yin & Yang… the center is only as healthy as its outer influences and the outer influences are only as centered as the core of its being. It is the dance of the elements in perfect harmony with the Universe.
- **Operative Words**: Centered, Balanced, Harmony, Grounded, Stability
- **Gemstones**: Citrine, Andalusite, Red Jasper, sapphire, topaz, and amber
- **Directional Flow:** The center is only as powerful as the external guas and the outer guas are only as strong as the center. The inner creates the outer and outer reflects the inner.
- **Imagery**: Items made of brick, ceramic, pottery, or concrete. Things that are square or flat. All items that are the colors of yellow, brown, terra cotta, orange, and/or earth tones. Items in groupings of five and photos of mountain ranges or desert landscapes.
- **Affirmation**: I am centered in life's journey
  I enjoy stability and I am grounded.

I am secure and I am safe.
I am beautifully connected and supported by Mother Earth.

## The Unity of the Bagua

*"If there is righteousness in the heart, there will be*
*Beauty in the character. If there is beauty in the Character, there be*
*Harmony in the home. If there is harmony in the home, there will be*
*Order in the nation. If there is order in the nation, there will be*
*Peace in the world."*
*- Celebrated Confucian Proverb*

Be Well and Be Transformed holds the energy of harmony and balance. It literally creates unity and wholeness. This wholeness is focused on being centered. In a world that is moving all too quickly, it is essential to be grounded and present.

Whatever is in the center of a home or room sets the precedent of the energy's movement. This middle area should be free of furniture and open to the other elements. The hub is only as healthy as the surrounding Guas and the surrounding Guas are supported by the center of the Bagua. This is where all of the energies are combined and able to achieve balance. In turn, this energy pushes out in all directions. The Tai Chi or Unity Gua is nurturing and is the support system for the other Guas. Below is an overview of the Guas and their values. They are as follows:

**Family: Be Strong**. The gift of strength allows us to trust the process and not be surprised by challenging events. Cultivating deep roots creates trust and just as the tree's branches sway, we should be flexible.

**Pure Abundance: Be Grateful.** Be deeply grateful for your numerous blessings. Honing your skills and talents enables you to prosper.

**Integrity and Illumination: Be Enlightened**. Living with integrity fosters poised confidence, and ushers in the illumination of clarity.

**Intimate Relationship: Be Receptive.** Embody the qualities of the people you want to see in your life. Be trustworthy, honest, faithful, committed, be love.

**Creativity and Children: Be Joyous.** Align yourself with the energy of creativity and joyous life experiences open up for you. Invite your inner child to express playfulness and see how fun life truly can be.

**Helpful People/Travel: Be Inspired**. Inspiration comes from within study the lives of masters to bring your genius forth. Be the helper and thus be helped. Walk in the field of synchronicity. Relish in being in the right place at the right time and embrace moving forward.

**Career/Life Journey: Be*lieve.** Courage is a bridge across the great abyss or the dark night of the soul. Walk past this darkness or fear that attempts to defeat your success. Navigate the uncharted waters of your career/life journey with courage and sincerity. Merging your private dreams into public responsibility expresses the depth of your being without comprising the desires of your heart.

**Self-Cultivation/Knowledge: Be Still.** The art of meditation is at the heart of this wise Gua. Silence beckons you to BE STILL. Gift yourself the sacred timeless-ness of the beyond and be one with wisdom.

## Closing Sage Meditation

Please stand in the middle of your home and envision that you are standing on the Yin and Yang Symbol. As you turn into the stillness, visualize all eight Sages standing in their relevant Guas. They move toward you to re*mind, re*enforce, and increase the blessings of strength, gratitude, generosity, integrity, illumination, love, creativity, inspiration, courage, and wisdom of your inner and outer home. Re*member, all of these values are within your awareness for time immortal. Each attribute has a keen and upbeat energy. Bow and thank the Sage for these treasures. The Sage now returns to infinity. Whenever you need assistance, please ask the Sage and cosmic helpers as they walk beside you. You are a pearl and you are connected within the web of life.

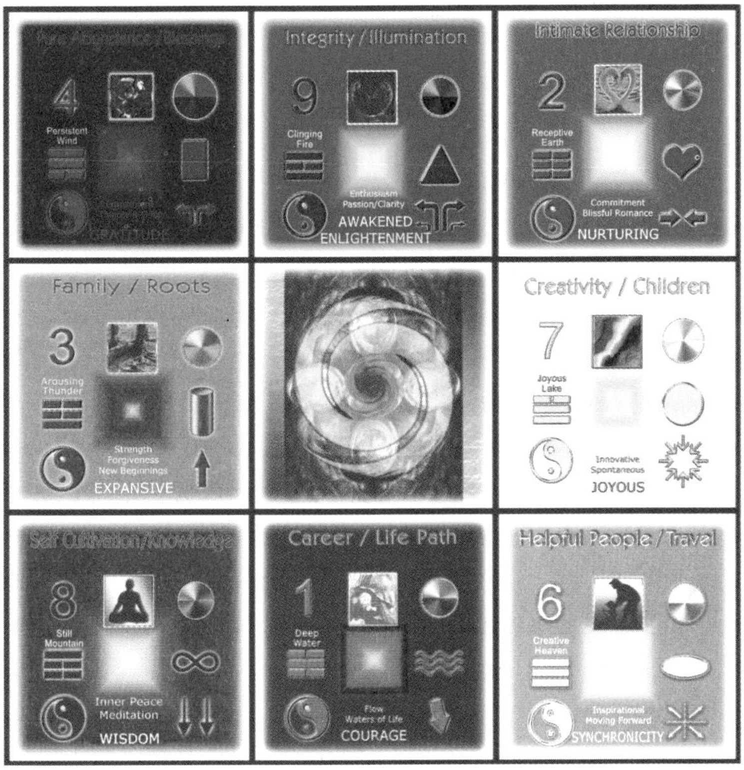


# 27

# -

# Matrix of Your Miracles

A matrix is a pattern that contains information. In mathematics, it is a rectangle that has rows and is multi-dimensional in its structure. The Bagua replicates a matrix in our three-dimensional space, as it is a form that provides a transformational map through its matrices by association.

A miracle is considered an event so out of the ordinary that its cannot be explained by the laws of nature. Such an event arouses awe, admiration, and wonder. It is an act that causes us to marvel, be astounded and recognize that it is supernatural. In fact, our everyday lives are the transmission of the miraculous. In 2002, my workshop, *Stepping Into The Miraculous,* encouraged the attendees to begin to see the extraordinary hidden within the ordinary. There has always been a strong movement to build such awareness and we are fortunate that this teaching shows up in many different places.

Please note the illustration at the beginning of this chapter. This includes all of the numbers, colors, five elements, and cycles - productive and controlling energies that are present within each Gua. As a matrix, the Bagua shows us how to map the energy of our physical space. When we balance the energies, we create a sacred space. As we have learned, a sacred space transforms and enhances the quality of our lives.

In this chapter, we will discuss how this matrix can support an even deeper aspect of our being. Each Gua has a corresponding Gua. As you look at the Bagua, notice the opposite side or diagonal correspondence to each section. They are the Family/Gua in relationship to the Inner Child/Creativity; Pure Abundance in relationship to the Helpful People/Travel; Integrity/Illumination in relationship to the Career/Life Journey; and the Intimate Relationship's association to the Self-Cultivation and Knowledge. Working in the reverse, you will see the importance of one to another such as the Career/Life Journey is supported by Integrity/Illumination to enhances one along life's journey by the high standards your adhere to.

The Inner Child and Creativity section is directly opposite the Family/Roots area. In order for creativity to freely pour forth, it does so more fluidly if we are supported by the strength of our family… our actual family, co-workers, our community, and/or our tribe. This relationship is two-fold in that the support of the family inspires the spontaneity of the inner child and thus, pure artistic ideas can be expressed. Inner Child and Creativity's mission promotes open mindedness. Being strong and rooted empowers us to create and speak from the treasures of our inner truth. In reverse, the more creative and fluid we are, the more supportive we can be to our Family/Group.

Diagonally, let's look at the Pure Abundance and Helpful People/Travel Guas. On so many levels, they are interrelated. We have already shifted our homes so that time after time, they are whispering nurturing and loving thoughts to us. So you might be asking, "How do we improve on that?" Just look at Helpful People/Travel. This is an infinite opportunity to serve and serve from the greatest of all places, generosity of self. The Helpful People teaching inspires us to be the highest ideas of ourselves, to walk in harmony and balance on the earth plane and to know the heavens are guiding us.

To be a helpful person and to have helpful people in our lives promotes the flow of good will, abundance, enrichment, and well-being. The travel part of this Gua reminds us to move forward and grow. When we experience our thoughts and hearts in the spiritual realm, we are open the new paradigm of an outstanding business model. We have insights that relate to wise investing and sound financial choices. We are safe, we are prosperous, and we are living in abundance.

Flip those two Guas around and notice that when we are prosperous, we can be an even more helpful person. We can donate our funds to worthy causes, we can bestow gifts upon children and grandchildren, and we can create a legacy that thinks about giving to our heirs for at least seven generations beyond us.

Being a helpful person to the heirs we will never see sets an example of the wealth of true generosity. Establish a foundation to gift your monies to causes that speak to you. Being abundant is a gift to the world, for truly, when you are generous and prosperous, others respond to that gift in you and recognize it in themselves.

Abundance in others actually belongs to humanity. One person could not achieve his or her abundance without the helpful people in their life. When abundance is shared abroad, others respond and this feeds their own ability to share. It creates a model of humanity being the highest idea of itself.

Integrity and Illumination is vertically opposite Career/Life Journey. We are known for what we do, what our profession is, and where our interest lies. All around our enchanted cottage, we have beautiful flower gardens. On numerous occasions, I have been tending to our gardens when a passing motorist has stopped to comment on how beautiful our home and landscaping is. I am grateful that we are known for creating beauty. It is the law of reciprocity, for having a garden gifts us with infinite blessings. It is an honor.

With passion and enthusiasm, you can enjoy earning a living doing what you love. No, you may not be able to quit your day job just yet. However, through the Career/Life Journey and Integrity/Illumination tandem, you can perceive enlightened awareness. The Career/Life Journey Gua influences our nighttime dreams. Prior to going to sleep, give thanks that you are earning a living doing what you love. Even if you do not like where you are presently working, give thanks for it.

Fall in love with everything you are doing now and this creates the ability for you to move through. Gratitude opens the portal to integrity's leadership and passion, and enables you to go with the flow of your life's journey. Being grateful is a glorious and mysterious energy that, when practiced, shows up as living a life you love. Step out of survival programming and begin to live with integrity. Illumination empowers you to create an enriching life path.

The Intimate Relationship Gua is associated with commitment, bliss, trust, and going beyond our present selves to dance in the perfection of giving and receiving. In order to enjoy a loving and reciprocal relationship with another, we must first know ourselves. Appropriately the diagonal energy for Intimate Relations is Self-Cultivation and Knowledge - don't you just love this stuff? When we nurture ourselves, we are then able to nurture another. It is not the other way around. Part of Intimate Relationship's teaching is learning to receive. Begin from the inside and know that as you cultivate your knowledge, wisdom comes forth. You are always in an intimate relationship with yourself and when you are deeply fulfilled and content, your ability to love is unlimited. Re*member what Robert Ogden said, “To love, love, and love is love’s greatest prerogative.”

Re*member what Robert Ogden said, “To love, love, and love is love’s greatest prerogative.” With yourself and others, cultivate relationships of abiding good will and loving trust. These values foster deep and sustainable contentment.

The center… ah, everything flows through the center. This hub is only as strong as the perimeter and the outside gains its strength through the center’s balance and harmony. This centrifugal force blesses, expands, and is in continuous movement, while simultaneously, it is rock solid and ever so still. Plus, the process of being useful is a proven way to stay youthful. Step into the matrix of your miracles and be the blessing, and in the course of events, you are also blessed.

| | | |
|---|---|---|
| PURE ABUNDANCE<br>4<br>Yin Wood<br>Eldest Daughter<br>Purple, Blue & Red | INTEGRITY & ILLUMINATION<br>9<br>Fire<br>Middle Daughter<br>Red | INTIMATE RELATIONSHIP<br>2<br>Yin Earth<br>Mother<br>Red, Pink, White & Yellow |
| FAMILY & ROOTS<br>3<br>Yang Wood<br>Eldest Son<br>Green & Blue | CENTER<br>5<br>Earth<br>Brown, Orange & Harvest Gold | CREATIVITY & CHILDREN<br>7<br>Yin Metal<br>Youngest Daughter<br>White, Pastels & Gold |
| SELF-CULTIVATION & KNOWLEDGE<br>8<br>Yang Earth<br>Youngest Son<br>Royal Blue, Green & Black | CAREER & LIFE JOURNEY<br>1<br>Water<br>Middle Son<br>Black & Deep Blue | HELPFUL PEOPLE & TRAVEL<br>6<br>Yang Metal<br>Father<br>Black, Silver & White |

# The Matrix of the Bagua

In the previous chapters, we discussed … nd each of the Gua's unique support systems. Within this wisdom is where … nced. It is time to learn how to decode the matrix of your miracles. Ea… nce and this determines how the energy flows through this area.

Family/Roots
Inner Child and Creativity Number.

Pure Abundance — Nu… ateful
Helpful People/Travel — +Numb… nspired
=10 Synchro… stic Good Fortune

Integrity/Illumination — Number #9 - Be Enlightened
Career/Life Journey — +Number #1 - Believe
=10 Stand in the Radiance of Self
Your Light Lifts Humanity

Intimate Relationship — Number #2-Be Love
Self-Cultivation/Knowledge — + Number #8-Be Still
=10 Receptive to Wisdom

In numerology, the 0 is the symbol for infinity. So to the power of 10, we drop the 0 and advance it to the state of being #1. One represents our life path, the journey our soul is making, the understanding that life is a winding path. The #1 represents the Career/Life Journey Gua. Water is its element, which is meandering or curvilinear. It is essential that we re*member we are supported, we are loved and we are being guided. We are One - we are connected.

Add in the middle number of #5 ~ Be Well & Be Transformed

When we add in the #5 that is in the middle and stands for Unity, to the sum of 10, we come up with 15 and 1 + 5 = 6. The number #6 is the path of service and represents the helpful person. For truly, whatever path we are on, we are here to serve.

# Part Four

-

# Feng Shui Gardening

# 28

# -

# The Art of Energy Gardening

From gardening in a container to having at your disposal generous acres, there are some very basic rules of green thumb for a Feng Shui garden. First of all, just like we have applied principles to our home and workspaces, we can now use those same tools and apply them to our outdoor rooms.

My husband and I arc avid gardeners and we know using the Feng Shui principles has enhanced our garden immensely. Honoring the Bagua map will enliven the Chi in your garden. It is most auspicious to create your beautiful garden in a perfect square or like we did, in a rectangular shape. This way, you will not have to fill in any missing corners, but if you do - you know the drill. Simply "plant" stones to complete your space.

When it comes to planning your garden based on the art of placement, it is simply delicious. Select a location for your garden by thinking about the elements. Consider its strengths. Sit in this chosen spot at different times of the day and get a sense of how the shadows (if any) play against the site. Notice if your outdoor room is partly shaded or full sun. This will come into play when you are selecting your flowers, plants, and veggies. Always site your garden in a stable area that does not have run off. We live at the semi-bottom of a hill and it is wonderful to have a soft stream running into our home. However, our neighbors are below us and in the monsoon season, their backyard resembles the rushing Brazos River.

**1. Site your garden on higher ground**

A garden is a place to reflect, connect, project, and simply dig your hands into the soil and be one with nature. There is a great sense of balance derived from gardening. To be certain that you will fulfill all of your gardening desires and needs, create a plan. Since our garden is already sited, the first decision we made for our garden was how we wanted it to function. Depending on our travel schedule, we fluctuate with our gardening variety. This year, we knew we would be home most of the summer to tend to it. However, we each had a great many projects (mine was to finish this book!) and so we limited our garden to allow us the time to enjoy the entire gardening process.

**2. Have a Plan and then work the plan.**

**Draw a sketch of your garden to be and research the flowers and veggies you want to plant. Using the Bagua, you can see where to plant what, so allow it to be your treasure map. Again, notice the sun and where to best locate your plants and veggies.**

The tilling of the earth is an excellent exercise of new beginnings and making ready for the rich soil of potentiality to bring forth blooms of wisdom and enrichment. When you begin this process, you will feel the excitement bubble up in your belly. And if you are getting your back into it, you will feel every muscle you have not felt in a very long while the morning after.

3. **Do the dirt work and always build up the soil with organic nutrients. Look into building a compost pile**

Since we have lived in our enchanted cottage in the woods for seventeen years, we have collected an interesting assortment of garden statuaries and outstanding rocks and memorabilia. In fact, many of our travels find us in garden shoppes where we select souvenirs for the garden. I have an amazing angel weather vane from Jamaica and a lovely garden globe from St. Augustine, Fl. This is just food for thought because these can add whimsy and personality to your out of doors room. So begin gathering up your treasure troves to place in your garden. You can walk through your home and see many items that can live out doors. Stay away from wooden objects as they weather too easily.

Viewing our garden from our kitchen window, our laughing Buddha makes me smile and the host of angle statuaries assures me they are watching over and blessing this sacred space. Upon another glance, I can see the little boy and girl (in metal) joyously flying their kite around a glass globe of blue swirls. They are located in our garden's Inner Child and Creativity gua. How delightful this is?

3. Statuaries, wind chimes, gazing balls, and Buddha give your garden a deeper meaning.

This is the main reason for gardening is to enhance your properties Chi and to raise your own vibration by being in nature. I created a meandering path into the garden by placing garden paving stones in a curvilinear fashion. This brings the element of water into play and is a soft way to enter. If you prefer to add more color, simply plant flowers in a curvilinear pattern.

Plan to have a water feature in your garden. In today's world, you can choose from elegant fountains to small ponds. To the scale of your garden, select the best suited for your space. Birdbaths or a sprinkler that rotates and is made in the shape of a butterfly is perfect too.

4. Be sure to have this path detailed during your planning stage and enjoy entering into your garden paradise via the way of water. Please include a water feature.

At the very back of our garden, we placed a red door that once graced our front door. It does go against the rules to avoid having wood, however it is mostly in shade and therefore it is protected. It gives the appearance of a portal into another world. Plus, it anchors the space with the feeling of a mountain.

Depending on the theme of your garden, you will now choose your colors and plant accordingly. Just as we chose red and purples, think about colors you love to live with the colors you love to wear. Bring these colors into the garden with flair. Think about the meaning of each selected color and simply be with those colors awhile. Re*member… green is growth, purple is enrichment, red is fame, pink is love, white is purity, silver is spiritual, black (great for containers) is water, royal blue is wisdom and yellow is unity.

*Choose your colors with conscious awareness.*
*Re*member each flower has a meaning or symbolism too. Refer back to the Pure Abundance chapter and select accordingly.*

When you plant trees, think about naming them. We planted two maples that turn crimson in the fall. We named one for my dad Jordan and the other Jack for my husband's grandfather. Each one of these wonderful men was ever so important to us. Since they each are now gardening in the heavens, this is a magnificent way to pay tribute to loved ones.

I have gardened with Feng Shui principles since 1995 and every year, our garden takes on an entirely new theme. One of the staples is that within the garden as a whole, we have a secret garden. It is by the abundant strawberry patch and within its space, there are two oversized garden chairs that welcome us to sit and take part in the paradise we have created. This is a perfect place for early morning tea and meditation and for the afternoon, reading a book in this quiet place is heavenly. Honor the Feng Shui principles you have learned in the book and you too will create heaven on earth.

A garden is where your dreams can come true. Please re*member-before tilling the soil and prior to planting, talk to the divas of the earth and ask them to work with you for the highest frequency to be emitted in this sacred space.

## A Jewel to Re*Member

*When the sun rises, I go to work.*
*When the sun goes down I take my rest,*
*I dig the well from which I drink,*
*I farm the soil which yields my food,*
*I share creation, Kings can do no more.*
*- Chinese Proverb, 2500 B.C.*

*What greater delight is there than to behold the earth appareled with plants as with a robe of embroidered works, set with Orient pearls and garnished with the great diversities of rare and costly jewels. But these delights are in the outward senses. The principle delight is in the mindful, singularly enriched with the knowledge of these visible things, setting forth to us the invisible wisdom and admirable workmanship of Nature's beauty.*
*- John Gerard, 1633, The Herbal*

## The Healing Garden

*"Inside the sacred fence before which I bow,*
*There must be a pond filled with clear water.*
*As my mind-moon becomes bright,*
*I see its shadow reflected in the water."*
*Daito Kokushi (1282-1337)*

The healing properties of a garden embody the same restorative abilities of a sanctuary. Its nurturing voice speaks wellness to the core of our being, soothing balm to our spirit, and transformation to our souls. We reflect on our challenges and know they are only in our path to be as stepping-stones. In the refuge of the garden place, we find solace and healing balm. Within our heart, we silently bow and know there is a bridge from shadow to wholeness. Creating a healing garden is the highest form of remedy in restoring health to body, mind, or spirit or all three.

It is essential for this garden to represent all five elements. Stand at the gateway or threshold of your garden as if it is your front door. Look to the left hand middle section and recognize Family/Roots. It is the area of growth-verticality. Plant Echinacea, Climbing Roses, trees Place a teak wood bench with a comfy cushion nestled in this area offers the opportunity to build inner strength. In the far back is the Fire. Re*member my red door? Red, purple and orange flowers. Day lilies and Red Trumpet vine trailing up a back fence along with torch lighting, a fire pit or a brick barbecue grill > is excellent food for thought. In the far right hand side, place a bench for two under an arbor. Statuaries of two children, a couple, or two cranes (longevity) are especially beautiful here. Pots of ceramic and terra cotta create a sense of stability and offer deep stillness to this secret garden of the heart. Plant Cosmos with their dazzling pink and white flowers. The mid-right hand side is Metal. Place a metal arch to oversee the growth of all things heavenly. Circular paving stones refine and adorn this area, as will saffron colored flowers, We have now gone full circle and are back to the beginning. This area is governed by Water. You can create a meandering path with paving stones, gravel, or flowers. To enhance the healing essence play a water feature here.

Design your healing garden with a water feature, a pond where clear water pools within it well. Water is symbolic of renewal and release. Allow the curative properties of plants, flowers, the fragrant soil, and trees to surround you. Their therapeutic value creates a lasting sense of the timelessness of nature. We are ageless, we are enduring, we are eternal, and we are everlasting. We embrace the transformation of our spirit into wellness… wellness of place; wellness of being present, and the strength that wellness gifts me. I rejoice in the process of healing. To symbolically call forth the transformation of healing, we can plant host plants to invite the butterfly to join us. They love Alfalfa, Butterfly Bush, Clover, Deer weed, Dill, Hollyhock, Parsley, Sassafras, Snapdragons, Sunflower, and Thistle.

Plants that denote medicinal qualities are the Aloe Vera, Angelica, Agave, Borage, Chamomile, Comfrey, Dandelion, Echinacea, Feverfew, Garlic, Lemon Balm, Rosemary, St. Johns Wort, and Yarrow.

The healing abilities of the simple tasks of tending a garden extend themselves to rake, hoe, and shovel. These tools are our assistants in the pursuit of wellness. Just being out of doors in the fresh air draws benefits untold and unexpected ways to us.

For our mind-moon to become bright, we must adopt affirmations of wellness. Such as I am well, I am whole, I am centered, I am grateful, and I live in harmony and balance. Affirming positive statements and being truly present with these powerful and healing words connects us to our inner wellspring of peace. To have brightness in our moon-mind, we can plant a nighttime garden.

This is a mystical journey that takes us into the skies to dance with the magical man in the moon and his attending stars of beauty. A good variety of these nocturnal flowers are Angel's Trumpet, August Lily, Citrina, Columbine, Day Lily called Moon Frolic, Dark Purple Petunias, Epiphyllum, Evening Primrose, Fairy Lily, Four O'Clocks, Greek Mulleins, Hemerocallis, Moonflowers, Nottingham Catchfly, Nicotiana, Night Bloomers, Phlox, Pinks, and Yucca.

When we can see our shadow reflected back to us in the water, we are at last free. At that moment, the grace of our awareness allows us to see the shadow or challenge that has lurks within our heart of hearts. We are at rest with the knowing that we can till the soil of our healing gardens of our mind, body, and spirit. We are at rest and as we will bow at the sacred fence, we are grateful and we are at peace.

## The Spiritual Garden

*Before creation, a presence existed,*
*Self-contained, complete,*
*Formless, voiceless, mateless,*
*Changeless,*
*With yet pervaded itself*
*With unending motherhood.*
*Thought there can be no name for it,*
*I have called it 'the way of life.'*
*Perhaps I should have called it 'the fullness of life.'*
*Since fullness implies widening into space,*
*In this sense,*
*The way of life is fulfilled,*
*Heaven is fulfilled,*
*Earth is fulfilled,*
*And a fit man is fulfilled:*
*These are the four amplitudes of the universe*
*And a fit man is one of them:*
*Man rounding the way of earth,*
*Earth rounding the way of heaven,*
*Heaven rounding the way of life*
*Till the circle is full.*

*The Way of Life-Lao Tzu*

Spiritual Gardening is the practice of attending to the soil while attending to the soul. The deep fulfillment derived from spiritual gardening encompasses every season of the year. Spiritual gardening is a way of life that offers deep and abiding contentment rich with the anticipation of tomorrow, delight of today, and acceptance of yesterday.

On a cold winter's day, I have found myself indoors feeling safe and warm with a cup of hot tea and my gardening book in lap. Cozying up in my favorite chair, I am envisioning the summer's garden and planning what flower will go where and what tree will someday give shade to an overly sunny spot. I dream of the coming spring when our lilacs will surely hasten the memory of Aunt Nita's rows of purple blooms of oh so many years ago in time, but yesterday in my heart. Each bush stood tall punctuating the air with an ever so sweet fragrance and the landscape with beauty. is simply a joy. To dedicate one's garden to the spirit is simply being one with spirit and listening to the garden Diva's and their whispers to you.

Gardening is a life affirming experience. It puts you in touch with nature. I have found that as I nourish my garden, it feeds me. This field of spirit gardening looms large within my spirit and has created space for my heart to hold so much more joy. As spring approaches, I not only think of the lilacs, but the messages the returning flowers will bring from their time of wintering over. Spring's homecoming is welcomed and she delights my spirit. This time of year is perfect for celebration.

In the soil of fertile possibilities, plant spirit food by sowing seeds of inspiration, marvel, joy, delight, compassion, serenity, wonder, insight, vitality, optimism, and love. Water them with kindness. Keep the weeds of fear, negativity, worry or anxiousness at bay by faithfully attending to your garden of your spirit.

Soul gardening embraces aromatherapy and creates a feeling of sanctuary. A sanctuary is a place where we feel connected. The flower fragrances waft through the air and each scent connects our emotional body to nature's mystical presence. Scent unfolds hidden memories that unfurl and take us to places of awe and amazement. We are at once present and yet we bend time and space. Once again we can see the world from the eyes of childlike wonder.

To allow the flower power of perfume to transport you, I suggest planting the following:

**Annuals:** Amaryllis, Evening Stock, Heliotrope, Marigolds, Mignonettes, Petunias, and Sweet Alyssum.

**Perennials**: Chocolate Daisy, Day Lily, Hyacinth, Lavender, Lilacs, and Swamp Vanilla Milkweed.

As we embrace the sweet fragrances of our spirit garden, we are returned to the circle of the heavens and of life. Breathing in her roundness of earth deepens the wholeness within our spirit and deeply enriches our lives. On every level, we are connected to nature and our spirit is content and full.

## The Helpful People Garden

*Gardening is a labor full of tranquility and satisfaction; natural and instructive, and as such, contributes to the most serious contemplation, experience, health and longevity.*
*- John Evelyn, 1666*

There is a certain glee that the sense of belonging bestows upon us. When we meet another kindred spirit along our life's journey, we recognize just how richly connected we are. This experience deepens our knowing are all one. For truly, being a helpful person strengthens our kindred spirit with all whom we meet. Underneath us one and all beats a same heart, it is only our culture or practices that might divide us up.

Create a Helpful People garden to bring together all walk this earth. Have a place to pray forth the blessings of forgiveness, the joy of togetherness, the dissolving of strife, and the melting away of judgment. Yes, gardening is a labor filled with tranquility and the sheer pleasure of creating a garden paradise evolves us into the person we were meant to be. Gardening enables us to extend ourselves into the assistance of humanity. Once we have been pressed into this special service, we find satisfaction. We recognize what we were put on this earth to do... till the soil and plant beauty. This is an intrinsically natural ability and in its process, we realize enlightenment.

The art of usefulness is truly at the heart of a Helpful People garden. This garden thrives with many vegetable varieties of the season in order to share with our friends and neighbors. We select flowers in a riot of color and thread throughout the garden tapestry. These flowers symbolize the diversity of humanity. As our multicolored flowers flourish side by side with one another, we create a haven within this haven. This secret place has a garden bench so tha may sit and simply celebrate nature and rejoice in her many gifts. This little place of peace earth enhances the Chi of the land.

Placing garden stones in our garden as a border or as an energetic chatzkie connects us t Mother Earth. Each garden stone is unique unto itself and communicates a vibration or energy to its beholder. They also transmit and provide healing, support, and return vital energy back to the earth. In fact, the crystal or garden stone holds the earth's DNA. Garden stones have long been acknowledged as a method of creating greater well-being and are a remarkable means of increasing one's life force or Chi.

Rocks or gemstones are known to enhance one's personal life path, augment clarity, enlarge one's perception, boost personal creativity, and promote compassion. These descriptions are but a few of a gemstone's properties. Through studying their abilities, please note that a gemstone is a naturally occurring crystalline form of a mineral and were created as the earth was formed.

Garden globes are symbolic of global peace. Their convex mirrored orbs elegantly decorate our gardens. They are agents of expanding the energy through reflecting Chi to surrounding areas.

The Helpful People garden is notable because it is filled with lovely statuaries. They honor the saints and mentors who went before us and set a higher standard of service. Statuaries of Buddha, Quan Yin, Angels, Children (when we see the world through a child's eyes, we are once again innocent and creative), St. Francis, the Virgin Mary, Mermaids (freedom), Cranes (longevity), Harvest Boy (abundance), and Fairies.

As in the spiritual garden, planting silver lamb's ear and cosmos throughout this garden reminds us to be of service. Serve with a willing heart and with an open mind. Serving the greater good makes a difference in this world and shifts our world from limitation to the unlimited.

The Helpful People garden resonates with lifting the energy to the heavens by way of joy, synchronicity, community, silver, and metal. Plant flowers in the colors of pink, yellow, white flowers around your deity in residence. Echoing Nature's cycles in the Helpful People garden, creates sacred space. You have woven within its pattern, a blessing or a mantle where kindred spirits can recognize one another in even the most distant of lands. The garden of Helpful People cultivates and regenerates the awareness that humanity is ONE.

225

t we
on

o

# End Word

In life, we have decisions to make and the choices we arrive at greatly determine the quality of our life's experiences. Living in harmony and balance and listening to our inner truth enables us to trust our intuition. Yes, we do have to walk our talk and there are some steps to follow in order to do so. When we focus inwardly in meditative reverence, we can hear not only our very own heart beating, but Mother Earth's strong pulse too. The earth's rhythmic pattern enables us to breathe in unison... we become one.

The labyrinth is the inner place of the heart and what we get from this experience is measured by what we contribute. We walk to labyrinth to find balance, peace, and inspiration. The labyrinth connects us with a sense of sacredness, of spirit where we know ALL IS WELL. We are once again one with Divinity, with the process of creation that renews itself within our being and within our lives. Awareness comes through walking the labyrinth and embedded in the experience are the following processes:

1. Mineral............................State of Being
2. Vegetable..........................State of Growing
3. Animal.............................State of Feeling
4. Human..............................State of Thinking
5. Angelic World......................State of Knowing

6. Divine Mystery........................State of Unknowing

Embarking on the labyrinth's walk, we must begin by letting go or shedding those things, thoughts, words, and deeds that no longer serve us. Mindfully walking the labyrinth enables us to be present with our deepest thoughts and hear what our inner truth is whispering in our heart of hearts. Once we do this, we can confidently walk into the labyrinth's center.

At the center of the labyrinth, just like our life, there is illumination to be found. Once we recognize the hidden treasures of our inner and outer home, the labyrinth draws us back to our center. Only then can we walk the return passageway knowing we are now one with all there is.

The labyrinth's elegant concentric paths ultimately lead to the deeper understanding of love, safety, and peace. Our inner truth creates and makes known the outer and the inner outer reveals the inner. This concentric truth is at the heart of beauty.

Re*member, we are pearls, and awakened illumination shifts humanity into who it is meant to be, to be in alignment with our cosmic self.

# In Summation -

## Discovering the Hidden Treasures of Your Heart & Home

These Feng Shui principles have worked in my life and, although a great deal of it is simply common sense, it always helps us when we have a point of reference. Energy work continues to surprise and delight me as I find it to be a multi-layered learning process. One of my students shared that she thought I had a gift for making this ancient and quite complex subject easy to understand. I considered that generous compliment high praise. It is from this spirit of Feng Shui Simplified that this book was created. The words of serenity, joy, bliss, balance, harmony, and belief lovingly threaded their way through each chapter. You now have a woven work that warms your heart, stills your mind and reveals the treasures of your inner and outer home. Listen to the whispers of your heart and of your home and BE WELL.

I believe with 'a clear heart and an uncluttered mind', we can accomplish anything we intend. Re*member, we are all energetic beings and you can walk in a greater light, with a skip in you step.

In closing, I want to share some of my favorite words with you. My workshop attendees will attest to their profound impact on their lives. On my website, I have a place called Inspirational Word for the Day. Each time you visit, you are given a word. This will be the perfect word for you to boost your spirits and focus on your highest best idea of yourself. This book and these words will help you discover the hidden treasure of your heart and home. Re*Member, live with the things that inspire and nurture you.

| | | |
|---|---|---|
| Abundant | Appreciated | Ageless |
| Accomplished | Awesome | Beauty |

Blessed
Calm
Centered
Clear
Contentment
Creative
Courage
Desirable
Enchantment
Energy
Enlightened
Enriched
Expectant
Exquisite
Generous
Giving
Grace
Graceful
Gratitude
Grounded
Honor
Hopeful
Inspire
Love
Nurtured
Open Heart
Peace
Playful
Poised
Prosperity
Prosperous
Purpose
Receptive
Refreshed
Rejuvenate
Renewal
Release
Rested
Revived
Safe
Secure
Stable
Surrender
Treasure
Unfolding
Valued
Wanted
Welcoming
Zestful

# The Western School of Feng Shui

Per their website, The Western School of Feng Shui provides innovative, career-based educational programs that enhance the health, wealth, and happiness of people around the world. Programs include a unique Feng Shui Practitioner Training 7-Day Immersion Program, Consultation Services, Workshops and a Feng Shui Speakers Bureau.

## Essential Feng Shui®

Our school and our services embrace Essential Feng Shui®, which fully honors the essence of its Form Feng Shui while focusing on the practical applications it has in our Western culture.

Feng Shui, the ancient system of environmental placement, sees the world as completely alive with everything, including buildings, streets and property, interconnected in a dynamic relationship that affects everything we experience. The growing popularity of Feng Shui is the direct result of the extraordinary effects it can have in peoples' lives.

This includes improved health, more rewarding relationships, and an increase in happiness and prosperity. Whether you wish to transform your home into a personal paradise, your office into a powerhouse of creativity, or you are searching for a rewarding addition to your career path, the Western School of Feng Shui can light your way.

The Western School of Feng Shui provides innovative, career-based educational programs that enhance the health, wealth, and happiness of people around the world. Programs include a unique Feng Shui Practitioner Training 7-Day Immersion Program, Consultation Services, Workshops and a Feng Shui Speakers Bureau.

Terah Kathryn Collins is the founder of the Western School of Feng Shui. It has been my personal experience to know Terah as a witty, generous, and wise Feng Shui teacher. She is a best selling author of such books as The Guide to Western Feng Shui, Feng Shui for Romance, and Feng Shui Prosperity. She is the originator of the essential (yin) approach to creating beauty in our lives through balance and harmony.

You can reach Terah via the school's website www.wsfs.com or by calling 1-800-300-6785 or 858-793-0945.